NAPOLEON AND THE AMERICAN DREAM

Napoleon and the American Dream

INES MURAT

Translated by Frances Frenaye

LOUISIANA STATE UNIVERSITY PRESS
Baton Rouge and London

Originally published in 1976 as *Napoléon et le rêve américain*
Copyright © 1976 by Librairie Arthème Fayard
Translation copyright © 1981 by Louisiana State University Press
All rights reserved
Manufactured in the United States of America

DESIGNER: Joanna Hill
TYPEFACE: Linotype Janson
TYPESETTER: Service Typesetters
PRINTER and BINDER: Thomson-Shore, Inc.

Library of Congress Cataloging in Publication Data

Murat, Inès.
　Napoleon and the American dream.

　　Translation of Napoléon et le rêve américain.
　　Bibliography: p.
　　Includes index.
　　1. Napoleon I, Emperor of the French, 1769–1821. 2. France—Relations (general) with the United States. 3. United States—Relations (General) with France. I. Title.

DC203.9.M8213　　944.05　　80–39681
ISBN 0–8071–0770–0

Contents

Preface   vii
Introduction   3
1 Abandonment of the New World   9
2 Two Brothers in Exile   17
3 The American Refuge   47
4 Some Lives in Exile Outside the Agricultural Communities   64
5 Grapes and Olives in Alabama   76
6 The "Field of Refuge"   101
7 Echoes of Napoleon in Latin America   151
8 At the Canadian Border   172
9 Itinerary of a Legend   179
10 The Napoleonic and the American Dreams Face to Face   199
Notes   227
Bibliography   231
Index   239

Preface

While celebrating the bicentenary of its birth, the United States proudly took account of its territorial, economic, and political importance.

Two hundred years ago, when the new country was a feeble fledgling as viewed from the great powers of Europe, the "American dream" had, nonetheless, a great place in Western imagination. It represented a dream of Europe fleeing from the weight and wounds of history, and the hope of living out, in a new world, the dreams that history stifled in the old.

Napoleon seemed to take hold of the world's dreams and submit them to destiny. His prodigious adventure is one with the tumult of history. Fascination of and escape from history: Napoleon's epic and the American myth represent two contradictory dreams by which men are alternately haunted.

Napoleon gave up America, and, by selling the Louisiana Territory to the United States, contributed to the creation of a great world power. Could he have imagined that, later, the American model would be compared and opposed to his historical dream?

After his abdication, he thought of going into exile in the United States and of embarking on a career as an explorer and a naturalist. But he could not save himself from history. On St. Helena the image of him as a political prisoner aggrandized his legend.

Some of his soldiers, rejected or exiled by the government of Louis XVIII, set sail for the New World, hoping there to revive their dead dream. The attempt was a failure. Their dream belonged to the history from whose demons America had fled.

Napoleon and America judged each other by the criteria of

their respective dreams. Napoleon and his legend face-to-face with America and its myth: we have tried, here, to imagine a dialogue between them.

NAPOLEON AND THE AMERICAN DREAM

Introduction

1803. The Tuileries Palace. The First Consul, in his bath, was waiting for a visit from Joseph and Lucien Bonaparte. Lucien was the first to arrive, and the two brothers spoke together of literature, poetry, and the theater. Lucien didn't dare to bring up immediately the matter that was upsetting him: was Napoleon thinking seriously of ceding the immense province of Louisiana to the United States? Meanwhile Joseph was at the door, asking for admittance.

"Let him in! I'll soak a quarter of an hour longer in the tub."

In his turn, Joseph questioned Napoleon as to his intentions about Louisiana. He and Lucien were astounded to hear that the First Consul was ready to cede the entire province without even consulting the legislative Chambers. Joseph was openly indignant, and violent words were exchanged. In his anger, Napoleon raised himself out of the water and slid back in, splashing Joseph's clothes. The valet who was holding the bathrobe fainted.

A few minutes later, in his study, Napoleon attempted to explain to Lucien what he frankly called his act of "Louisianicide." Lucien replied testily:

"Citizen Consul, you pledged allegiance to the Constitution of 18 Brumaire before me, as president of the Council of Five Hundred. But now that I see how totally you disregard it, I can only conclude that, were I not your brother, I'd be your enemy."

"My enemy? Unthinkable! But if you were, I'd break you like this box." And the snuffbox he was holding in his hand rolled across the rug.[1]

Louisiana, as the possession of a European country, brought the Old World closer to the New. This vast territory, stretching from the Gulf of Mexico to the Great Lakes and the border of Canada, and from the Mississippi to the Rocky Mountains, seemed to hang, almost oppressively, over young America, to limit its dreams of expansion and stifle its vitality.

If America were to buy this area from Napoleon, it could look toward the immense, unstoried lands of the West, proportioned to its faith and hope in a free world. The American myth, protected by oceans, forests, desert wastes, and land as yet unexplored, would expand, far from the brilliant but tragic epic that was being played out in Europe.

Napoleon would double—and more—the surface of the United States. Just as he was launching his armies in the pursuit of glory, he offered America one of the greatest acquisitions France had ever made. What manner of man was this, a liberator or a despot? An heir to the Revolution or its gravedigger? Hated or admired, feared or loved, he fascinated Americans, even if they were of two minds about him. As in the past, relations between France and the New World were subject to the sway of passion. Now, in 1803, the people of Louisiana learned for the second time, without having been consulted, that France was ceding their province to another nation.

Forty years earlier, Louis XV lost the war he had waged against England on American soil. After Montcalm's defeat at Quebec, the king hastened to sell Louisiana to Spain before it could fall into the hands of the English. France had settled Louisiana under Louis XIV, and its inhabitants, who were deeply attached to their French roots, learned with despair of his successor's decision. They sent a delegate to Paris, who threw himself at the feet of the foreign minister, the duc de Choiseul, and, with tears in his eyes, begged him not to give up the province to Spain. Choiseul's reasoning was exactly the same as Napoleon's: it was based on the necessity of blocking the ambitions of England.

By an accomplishment unique in the Western world, the English aristocracy, which wielded political power, had absorbed the upper stratum of a mercantile middle class, which had the money. The money-making and sea-trading activities of this hybrid group, half-noble, half-merchant, constituted a serious threat to continental Europe. The American policy of Louis XV and Louis XVI, and of the Directory and Napoleon after them, was aimed at holding in check this moneyed oligarchy and its despotic rule of the seas.

The comte de Vergennes, foreign minister of Louis XVI, proposed to help the American colonies win their independence in order to thwart England's attempt to monopolize world trade and wealth. And there was another element in the struggle. In the eyes of the French volunteers who thronged to join the "insurgents," America was fighting for the freedom and other ideals of the century of the Enlightenment. When they landed ready for combat on American shores, they came to defend their own dream.

While the marquis de La Fayette covered himself with glory alongside Washington, the fifteen-year-old Napoleon Bonaparte was trying to obtain a lieutenant's commission. He had a chance to observe the enthusiasm aroused in France by the American experience, and we may wonder whether he shared it. A few years later, as a young officer, he summed up what he had read about America as follows:

> The English colonies measure 800 miles by 150, a surface of 120,000 square meters. In 1780, 2,500,00 whites and 450,000 blacks made up the population. This has doubled every twenty years, so that now it comes to a total of 4,000,000. In France a man needs four acres to live on; in America he needs forty. The mean temperature is ten degrees warmer in London than in Boston.
>
> North America has recourse to fishing for its subsistence. There is plenty of wood for building, but distance prevents its importation to France or makes it very expensive. The fur trade is tapering off; as of today it brings in no more than 35,000 pounds sterling.... They trade with the Antilles, but not advantageously. They have industries, including branches of the iron foundries of Dartmouth. Mulberry trees flourish. Cotton plants are large and produce very strong fibers. In the central region there is tobacco, but this voracious plant has exhausted the soil.
>
> In the Carolinas, Georgia and Florida, there are rice fields, and cotton trading is in the process of development. Rain and fog are adverse to the cultivation of grapes.

Napoleon saw America in geographical terms; his New World imagery evoked forests, cotton fields, and trade. After his defeat at Waterloo, he had an urge to go to America; together with the famous scientist, Gaspard Monge, he planned to study the flora, fauna, and climate of the North American continent. In Europe, as in the Near East, Napoleon was carried away by his dream of history. America, on the other hand, impressed itself on his imagination by its overwhelming size and variety—as if he had a presentiment that his epic dream would never extend over the lands of the New World.

General Washington, as president of the United States, followed with attention and mistrust the bloody unfolding of the French Revolution. His ambassador to Paris, Gouverneur Morris, said that revolutionary orators "have taken Genius instead of Reason for their guide . . . and wander in the Dark because they prefer Lightning to the Light." For the duration of his presidency, the calm and coolheaded Washington sought to save his country from the storm of a revolution of which he did not approve and about which the opinions of his fellow citizens were divided.

He managed, not without difficulty, to persuade his countrymen to adopt a policy of American neutrality in case of a war between England and France. The incredible clumsiness of the French National Convention's envoy to the United States, Edmond Genêt, strengthened Washington's aversion to the Paris régime. Genêt, an ardent revolutionary of aristocratic origin, arrived in the United States in 1793 and immediately embarked on an extraordinarily rash policy of interference in American domestic affairs. In the hope of arousing support for American participation in a war against England, the fiery ambassador successfully inspired numerous democratic groups known as "Genêt clubs." Moreover, he recruited frontiersmen and, on his own initiative, armed pirates or privateers in the Gulf of Mexico for organizing forays into the American West in order to snatch the mouth of the Mississippi from Spain and, eventually, to reconquer Louisiana. When Washington proclaimed a policy of neutrality, Genêt accused him of violating the Constitution and threatened to go over his head to the people. This was too much! Washington declared the Genêt clubs illegal centers of agitation and successfully demanded of the French revolutionary government that Genêt be recalled.

During the Reign of Terror, various Frenchmen—Talleyrand, who was later to play an important part in Franco-American diplomatic relations, among them—sought refuge in the United States. Talleyrand asked for an audience with General Washington, but it was denied him. "I can perceive very clearly," Washington wrote to Alexander Hamilton, "that the consequences of receiving these characters into the public rooms will be driving the French minister from them." In other words, there must be no question of offending the French government by welcoming its banished opponents. However, he went on, "These emigrants, if people of good character . . . will be entitled to all the benefits of our laws."[2]

In 1794 Washington seemed to abandon his neutral attitude toward events in Europe. In that year John Jay, the Anglophile envoy to London, signed a treaty very favorable to England. In wartime the British navy did not respect the neutrality of ships trading with France, such as those of the American merchant marine. Backed by Jay's Treaty, England, to the fury of New England shipowners, now claimed the right to seize all American cargoes on the high seas. The treaty created a scandal in the United States, and Washington was severely criticized.

John Adams succeeded Washington and, in France, the Directory put an end to the Terror. Jay's Treaty was still in force, and the new French government, convinced that American shipping was under English control, decided to attack the United States merchant marine by all the means at its command. Fear of losing the right of free navigation on the Mississippi and of access to the mouth of the "father of waters" haunted American merchants and shippers. Spain, which at this time possessed the western part of the future Louisiana Territory, had granted the United States temporary permission to use the river and to set up a commercial depot at New Orleans. The Directory's first aim was to buy back Louisiana from Spain in order to obtain jurisdiction over the traffic, but exaggerated claims on the part of France caused negotiations to fall through.

Although American shippers no longer had to face the danger of a French return to Louisiana, they were still up against the threat of French corsairs or privateers based in the Antilles. Three hundred American ships were seized by privateer vessels on the Atlantic and in the Gulf of Mexico. The United States and France were engaged in a cold war. Talleyrand, artificer of the Directory's foreign policy, tried in vain to bribe the indignant emissaries of

President Adams. In America, there was violent anti-French feeling, and war seemed imminent. General Washington himself was drawn out of retirement to take command of the army. But the old general, more coolheaded than his compatriots, did not believe in the possibility of a French invasion as long as France was warring with England. The English blockade, he wisely thought, would make it out of the question for France to transport troops and munitions across the Atlantic.

In the end, Adams came to an agreement with Talleyrand. But what if no such agreement had been effected? We can imagine an incredible picture: 1798, and Bonaparte, hero of the wars waged by the Directory, leaving Egypt in order to fight the army of General Washington! Washington and Bonaparte pitted against each other on the field of battle! The reader may draw his own conclusions as to the outcome of such an encounter.

CHAPTER 1

Abandonment of the New World

On November 10, 1799, Napoleon Bonaparte made himself First Consul. George Washington died on December 14 of the same year. A six-day mourning period was decreed in France, black crepe was attached to flags, and a funeral oration was delivered on the Champ-de-Mars. The conspicuous solemnity of the ceremony served to cover up a succession of crises that had poisoned the relationship between France and the United States. Hence the First Consul proclaimed an attitude of peace toward all nations.

In Washington, under President John Adams, the Federalist party was still in control. Its founder, Alexander Hamilton, had an aristocratic manner and a pessimistic view of the human race as composed of "reasoning rather than reasonable animals." Indifferent to public opinion, he believed in a strong central government and a state run by bankers, businessmen, rich lawyers, shipbuilders, and a few prosperous landholders in the vicinity of the big cities. He mistrusted the mass of the people, made up largely of small-scale farmers. Yet, although he did not share the deep-laid optimism of the American dream, he foresaw the country's future capitalistic power. Economic growth calls for investment, that is, capital, which, at this time, the United States did not possess. England was the foremost capitalistic state, and it was with her that American businessmen traded. The Hamiltonian and Anglophile business class was quick to take a stand against the French Revolution, and the Reign of Terror confirmed its view that any mass movement was bound to commit excesses.

Since the United States had no aristocracy, its businessmen thought of themselves as constituting the upper class. For this reason, most likely, they underestimated the important part played in the French Revolution by the middle as well as the lower class of the big cities. France, like other European countries of this time, was more industrialized than the United States and had an urban proletariat with a strong revolutionary bent. For Napoleon, the "people" meant not so much the peasantry as the workers who cheered him under the windows of the Elysée Palace after the defeat at Waterloo. On the road to exile, between Malmaison and the Atlantic, he saw that he was more popular in the cities than in the countryside. In the United States, he knew, the reverse would probably have been true: farmers would have hailed him more enthusiastically than city businessmen. The Federalists considered Napoleon a direct heir of the Revolution and disapproved of President Adams' conciliatory diplomacy.

In 1800, when England and Austria rejected the demand of First Consul Napoleon for peace, he turned to fight again against a new coalition. In America, the Hamiltonians, with their belligerent feelings toward France still unsatisfied, hoped that Bonaparte would be defeated. The French victory at Marengo, on June 14, 1800, was considered a setback for their party.

In his effort to defeat England at sea, the First Consul sought to obtain the neutrality of all the great maritime powers. A convention of friendship with the United States was signed on October 3, 1800, at the residence of Joseph Bonaparte at Mortefontaine. On this occasion, Napoleon's brother organized unforgettable festivities for the hundred and eighty distinguished guests from both countries, among whom was General de La Fayette. The magnificent ponds and pools of Joseph's estates were illuminated, and the best-known actors of Paris put on a performance. The solemn pledge was made against a grandiose Roman background, built expressly for the event.

The First Consul, when he had to admit that the English had the upper hand in the Mediterranean and that the Egyptian expedition on which General Jean-Baptiste Kléber had been assassinated was a failure, abandoned his Middle Eastern projects and turned his thoughts toward America. He would fight Britain's rule of the waves from the far side of the Atlantic, from strategic points that he hoped to acquire in the Gulf of Mexico. Thirteen days after the ceremony at Mortefontaine, Napoleon secretly bought the western part of the former French Louisiana from

Spain.[1] The United States was not informed and did not learn of the sale until a whole year later. Spain was France's ally against England, and the First Consul was in no hurry to dispossess it. The secret treaty of San Ildefonso stated that "the French Republic may postpone the takeover until such time as is convenient."

1801: Revolt of the blacks of Santo Domingo (Haiti). Their leader, Toussaint L'Ouverture, was a former slave who had risen to be a general in the French army. He promulgated a constitution and imposed his rule, defying the authority of the French government and the white plantation owners. Toward the end of the year, General Charles Leclerc, husband of Pauline Bonaparte, was appointed commander of an expeditionary force, and the First Consul instructed him as follows: "I count on you to send us all the black leaders [as prisoners] before the end of September. Otherwise, we shall have accomplished nothing; an immense and beautiful colony will still be on the edge of a volcano and will inspire no confidence in investors, settlers, and traders. . . . When the blacks have been disarmed and the leading generals despatched to France, you will have done more for European civilization and commerce than the most brilliant European campaigners."

The Peace of Amiens (March 27, 1802) established a temporary truce between England and France, and the time seemed ripe for using Santo Domingo as a bridgehead for the rapid colonization of Louisiana. "My intention," Bonaparte wrote to Navy Minister Denis Decrès, "is that we take possession in the shortest time possible . . . and that the expedition be made in deepest secrecy." Government offices got busy putting together a colonial army, drawing up a map of the Louisiana coast, and preparing "a plan for the military and administrative organization of the colony." Consular decrees promptly established the future governmental structure of Louisiana: high tariffs on imports and a strict separation of the executive, legislative, and judiciary powers. The former royal province was to benefit from the solid, centralized core of the Napoleonic regime and would be ruled by a captain-general, a prefect, subprefects, and commissioners. The office of captain-general was bestowed upon the ambitious Marshal Bernadotte in order to remove him from the metropolitan scene.

In the United States, Republicans had succeeded Federalists, and Thomas Jefferson, founder and leader of their party, was president. Jefferson was as tall and powerfully built as Hamilton was short and slim, as casually dressed as his adversary was elegant. A minimum of protocol and etiquette distinguished his presidential receptions. Jefferson had an optimistic view of human nature, and his manner reflected a taste for democratic simplicity. His ideal was to limit the power of the central government and to offer the average man a chance to participate in public and political affairs. He mistrusted the mass of city-dwellers, who attracted demagogues and, by their excesses, provoked the strengthening of the central government. This is why, at least at the beginning of his career, he had reservations about Hamilton's projects for industrialization, which threatened to spawn big cities peopled by the very rich and the very poor.

Jefferson was the man of the planters, the farmers, and the craftsmen, for the most part rural and simple folk who feared that Hamilton's less numerous but more moneyed bourgeoisie might turn into a privileged and tyrannical aristocracy. The Republicans, with Jefferson at their head, did not hide their sympathy for the French Revolution. Yet, paradoxically enough, they seemed, in a way, to understand it no better than the Hamiltonians, who, in spite of their leaning toward a strong, centralized government, mistrusted the centralizing trend of the city-dwelling French bourgeoisie that supplied the revolutionary leaders. Jefferson's moderate idealism did not harmonize with the Revolution's romanticism or his agrarian concept of democracy with its city-born ideology. And his opposition to any reinforcement of the federal government conflicted with the centralizing process taking place in France.

Yet the Jeffersonian Republicans' enthusiasm for the French Revolution verged on delirium. The question was not so much one of political theory as it was of the contrast between optimism and pessimism in regard to the human race. The equalitarian American farmers instinctively appreciated the French revolutionaries' faith in a human race capable of getting along without the guidance of a privileged upper class. As for the Hamiltonians, could they have read the future, they would have seen today's European leftists, to whom the French Revolution seems like the first step toward the achievement of a socialist ideal, attacking the American capitalism of which they, the Federalists, were the forerunners. In short, their misgivings about the course of events in France was largely justified and prophetic.

To Jefferson's followers, the First Consul was a republican hero, the liberator of oppressed peoples, and their newspapers voiced enthusiasm for the "republican arms" with which the French defended freedom against a coalition of tyrants. They were concerned, however, by the disregard for constitutional law that was opening the way to dictatorship. Jefferson remarked that the French people's blind trust in Bonaparte had enabled him to subvert the law and bend them to "his will and his life," and he enjoined his countrymen not to change a comma of their Constitution. In typically American fashion, he could not conceive of a government that subordinated economic to political considerations. Nothing could have been more fearful to Americans and more at odds with their dream than the presence on their continent of a Caesar come to impose his politics on their free trade.

It is easy to imagine Jefferson's consternation when, in spite of official denials, he learned from diplomatic indiscretions that Bonaparte had bought Louisiana: "There is on the globe one single spot," he wrote, "the possessor of which is our natural and habitual enemy. It is New Orleans, through which the produce of three-eighths of our territory must pass to market. . . . The day that France takes possession of New Orleans . . . we must marry ourselves with the British fleet and nation."

Two envoys, James Monroe and Robert Livingston, were dispatched by Jefferson to Paris, where they met Talleyrand, then minister of foreign affairs. Would France sell New Orleans? they asked him. They choked with astonishment when he answered, "You want to buy New Orleans? Why New Orleans? Wouldn't you rather have the whole of Louisiana?"

For the First Consul had decided, in these early months of 1803, to give up America. He was much affected by the disastrous end of the expedition to Santo Domingo, where fifteen hundred officers, twelve thousand soldiers and sailors, and two thousand civilians had died of yellow fever. Pretty Pauline Bonaparte had brought back the dead body of her husband, on which, following an old Corsican custom, she had laid her shorn hair. Moreover, war with England was imminent, and the British navy was indisputably stronger than his.

And so, on April 30, 1803, Napoleon Bonaparte sold Louisiana to the United States of America for the sum of sixty million francs. This money, so paltry an amount for such a vast territory, was never to be paid, for it was chalked up against France's outstanding debt. On July 14, the United States Congress heard with amazement of the acquisition. Didn't the Union risk going in for "abnormal development" in the direction of the Pacific? But by twenty-four votes to seven Congress approved the Franco-American treaty. The French flag was hoisted at New Orleans on November 30, 1803, and solemnly replaced by the American flag on the 30th of December. The effective possession of Louisiana by Napoleonic France lasted only a month.

"I've given England a rival that, sooner or later, will break its pride," said the First Consul.

And Robert Livingston rejoiced: "From this day on, the United States take their place among the powers of the first rank."

Although taken aback at first by the unexpected and sudden enlargement of their country, Americans soon adapted themselves to the new situation. Napoleon had opened the way to the West and laid the groundwork for a great epic, for a whole mythology, uniquely American in character.

Jefferson, usually so jealous a defender of regional autonomy, broke with his own principles and himself named the governor, the members of the legislative council, and the magistrates—in short, a territorial government in which the local people had no voice. Years later, Henry Adams passed judgment on this presidential initiative: "He made himself monarch of the new territory and wielded over it, against its protest, the powers of its old kings."

1804: Napoleon was proclaimed Emperor of the French. Throughout the United States, there was anger and consternation. To the Jeffersonians, the title of emperor was a betrayal of republican principles. The Federalists, sarcastic in their comments, were more than ever persuaded that Napoleon was a threat to the peace of the entire world, including North America.

The following year, Admiral Horatio Nelson annihilated most

of the Franco-Spanish fleet at Trafalgar, and the Continental powers found themselves under siege by Britain and its accomplice, the Atlantic Ocean. Because of the European wars, Americans began to take the place of the British and Dutch as "wagoners of the seas." The American merchant marine was one of the largest in the world; in 1806 its tonnage went over the million mark. In the face of the mortal combat between Britain and Napoleonic France, the United States proclaimed its neutrality, but neutrality, under the circumstances, was intolerable. To trade with the Continent at the risk of being captured by the British navy, or to trade with Britain at the risk of being captured by the French: this was the impossible dilemma.

The Federalists were unanimous in their hatred of the Emperor, whom they called the "imperial Jacobin." The Philadelphia *Publick Ledger* said that "in France, legislation is mockery." The Republicans, nonplused, were hesitant. For many of them, Napoleon was still the champion of freedom of the seas against tyrannical Albion. After all, the Emperor of the French had not reestablished the privileges of the *ancien régime*. The Richmond *Virginia Argus* congratulated Napoleon for having given equal rights to Jews.

Up against the paradoxical character of Napoleon and the complexities of European ideologies, Americans, on the whole, congratulated themselves on the purity and simplicity of their democracy. Jefferson compared the Napoleonic empire to that of Rome, whose peace was predicated on slavery, and proclaimed that the United States was "the sole repository of the sacred flame of freedom and self-government." Nevertheless, the new French despotism seemed to him less threatening to the United States than that of the English "oligarchy."

James Madison, who succeeded his friend Jefferson in the presidency of the United States, has a place in history for having declared, in 1812, a "second war of independence" against England. As John Quincy Adams told Secretary of State James Monroe, France "had laid the trap which she concluded would catch us in an English war." The Emperor proposed that the decrees offensive to the American merchant marine be abolished, but in return, said Napoleon, the United States must break off commercial relations with Britain if the latter refused to annul the

Orders in Council, which violated the rights of neutrals. As it happened, London did annul the Orders in Council, unaware that, just the day before, the United States had declared war upon it.

1814: Napoleon's first abdication. A short time after, British troops ravaged the city of Washington. Finally the Atlantic war subsided, and Britain and America made peace. Two weeks after the signing of the peace treaty, of which he was not aware, General Andrew Jackson scored a brilliant victory over the British at New Orleans. The eight thousand British soldiers who lost this battle went on to reinforce Wellington's troops at Waterloo.

No treaty linked the United States with Napoleonic France. Young John C. Calhoun, a future secretary of war and state, spoke before gatherings of businessmen against the continental blockade that was one of the chief weapons of Napoleon's war: "Burning and confiscation are the only effective securities. . . . In such a state of things the honest merchant must retire. . . . The desperate adventurer and the smuggler will succeed." No, a Caesar's dream could not harmonize with the mercantile ideal of a free America.

The War of 1812 cut whatever bonds were left between Europe and America, and the United States entered a period of isolationism that was to last a hundred years, until World War I—a hundred years in which the young nation became a great economic and military power, learned to define itself and to fulfill its destiny. The political turmoil, bloody battles, and violent emotions thrust upon Europe by a man with the uncommon and compelling personality of Napoleon drove the Americans to attach themselves to the constitutional stability, republican simplicity, and peaceful isolationism that are the components of their dream. Unconsciously they learned from him something of the fate of nations. And, by abandoning all territorial ambitions in the New World, he left them to their myth.

CHAPTER 2

Two Brothers in Exile

1815

June: Napoleon was staying at Malmaison. After the disaster at Waterloo, the pressure of the Chambers forced him to abdicate, and he contemplated going into exile in the United States under the name of Colonel Muiron.[1]

As the advance of the allies became more and more threatening and Field Marshal Blücher, with his Prussian troops, was approaching his retreat, Napoleon was absorbed in reading Alexander von Humboldt's *Voyage aux régions équinoctiales du Nouveau Continent*, a treatise on the geography and botany of the New World, devoid of historical and political considerations. Napoleon was contemplating a barometric scale and various algebraic formulas; he was interested in the descriptions of *Ambothorium* (the cinchona or quinine tree), *Melastoma* (with its violet flowers) and *Alistonia* (whose dried flowers have some of the healthy quality of tea). As he wrote to Gaspard Monge, an illustrious member of the Académie des Sciences,

> For me idleness would be the cruelest torture. Without armies or an empire, I see only science as influencing my spirit. But learning of the achievements of others is not sufficient. I want to embark on a new career, to leave worthy undertakings and discoveries behind me. I need someone who can speedily bring me up to date on the present situation of the sciences. After this, we shall travel through the New World from Canada to Cape Horn and, in the course of this long journey, we shall examine all the phenomena of physics and of the globe.

A fortune was spent on the purchase of apparatus for the study of physics, meteorology, and astronomy. Napoleon imagined himself in America, surrounded by his family. His mother was ready to go with him, and his brother, Lucien, wrote to Princess Pauline: "You've surely heard of the latest misfortunes of the Emperor, who has just abdicated in favor of his son. He's going to the United States, where we shall all join him. He's quite calm and courageous." Indeed, Napoleon summoned his two illegitimate children, the future Comte Léon and the son of Marie Walewska, to Malmaison, with the idea of taking them to America with him.

When Napoleon imagined his life in the United States, it was as a private individual and a devotee of science. He had written in his act of abdication that his "political life was over." His treasurer, the baron de Peyrusse, was to transmit three million gold francs to the banker Jacques Laffitte, who would transfer them to America. General Henri Bertrand organized the transportation of most of the imperial library, the china and linen of Malmaison, furniture sufficient for a city house and a country one, and twenty hunting guns. The groom Chauvin was to sail with fifteen stableboys, horses, harness, and saddles. Subscriptions were even taken out to the *Moniteur* and other Parisian papers, which were to be sent to Bertrand, in care of General Delivery, New York.

One evening when Napoleon was walking in the gardens of Malmaison, he looked for his star, between two branches of a tree where he had seen it once before, on a winter night.[2] It was not there, and any prescience of his future fate seemed to elude him. Was his historical role really over? He could not make up his mind to believe it. Until the day when he gave himself up to the English, he hoped or, rather, he dreamed that France would call him back to power.

Joseph Fouché, former chief of the imperial police, was directing the provisional government commission and had sent emissaries to the duke of Wellington to discuss a cease-fire. Wellington wrote to Talleyrand, who was then with Louis XVIII, to report on his meeting with Fouché's envoys:

> I explained that Napoleon's abdication was not a guarantee sufficient to justify suspension of my operation. I told them that my purposes would be fulfilled if Napoleon were to turn himself over to the Allies and if an advance-guard of our troops were to enter Paris. [As to the future government of France] I told them that I had no authority to speak on this subject but

that, in my purely personal opinion, the King should be called back, unconditionally, and that French honor demanded his immediate recall, before it could be attributed to pressure on the part of the Allies.

To force Napoleon to surrender himself to the English and to favor the return of Louis XVIII—it was all quite clear in Fouché's mind. He granted Napoleon two frigates for going to the United States but no guarantee of safe-conduct. The Emperor, alert to the likelihood of a trap, refused. Fouché promised to send safe-conduct papers to Rochefort, where the frigates were waiting.

Napoleon scrutinized a map and detected the enemy's weak points. The Emperor had abdicated, but General Bonaparte could still lead a French army. He came down from his room in uniform and informed the provisional government of his intention to crush the Allied army and, "once this was done," to pursue the road to exile. When Paris gave a categorically negative answer, he left Malmaison, wearing a brown frock-coat and a round hat. Later, aboard the frigate *Saale*, he found out about the secret orders that the captain had received from Fouché. The frigate could not set sail, and the former Emperor could not disembark anywhere on French soil. On the same day, Napoleon learned of the capitulation of Paris. He was seen to stifle a sob, to throw down the newspaper, and to retire to his cabin.

All along the road to exile, various escape plans were submitted to him, but he turned them all down. Decrès, minister of the navy, transmitted the offer of an American captain whose ship was to sail from Le Havre the next day, but Napoleon took offense at the idea of being "got rid of" so quickly. Captain Baudin proposed that he embark aboard an American privateer that had consistently outdistanced English cruisers. In case of an encounter with the enemy, two French corvettes—the *Bayadère* and the *Infatigable*—would bar the way, while the privateer headed straight for the American coast. At a certain point, Napoleon accepted this plan, but then he remained at Rochefort. A Lieutenant Besson, who commanded a Danish schooner, invited him to come aboard with a cargo of brandy and to hide in a padded barrel, from which he would breathe through a rubber tube. This solution Napoleon rejected as ridiculous.

When he did embark on the *Saale*, the tide was so low that he had to be carried on a sailor's back. On the way, an old navy officer approached him and said:

"Sire, be wary of treason. My lugger would carry you through the line of English cruisers."

"We'll see..."

The brave Captain Ponée, commander of the *Méduse*, the second frigate that the provisional government had put at Napoleon's disposal, proposed attacking the British *Bellerophon*, which was watching over the roadstead. While the *Méduse* waged a hopeless battle, the *Saale* would carry Napoleon to safety. Although touched by the offer of this sacrifice, Napoleon could not accept it. When, aboard the *Saale*, he realized that he had fallen into a trap set by Fouché, he asked to disembark at the island of Aix, where Joseph Bonaparte came to join him. Joseph had a high rank among the Freemasons, for which Napoleon had often teased him. Tradition has it that, on this occasion, Joseph recalled such episodes at the same time that he came forward with a proof of Masonic brotherhood and loyalty—namely, an offer on the part of a former Master of the Grand Orient Lodge to procure an American ship for the former Emperor. And Joseph proposed that, in view of the close physical resemblance between them, he take his brother's place on the *Saale*. Again, Napoleon refused. Joseph went to Royan, set sail for the United States, and arrived there in safety.

Officers of the Fourteenth Navy Regiment had a plan to take Napoleon aboard one of the two luggers anchored in the harbor, to sail along the coast by night to La Rochelle, and, once at sea, to force a merchant ship to convey him to the United States. Napoleon hesitated. On the evening of July 13, 1815, the two luggers and Besson's schooner, which had not yet set sail, were ready to go. Luggage was loaded on the schooner, and Napoleon ordered his valet Saint-Denis, called "Mameluke Ali," to see that all his arms were in a state of readiness. At eleven o'clock in the evening, General Becker, who had escorted him from Malmaison, came to report.

"Sire, all is ready. The captain awaits Your Majesty."

Napoleon was silent for a few minutes, and then he announced his decision: "There's always a risk in putting yourself in the enemy's hands. But it's better to trust in his honor than to remain his prisoner. Say that I've given up the idea of embarking and am spending the night here."

On July 14 he wrote the famous letter to the Prince Regent: "I come, as Themistocles did, to claim a seat by the hearth of the British people."

The next day he embarked on the *Bellerophon*, wearing the green uniform of the Chasseurs de la Garde, a bicorne hat with a red-white-and-blue cockade, the grand cross of the Legion of Honor, and the Order of the Iron Crown.

In August, news arrived in America from England, announcing Napoleon's defeat at Waterloo. Most American newspaper editors couldn't believe it was true; many even headlined a French victory.[3] When Americans finally gave in to the evidence, they realized, with a rude shock, that the coalition of the old European powers, together with their former mother country, had won the war. "The public mind feels anxious to know," said a paper from Norfolk, Virginia, "what is to be the fate of a man who, for more than twenty years, has, more than any other mortal who has preceded him, attracted public attention."

Wild rumors were rife. There were reports that Napoleon had been beheaded in Paris. A Baltimore paper said: "If the Parisian savages have massacred this man, eternal infamy must be their portion."[4] But this rumor was soon denied. From New York it was announced that Napoleon had embarked from France, with a few faithful followers, for the United States. "If he has not fallen into the hands of the British cruisers, this celebrated man is, at this moment, near our shores to seek asylum from the persecutions of the Old World." As word spread that Napoleon was approaching the coast of Virginia, Colonel King, commander of the militia of Somerset County in Maryland, summoned his men and hurried off to greet the hero of the day.

It was with stupefaction that America received confirmation of the news of Napoleon's surrender. Such was the public's disappointment that Napoleon was accused of cowardice, and certain newspaper writers went so far as to deplore the fact that he had not chosen to kill himself.

On July 26, aboard the *Bellerophon*, Napoleon heard that he was to be deported to St. Helena. Confining himself to his cabin, he read a life of Washington and continued to hope for a safe-conduct to America. After the first moments of uncertainty, Americans returned to their preoccupation with the fallen Emperor's future. A citizen of Raleigh, North Carolina, foresaw that "imprisonment for life will doubtless be the destiny of this extraordinary character, for neither the Prince Regent nor the Allies would jeopardize their popularity by putting him to death." On July 31, Napoleon learned what his fate was to be. "It's a death sentence," he responded. The horses and equipment that were to go with him to America arrived at Rochefort, where they remained, forgotten, for three months before they were brought back to Paris.

The majority of Americans were indignant over England's decision. To them, Napoleon was still the man with new ideas who had risen up against the old Europe in behalf of national independence. They were aware, above all, of his stature. "Victor and victim," said a newspaper in Lexington, Kentucky, "one is induced to view him as a strange production of a fabulous age, the like of whom never was—the like of whom may never be again."

Two Bonapartes crossed the Atlantic, the one to St. Helena, the other, under the name of Monsieur Bouchard, with a passport obtained for him by the chargé d'affaires of the United States in Paris, on an American brig, the *Commerce*, destination New York. Prince Joseph's conversational ability and his gift for reciting French and Italian poetry charmed his traveling companions. They also had some moments of excitement during the voyage. Twice, while it was still near the French coast, English ships stopped the *Commerce* and examined the passports of all those aboard. But the British officers harbored no suspicion of "Monsieur Bouchard," who, during the second search, stayed in his cabin on the plea of seasickness. The brig completed its voyage without mishap. The captain did not know that "Monsieur Bouchard" was Joseph Bonaparte, but took him for General Lazare Carnot, Napoleon's minister of war and a noted mathematician.

On August 27, New York was in sight. The arrival by sea was spectacular. "A forest of masts announces the city from a distance, as one of those places where world trade congregates," says the intrepid traveler, Edouard de Montulé.[5] Joseph had still some uncertainties to face; two English frigates barred the entrance to the harbor. A young American pilot, outraged by the English claim to the right of search in time of peace, leaped aboard the brig and, with all sails unfurled, forced the barricade. The frigates sailed away, and Joseph learned that they had been mounting guard for the last ten days in the expectation of seizing Napoleon, who was supposed to be on his way to the United States.

On August 28, the *Commerce* disembarked its passengers at an East River pier. Commodore Jacob Lewis, one of the guests in the boardinghouse where Joseph went to stay, recognized him as the Emperor's brother but promised not to reveal his identity. New Yorkers and their mayor were persuaded that the newcomer was Lazare Carnot. After a short visit to Commodore Lewis' home in New Jersey, Joseph returned on September 5 to New York. Even at this date, New York was a city unique in the United States. Says Montulé: "The large number of foreigners lends New York the liveliness of a combination of European cities, a liveliness which is not to be found elsewhere in America. The streets are straight, bordered by sidewalks; the houses, most of them built of brick, are often repainted. There are several cafés, but such establishments, typical of western Europe, are here not very successful. They suit idlers, and here, everyone is occupied with business."

On September 6, in the middle of Broadway, Joseph ran into a former officer of his Guards, who threw himself at his feet. "Your Majesty here! . . . How happy I am to see Your Majesty again!" This scene attracted a crowd, and the next day Joseph learned from the newspapers that his incognito was broken. On the advice of the mayor of New York, he went to Washington to ask an audience of President Madison, in order to confirm his right to live in the United States. He took and kept until the end of his life the title of "comte de Survilliers," in memory of a little village on the edge of his estate at Mortefontaine.

On the way to Washington, beyond Philadelphia and Baltimore, Joseph was informed by an emissary that President Madison could not receive him. The secretary of state and future President James Monroe recalled that, some years before, George Washington had refused to see Talleyrand. Later Madison explained:

"Protection and hospitality do not depend on such a formality; and whatever sympathy may be due to fallen fortunes, there is no claim of merit in that family on the American nation; nor any reason why its government should be embarrassed on their account. In fulfilling what we owe to our own rights we shall do all that any of them ought to expect."

In other words, Joseph Bonaparte would enjoy all the rights that the American Constitution granted to those desirous of setting up residence in the United States, but there would be no official relationship between the government and the former king of Spain. Like his predecessor, Jefferson, President Madison belonged to the Republican (later Democratic) party, which was to remain in power for many years. Its ideology was republican and hence not favorable to the Bourbon restoration, and its general policy was one of strict neutrality toward the European powers. The harm done to American trade by the wars between England and France was still fresh in mind; obviously the Napoleonic epic had represented a constant threat to the tranquillity of the New World.

Another reason for Madison's reluctance to lend importance to Joseph Bonaparte as a public figure was the fact that, in his former official capacity, Joseph had had dealings with the American government. It was at Joseph's estate at Mortefontaine, on October 3, 1800, that a convention between the United States and France was signed. Later, when Joseph became king of Spain and theoretically master of the Spanish colonies in Central and South America, Washington deliberately chose to ignore any connection between them.

Now Joseph, assured of a refuge as a private citizen, went about organizing his new life. The first thing he did was to rent a house in the center of Philadelphia, which, at this time, was a charming town with tree-bordered streets and coffeehouses filled with animated conversation. Another French traveler, Montlezun, remarks that the inhabitants were "strongly imbued with democracy" and thought, like their newspapers, that the Napoleonic exiles were the true French heroes. In short, the city was ready to welcome Joseph Bonaparte. The women, it seems, were particularly pretty and "wasted their time shopping." Montulé describes Philadelphia as:

the largest and finest city of the United States. None other in the world, perhaps, is so regularly laid out: all the streets are parallel or perpendicular to the Delaware, at least forty feet wide and paved with round little pebbles. As in many towns in the south of France they have eight- or ten-foot wide sidewalks, paved with bricks set edgewise and kept very clean. At intervals of about a hundred yards there are pumps, topped by lamps. Add to all this that the sidewalks are trimmed by poplars and plane trees, whose greenery, in the summer, must agreeably break the monotony of the single-color houses. Most of these are built of bricks; the door, usually very ornate, gives onto a white marble stoop, decorated with a spotlessly clean iron railing.

In September, Joseph's wife Julie (née Clary, the sister of Napoleon's former fiancée, Désirée) learned that her husband had arrived in the United States. In November Joseph rented, for a while, an agreeable country house on the Hudson River, eight miles from New York. The owner, Lord Courtenay, according to the French consul, Cazeaux, had embellished and furnished it at great expense at a time when he was exiled from England on charges of moral turpitude. Here Joseph lived a retired life, seeing few people. Occasionally he drove, incognito, to New York in a hired carriage.

Toward the middle of November, Coxe, the American consul at Tunis, informed the Bonapartes' mother, who was familiarly known as Madame Mère, in Rome, of her son's arrival in the United States. On the 20th of this month she wrote him: "You can imagine how glad I am to know that you are in the United States, safe from harassments and from pursuit on the part of the enemies of my family . . . (while) my very dear Napoleon. . . ." By the end of the year, Joseph had formed a favorable idea of the United States, as is shown in this letter to his secretary, dated December 15:[6]

> The place where I live is very beautiful and has a good climate. There are perfect peace and quiet, no sign of judges or policemen or criminals. Everyone works and enjoys such general respect that we detect no bothersome gesture, no wounding discrimination, no revolting injustice, no offense painful to ourselves or others. Liberty is complete. Domestic morals are

perfect, practical skills very advanced, the arts still in their infancy. Essential goods are fairly cheap, luxury items overpriced. In Switzerland they hide their wealth, here they display it. Here they live on work and credit, in Switzerland on work and savings. The Swiss works and saves, the American works and spends. Americans are cold but hospitable and kind, not ceremonious like Spaniards or polite like Frenchmen, but more cordial and obliging to foreigners. Generally speaking, I like the country and its inhabitants. As soon as my dear ones are with me I shall be quite content, and better off than in Switzerland.

1816

On January 18, 1816, Napoleon read in Brazilian newspapers of his brother's arrival in the United States. At this point the Emperor seemed to be in a weakened condition. Historian Comte Emmanuel de Las Cases, who accompanied Napoleon to St. Helena and was the author of the famous Mémorial de Sainte-Hélène (1823), noted: "His gait is heavy, his feet drag, and his features are changing. The resemblance to Joseph is striking, to the point that, a few days ago, when I went to meet him in the garden, I'd have sworn until he was very close that he *was* Joseph."

Joseph, Napoleon's elder brother, did indeed, except for the fact that he was taller, resemble him closely. In the United States, he led the comfortable private life to which he had always aspired, while Napoleon, as a political prisoner on St. Helena, suffered the fate of the public figure he had always wanted to be. Their lives in exile were as different as their natures, for, if Joseph was the one of Napoleon's brothers who most resembled him physically, he was the least like him in character and mental makeup. The contrast between them was so evident that it often gave Napoleon a dialectical support for defining his own personality and fate. He described Joseph to Las Cases as follows:

> Joseph has been of little help to me, but he's a thoroughly good man, and his wife, Queen Julie, is the best creature that ever existed. Joseph and I have always cared for each other and got on together; his feelings for me are sincere. I know he'd have done anything in the world for me, but his qualities are those of a private citizen. He's gentle and kind, educated and witty, extremely agreeable. In the positions of power where I

placed him, he did all he could; he had the best of intentions. His shortcomings were not his fault but mine, for pushing him out of his natural sphere. Amid overwhelming circumstances, he found himself up against a task beyond his powers to accomplish.

During their years of exile, the brothers received news of one another and even managed to exchange some clandestine letters. Napoleon imagined what his life might have been in America. He was a man in the depths of woe, hoping for a bit of happiness with his family, a prisoner confined to a narrow island, dreaming of freedom and open spaces, of the mirage of "a true refuge in every meaning of the word . . . a vast continent that enjoys a special kind of liberty. If you are sad you can jump into a coach and ride a thousand miles as an ordinary traveler. Everybody is equal, and you can lose yourself in the crowd, with your customs, your language, and your religion."

At the beginning of the year, Joseph wrote to Julie to ask her to come with the children to join him. But Julie was frail and fearful of the Atlantic crossing, which was indeed uncomfortable and dangerous at this time, so she never came. Meanwhile, the comte de Survilliers, as he was now known, rented Landsdowne House, near Philadelphia, built by John Penn, a descendant of the founder of Pennsylvania. Like Napoleon, Joseph spoke poor English and tried to avoid all occasions for speaking it at all. In February, Las Cases noted that Napoleon had made some progress. We can imagine that, had he managed to get to America, he would have made much more effort than did Joseph to talk to Americans in their own tongue.

One April day, Napoleon voiced to Las Cases his regret at not being in America, where he could have "protected France from her detractors. . . . The fear of my presence would have checked their violence and unreasonableness." And here is Las Cases' account of June 7:

> Today, in a long private conversation during the morning, the Emperor went back over the horrors of our present situation and ran through the hopes for a better future.
> After all these considerations, which I cannot reproduce here, he abandoned himself to his imagination and said that there was no place where he might live other than England or America. And his preference, he said, would be America, because there

he would be truly free and he wished only for independence and rest; for at this time he was writing his novel. He imagined himself near his brother Joseph, surrounded by a miniature France.

It was on a June day that Joseph finally found a house to buy in view of a prolonged stay in the States. Point Breeze—such was its name—was surrounded by 211 acres of land and ideally situated where Crosswick's Creek runs into the Delaware River, near Bordentown, some thirty miles north of Philadelphia and seventy miles south of New York. Napoleon, it seems, had advised his brother to settle between these two cities, close enough for receiving news from France and yet far enough away to discourage importunate visits. The sale was closed in August, with an American friend acting as the buyer, because according to the laws of New Jersey no foreigner could own land.

During this same summer, Joseph received the first offers from Latin-American insurgents who wanted him for a leader. As early as July he wrote to Napoleon on St. Helena to ask his advice. But Napoleon knew his brother. Even before he heard of the propositions from Latin America, he said to General Charles de Montholon, who had accompanied him into exile, about Joseph's arrival in the United States: "Joseph will found a great establishment over there, where all dear ones will find refuge. If I were in his place, I'd weld all the Spanish Americas into a great empire. But Joseph—you'll see—will make himself into an American burgher and spend his fortune on laying out gardens."

Napoleon was right. Joseph, delivered at last from political preoccupations, did not dream of accepting the insurgents' offer but dedicated himself to improving his house and the surrounding land, whose acreage he increased with a succession of acquisitions. He was inspired, as often as not, by his estates at Mortefontaine and at Prangins (in Switzerland), whence he brought his library, fine china, and superb art collections. Plans were drawn up for an artificial lake, the planting of trees, and road construction. From the house there was a magnificent view over the Delaware.

The great distraction at Bordentown was the arrival of steamboats from Philadelphia. There was every convenience aboard the boats, Montulé tells us, and "the food and service were up to those of a reputable inn." We can imagine Napoleon arriving at his brother's house on one of these steamboats, whose introduction to France he himself had, alas, discouraged. In 1803, just when preparations for the invasion of England were under way, the president of the Tribunate presented Fulton's invention to the First Consul who, it is now established, rejected it. Beginning in 1807, there was steamboat service on the Hudson River. Actually it is strange that, in his many observations on the United States, Napoleon never mentioned this country's gift for technology.

Joseph possessed an immense fortune, and many of the needy refugees from France came to him for aid. Joseph gave them help, even if not always all they wanted, but, above all, although the fact is not sufficiently mentioned, he paid for most of the servants and household expenses at St. Helena. It was in Joseph's name that General Bertrand, the Emperor's faithful companion in exile, made out the drafts for domestic payments.

A new ambassador from France—the royalist Baron Jean Guillaume Hyde de Neuville—came to Washington in June. He knew the United States well, having lived there during the period when Napoleon, to whom he had never rallied, was in power. For royalists, the return from Elba had been a veritable trauma; as long as Napoleon was still alive, they feared that anything might happen. The new ambassador was received by President Madison with courtesy but reserve. He brought with him special instructions from the minister of foreign affairs, the duc de Richelieu, in regard to French refugees and their new circumstances. "The presence in the United States of Joseph Bonaparte should make us particularly cautious." Rumors of a plot to liberate Napoleon and place him at the head of the Mexican insurgents quite naturally alarmed the new ambassador. Joseph, it seemed, would finance the operation; perhaps the two brothers were communicating secretly with each other. In July, Napoleon said to Bertrand, about a letter from his mother, "Madame says that Joseph is in America, where his wife and children will join him. I have an idea that he has some twenty million francs, because he is in possession of the royal diamonds of Spain. They were the objects of a long search. For a long time it was thought that they were in the hands of Murat, but not so: the owner is Joseph, as he himself has told me." And he went on to imagine Joseph's life among the exiles, showing how carefully he had followed their movements:

It seems that Joseph will set up a city. There are already three hundred French families, more than in any other country. Aside from those we read about in the newspapers as setting sail from various places, we may name such personal acquaintances as Regnauld, Savary, Marlin, Chaptal, Grouchy, Lefèvre, and others. What other country could produce so prestigious a group? If, in the town where Joseph lives, there are intriguers, they can be escaped from in Philadelphia. The emigrants are waiting to see what may happen. If events change for the better, they will return to France. That's the best place to be, but America comes next.

In these suppositions there was less truth than imagination. Joseph was not involved in politics and still less in setting up a city. There is witness to his detachment in a letter dated October 10 from the French consul in Philadelphia about the project of a settlement for French refugees: "Monsieur Joseph Bonaparte was asked to take part, but he refused in order to stave off any suspicion of political ambitions."

Joseph's democratic ways were pleasing to Americans. He seemed at ease in his role of gentleman farmer, chatting with the people he met on his walks and leaving a gold coin to those who offered him a glass of cider. Thus we read in *Niles' Weekly Register* of September 28: "Joseph Bonaparte seems determined to conform to the manners of our country. When assisting personally to unload the furniture brought to his house, to a person who said something about sending for other hands, he said: 'No, everybody worked here.'"

In October, Napoleon, who had always believed in the United States' capitalistic efficiency, was considering the investment of some money there. As Santini was leaving St. Helena, Bertrand gave him "three notes regarding the Emperor's funds and the sending of them to America." Napoleon asked to see the texts and was annoyed. The proper wording should have been: "*If* there are any funds at the Emperor's disposal, they should be invested in his name in American government bonds."

On December 3, Joseph received Edouard de Montulé and "asked him some discreet questions about the effects produced by the execution of Marshal Michel Ney, the affair of Grenoble, etc."[7] He spoke of the pain he felt over his brother's exile and the regret that he had not been able to come to America. "Then," says

Montulé, "he asked me if I could draw. When I said yes he asked me to look at some of his own landscapes and, without flattery or consideration for the fact that he had been a king, I was able to compliment him. We went on to speak of the fine arts, and I realized that he cultivated them. Fortune, which raised him so high and then so quickly abandoned him, seems to have brought him, in the last analysis, to a place of peace and quiet in harmony with his character."

On December 9, on St. Helena, Napoleon spoke to General Bertrand of Joseph, who, he mistakenly thought, had his family around him. "Joseph's family has arrived in America. This is a happy circumstance, one that he desired. He must have the diamonds of the royal crown of Spain, since they are not in the hands of either Charles or Ferdinand."[8]

1817

In January, the New Jersey legislature issued a special document authorizing Joseph Bonaparte to own land in spite of the fact that he was not an American citizen. Beginning with the month of April, Point Breeze was in his name.

Joseph enjoyed spending the winters in Philadelphia. Petry, the French consul, wrote to Richelieu in February that Napoleon's brother "receives invitations to dinners, teas, and private social gatherings. Up to now he has turned down those to public balls, including the one given yesterday to celebrate Washington's Birthday. He himself entertains local businessmen and other wealthy people. Generally speaking, he leads a quiet life and does not make himself conspicuous. He shows great respect for local customs and manners, saying quite often that he prefers his residence here to the flattering and distinguished places offered him in Europe."

At this time James Monroe was president. He was a Democrat who for several years had represented the United States in France, a country that he esteemed for its republican slogans. His daughter had been a pupil, along with Hortense de Beauharnais, of the celebrated Madame Campan; he spoke fluent French and maintained cordial relations with French ambassador Hyde de Neuville. His policy of neutrality toward the Old World was embodied in the famous Monroe Doctrine, which bears his name. As for Joseph

Bonaparte, the comte de Survilliers, the American government prudently ignored his presence.

On March 11, as we learn from General Charles-Tristan de Montholon, chief of the former Emperor's household, Napoleon received a letter from his brother. "In July, 1816, Prince Joseph wrote to ask the Emperor what attitude he should take toward the various offers he had received from Spanish America and also toward the Frenchmen with burgeoning hopes in France. The Emperor was stirred by these prospects."

In May, two of the four men expelled from St. Helena in October, 1816—the steward Rousseau and the groom Archambault—arrived in the United States and brought Joseph direct news of his brother. To Archambault, Joseph gave employment.

In the course of 1817, Joseph undertook to travel. In July he visited New England and in September Niagara Falls. At a certain point during the summer, he gave a large reception at Landsdowne, his residence near Philadelphia, which was enjoyed by the notables and pretty women of the city.

Joseph had a considerable number of American friends, many of them introduced to him by his wealthy banker, Stephen Girard. Girard, born in Bordeaux, had been a steward, sailor, and captain of a ship, then a grocer, dealer in spirits, and shipbuilder before turning to banking and amassing one of the greatest fortunes in the United States, which enabled him to make loans to the federal government and to give it financial support during the War of 1812.

Other friends of Joseph were the statesmen Henry Clay, Daniel Webster, John Quincy Adams, and Edward Livingston, and his neighbors, Admiral Charles Stewart, a hero of the recent war, Senator Richard Stockton, and Colonel Cadwalader. He was especially close to U.S. congressman and Pennsylvania judge, Joseph Hopkinson, to whom he left a power of attorney when he was away, eminent medical doctor Nathaniel Chapman, diplomat William Short, and historian Charles Jared Ingersoll.

Had Napoleon come to the United States, would he have made friends with the New York literary society of which he was an honorary member? On April 5, 1804, as First Consul, he wrote to the United States ambassador: "I was interested to learn, from your letter of December 24, 1803, of the New York literary group. Since it has pleased this academy to make me one of its members, kindly pass on the word that I accept with pleasure and that I appreciate the esteem in which it holds me."

In the same summer of 1817, Joseph received Francisco Javier Mina, representing the Spanish-American insurgents, who asked him to take over their leadership and to accept the throne of Mexico. This was not the first time that the insurgents had offered him this crown. Early in the year, Napoleon had read in the papers about such an offer and said to Montholon: "Joseph will surely refuse. He has the intelligence, talent, and all the other qualities with which to make a nation happy, but he cares too much for his freedom and for the pleasures of a bourgeois life to plunge again into the stormy life of royalty."

Napoleon was right, for Joseph wrote to Mina: "No better recompense could crown my public life than to see men who would not recognize my authority when I was in Madrid come to me in my exile. But with every day that I spend in this hospitable country, I am more and more convinced that a republican form of government is the one most suited to America. Keep it in Mexico, as a gift from heaven."

In August, Joseph decided to send his faithful secretary, Louis Mailliard, to his estate at Prangins to recover the precious objects that Joseph had buried there before going to join his brother in Paris during the Hundred Days. Among these objects there were diamonds, perhaps those of the crown of Spain to which the Emperor so frequently referred on St. Helena. Mailliard was the only person besides Joseph to know the hiding place. As a passionate hunter, he had picked out an area of foxholes, where dogs always lost their way.

After a shipwreck off the coast of Ireland, he arrived, finally, at Frankfurt, where the former Queen Julie was living. She, however, definitely refused to follow her husband to the United States. Mailliard went on, disguised as an English tourist, to Joseph's Swiss estate, where the administrator, Monsieur Véret, failed to recognize him until he had taken off his red wig and dropped his British accent. Two workers, engaged by an English speculator to prospect for coal and metal deposits, were set to digging up the ground. During the night following the second day, Mailliard and Véret in person extracted the case they were looking for.

Mailliard returned to America after an uneventful voyage, with the diamonds concealed in a special belt and with some important papers, such as the letters exchanged between Joseph and Napoleon.

On St. Helena, on August 15, there was a celebration of the Emperor's forty-eighth birthday. In answer to Montholon's expression of good wishes, he said: "People lull me with illusions, and that's not a good idea. The awakening is too painful. If, in the two years I've been here, I hadn't hoped for a change in my luck, I'd have made up my mind to fall into the ways of a prosperous colonist."

Meanwhile, the comte de Survilliers was taking an active interest in the improvements of Point Breeze. He added two wings to the mansion, relished the idea of creating an artificial lake, staked out the gardens, marking the trees to be cut down and the places where new ones were to be planted, set statues here and there, and observed the growth of rhododendrons, pines, and magnolias around a vast lawn.

How, we may ask, did Napoleon imagine the life of a "prosperous colonist"? Joseph, as we have seen, was leading the life to which he had aspired, when his official duties permitted, on his European estates. Napoleon, on the other hand, would probably have applied his creative talents to the domains of agriculture, industry, and science, rather than to mere landscape gardening. On October 28, 1817, he said to General Bertrand: "My great mistake was to turn to the English and to wind up on St. Helena. If I were in America, everything would go well, whereas here everything goes badly. It's all an error."

On November 11, Baron Gaspard Gourgaud, another of Napoleon's companions in exile, noted that the Emperor had received a message in code from his brother Joseph. It read as follows: "She's from July. He asks for news. High hopes. Written in △." Was this an answer to messages from Rousseau and Archambault?

1818

At the beginning of the year, through the good office of a Mr. Tilghman, Joseph sent a letter from Philadelphia to his brother. "My last letters from mother were written in October. She was in good health but still unreconciled to your being so far away. . . .

This country is good, and the people excellent. I shall say no more on this subject for fear of increasing your regret that you were unable to come to it. I am hoping that you can give me news of your health and situation."

On February 21, Las Cases, recently expelled from St. Helena, wrote from Frankfurt to Joseph: "Sire, when I was snatched from him, your august brother was doing poorly in every way." The next month General Bertrand wrote directly from St. Helena: "The Emperor has a liver disease, which in this unhealthy climate is fatal. If they keep him here, they are willing his death."

In May, the Emperor spoke to Bertrand of his intention to make investments in America, in order to prepare a refuge for his son, should the boy be forced to go into exile. Here is the purport of this curious conversation:

> I have six million francs. Call it nine, counting the accrued interest, the amount I am asking from Prince Eugène and the appeal to Madame Mère. With this sum I shall buy land in America, entrusting its administration to the three following people: You, Grand Marshal, first; Montholon second; and Las Cases third.
>
> Finally, in a special disposition, I shall name the twenty persons who are to share this revenue. The trusteeship is to last fifteen years, until 1835, after which time it is to be dissolved.
>
> Half the revenue is for the King of Rome, but only when he is twenty-five years old, that is, in 1835, when the trusteeship is over. In the meantime, interest will accumulate. When he is sixteen, he is to be told that this money in America is his, so that, in case they try to force him into the priesthood or restrict his liberty, he may know that a great fortune and independence await him in the United States.

In this same year, Joseph, too, was concerned with his American investments. In 1814, he had given Le Ray de Chaumont two hundred thousand francs to be invested in the United States, against a receipt that was among the papers he took with him when he fled to the United States himself, aboard the *Commerce*, a year later. Le Ray de Chaumont put the money into land along the Black River, near the Canadian border. In July, 1818, Joseph Bonaparte decided to visit this northern property and arranged to meet Le Ray de Chaumont on the shore of Lake Ontario. *Poul-*

son's American Daily Advertiser of August 3 reported: "On Tuesday, accompanied by his suite and by Monsieur Le Ray de Chaumont, he went through the village. For two hours he inspected the cotton mill, the mill at Goulon, the paper mill, the grounds and so on. He seemed satisfied with his first-hand view of the improvement of the terrain, brought about in less than four years."

Joseph was so impressed that he bought 630,000 francs' worth of additional land, bringing his total holdings to about 25,000 acres. At the center, there was a big 1000-acre lake, soon known as Lake Bonaparte, with steep banks and a multitude of wooded islands. In its icy, transparent waters was an abundance of fish. There was game of all kinds in the environs, and Joseph undertook to build roads and a lodge and to organize hunting parties.

Judging by Joseph's holdings in Europe, his properties in America, his household and other expenses, his biographer Gabriel Girod de l'Ain calculates that Joseph had "if not the twenty million francs ascribed to him by his brother Napoleon, at least half this amount, the equivalent of thirty millions [six million dollars] today, without counting his books, paintings, and memorabilia."

During the year 1818, there was considerable correspondence among the members of the Bonaparte family. From Baden-Baden, Las Cases wrote to Joseph on August 16: "The Emperor thought that numerous Frenchmen, separately or together, would employ their talents in combatting the calumnies of our enemies about the splendid cause whose triumph we so long ensured." On June 23, his mother wrote to Napoleon: "From time to time we have news of Joseph. He is doing well." And on July 10, Joseph wrote to his uncle, Cardinal Fesch: "I have heard from Monsieur Las Cases [to whom Joseph sent money], but not from the Emperor. I wrote to Mother about this a month ago. From what I have written to her, you'll be informed of my decision to send for my family. It's impossible to live alone in a country where men seek happiness within the family and spend the rest of their time on business."

In July, Dr. O'Meara had to leave St. Helena. During a last talk, the Emperor gave him a note for Joseph, who did not receive it until the following year. The *Mémoires* of the valet Marchand tell us what Napoleon told the doctor to say to his brother: "Tell him to give you the private and confidential letters that the Emperor Alexander [I of Russia], Emperor Franz [II of Austria], the King of Prussia, and other European sovereigns addressed to me. Their publication will hold the writers up to shame, by demonstrating to the world the homage they paid me when it was a question of begging for favors and imploring me to leave them on their thrones." More than once Napoleon asked his brother to publish these letters, which he had turned over to him at the time of his second abdication. But Joseph always answered that he did not have them.

1819

The fear that Napoleon might escape from imprisonment and make his way to the United States haunted not only Sir Hudson Lowe, governor of St. Helena, but all of the former Emperor's enemies as well. At this point, the American dream, with its consecration of liberty and the immunity that it promised to all and sundry, was at one with the Napoleonic legend. François René de Chateaubriand understood this quite well. Early in January, Napoleon received an article that the great writer had published in *Le Conservateur*, saying:

> Bonaparte was born on one island and sent to die on another, at the far ends of three continents, tossed out amid the seas onto a place where Camoëns seems to have foretold him when he made it the abode of the spirit of storms. And, even now, he cannot stir upon his rock without our feeling the repercussions. A single step of the new Adamastor at the opposite pole is felt at the near one. If Napoleon were to escape from his jailers' hands and to retire to the United States, every look he might cast upon the ocean would trouble those on the other side; his presence on the Atlantic's American shore would force Europe to bivouac across the way.

Heretofore Napoleon had judged Chateaubriand adversely, but now it was plain that the writer understood the former Emperor's latest grand plan: the creation of his legend. It was after he had read Chateaubriand's article that Napoleon said: "Nature has endowed Chateaubriand with the sacred fire; to this all his works bear witness. His style is not that of Racine; it is that of a prophet. No one else could have declared with impunity before the Paris tribunal that 'the hat and the gray overcoat of Napoleon, displayed at the end of a stick on the coast of Brest, would call all Europe to arms.'"

On January 21, Dr. Stokoe, friend and successor of O'Meara, in his turn left St. Helena, "because," he said, "of the disagreeable circumstances in which he found himself." Napoleon gave him a note for Joseph, saying: "Please give Dr. Stokoe the thousand pounds sterling that I owe him. When he brings this letter, he will give you all the news of me that you could wish for. Napoleon."

Generally speaking, all the messages that Napoleon sent to his brother through the intermediary of those who, for one reason or another, left St. Helena (Rousseau, Archambault, Las Cases, O'-Meara, Stokoe) were concerned with either money matters or the Emperor's correspondence with the sovereigns of Europe. Napoleon was convinced that Joseph had no connections with the colonies that the exiled half-pay (*demi-solde*) officers had set up on the Mexican frontier or with the disquieting projects of these veterans of the Grande Armée, which we shall examine in a later chapter. Indeed, Joseph made a point of preserving the purely private character of his stay in the United States.

It was, perhaps, as a reward for Joseph's discretion that the ambassador Hyde de Neuville decided to turn over to him Gérard's portrait of Napoleon, which he had found in the Washington legation. On March 5, 1819, he wrote to Joseph Hopkinson, who had the comte de Survillier's power of attorney: "Political events shift and destroy fortunes, but they do not break the ties of blood. And so I take it upon myself to send, through you, to one of your friends, the portrait of his brother." Although Hyde de Neuville was criticized by his superior, the minister of foreign affairs, for this gesture, Louis XVIII maintained that "here is something noble and chivalrous and essentially French." Joseph had the painting cleaned and gave it to the Philadelphia Academy of Fine Arts, of which he was a member and Hopkinson president.

On St. Helena, in February, Napoleon said to General Bertrand, "If I were free I'd go to America and gather my family around me." The verb was in the conditional tense, and Las Cases says that the Emperor may have been "fantasizing" when he imagined life in America with his family. It was more realistically that he told Bertrand, in the course of the same conversation: "My family should settle in Rome. There they should marry off their children and take over the city. Perhaps some day we shall see a Bonaparte on the papal throne. This would be of considerable advantage to them. . . . And the name of Bonaparte will always be popular in Italy." In other words, Napoleon considered America as an agreeable refuge, affording total independence, but he knew that his family could never exercise an important public role there. The official attitude of the American government toward his brother confirmed this feeling.

In the month of May, the comte de Survilliers traveled, as a private citizen, first to Baltimore and then to Washington. The capital of the United States was surprising to European visitors. One such visitor, the young French diplomat, Bourquenay, wrote to his brother: "Imagine a city with a perimeter much longer than that of Paris; a river with a width a quarter that of the Seine—and known as the Tiber—a hundred or so houses in an area that could contain five hundred thousand; herds of cattle, sheep, and pigs; a fine building, half burned down, modestly called the Capitol, where the Congress holds its meetings. . . . Here is a summary picture of the capital of the United States."

Hyde de Neuville, likewise, was "surprised to find a half-built city extending over so vast an area that, in order to go from one place to another, it is necessary to cover distances where few arteries can be called streets, since the houses along them are so scarce. As for Joseph, he went from Washington to Mount Vernon, where he visited the house and grave of George Washington. Legend has it that he plucked a flower close to Washington's tomb and put it carefully into his wallet. Along the way, he happily recalled the ceremonies that his brother, as First Consul, had ordained in mourning the death of America's first president.

On September 20 Joseph wrote from Philadelphia to Dr. O'-Meara: "Sir, I have received your letter of July 31 and the note of July 26, 1818, bearing the first signature of my brother that I have seen since our separation. I took steps immediately toward the fulfillment of his wishes in Paris."

1820

On January 4, upon his return from a trip to New York, Joseph Bonaparte found his house afire. Servants, workers, and neighbors managed to save most of the furnishings, books, and objects of art, but by the end of the day the house itself was practically burned to the ground. With amazing serenity, Joseph spoke at once of building another house a little lower down. He wrote a letter to a Bordentown official—later printed in the local newspaper—expressing his gratitude to the townsmen for their efforts on his behalf.

On March 22 he wrote to his brother Lucien in Rome: "I am still well, in spite of the discomforts stemming from the accident that, in four hours, dislodged me from a house that was four years in the building. Under these circumstances the local people showed great concern."

The conflagration was supposedly the result of some carelessness in regard to a fireplace. But rumor had it that a servant in the pay of a foreign embassy had set the fire for the purpose of burning up the correspondence between Napoleon and various European sovereigns of which we have spoken above. But Joseph insisted, in answer to his brother's demand that he publish this correspondence, that it was not in his possession. So he said, quite clearly, in a letter of May 10, 1820, to Dr. O'Meara:

> Sir, I have received the letter that you kindly wrote me on March 1. I must ask you to deliver the two enclosures, one for the Emperor and the other for Madame de Montholon. I am sorry for the delay in the payment of her due, and I am writing to her in this connection, as well as to the Emperor.
>
> I did not receive, at Rochefort, the letters of which you speak and which the comte de Las Cases mentioned to my wife. Indeed, I am writing to ask by whom and to whom these letters were handed over. In the fire that burned down my house on January 4, I lost a great many papers. The letters of which you speak might have been lost in this way, but fortunately they had never been handed over to me.

Joseph's mind was taken up with the building of a new house in the Italian style, destined to be one of the biggest and most beautiful in the United States, by his trips to inspect the property near the Canadian border, and by his calls upon charming American ladies who, from time to time, received a sonnet written by the former King of Spain. Thus, one August day, he wrote to his friend Livingston: "Today I expect to pay a visit to Madame

Louis; tomorrow I hope to find you at your house and to go with you to see Madame Henri. . . . After which I shall continue on my way to Black River."

1821

In March, news reached St. Helena of forthcoming changes in the English government, with Lord Holland slated to be prime minister. Napoleon, who was to die only two months later, had fresh hopes of leaving the hated island. The possibility of being allowed to go to America crossed his mind. At other times, says General Bertrand, he imagined that "the English wouldn't want to do without him; they'd confine him to a beautiful park in England." And "if the Emperor of Austria were to write and offer him asylum in his states, as the Empress had hinted, he would go, quite confidently, to Trieste, in order to regain his wife and son." If the choice had been up to him, he would have opted for America: "I'd be happy in America. First I'd mend my health, then I'd spend six months traveling throughout the country; to cover a thousand miles would take quite some time."

"The Emperor's busy all day long," notes Bertrand. "He's in good spirits and hopes to leave this unhappy place at last." Napoleon was reading La Rochefoucauld's *Voyage dans les Etats-Unis d'Amérique*: "He hasn't learned much from it. What he needs is a more recent account, because the country changes very fast. To cover a thousand miles of it would be a pleasure." At the same time, he was reading the Abbé de Pradt's book on the American colonies[9] and daydreaming of how he would set up his life with Joseph.

> Upon arrival at New York, I'd send a messenger to my brother. I'd get the British consul to come aboard, asking him to keep the whole thing under his hat. A few hours later, Joseph would turn up, and we'd disembark.
> We'd make use of Joseph's staff. It seems that his house is on a river, near Trenton, twenty miles from Philadelphia and forty from New York. Soon many French families would cluster about me.

On March 13, Napoleon learned from the newspapers that there was no change in the government in London and that the election in France had gone against the Liberals. "We were building castles in the air," he said to his aides the next day. On the following days, in the course of his morning and evening walks, he was "weak and downcast," Bertrand tells us, and said nothing about the latest news to his faithful companions. On March 27, Napoleon had a presentiment of death and could no longer imagine any future happiness, even in America: "If now I could end my career, it would be a happy thing. At times I've wished to die, and I'm not afraid. I should be happy to die within a fortnight. What can I hope for? Perhaps an end even more unhappy. . . . If I were in America I might still vegetate. Actually, I don't want to die, I don't long for death, but, as of today, I attach little worth to life."

On April 24, ten days before his death, Napoleon spoke to General Bertrand, who was at his bedside, about his brother Joseph and about what his own family could hope for from America. He reiterated the necessity of publishing his correspondence with the European rulers: "It's a document, a monument for history. If Joseph has it, he should get it printed in America; if it's in the Archives, then it must be got hold of, somehow." His opinion of the place that his own family, particularly his son, might obtain in America was clearsighted: there was no future for the Bonapartes in the United States. He said to Bertrand that if his son were forced to leave Austria,

> Switzerland would seem to be the country where he might the most advantageously settle. He should inscribe himself in the register of the oligarchy of Bern; there he'd be better off than in America. It's somewhat of a shock to change climate and hemisphere. . . . Joseph, of course, might choose to stay in America, to set up his daughters there, marry them off to Washingtons and Jeffersons and have presidents of the United States for his kin. But his own dear ones could not live with dignity except in a theocracy like that of Rome or in a republic with a solid tradition and independence, like Switzerland.

Meanwhile, Joseph continued to lead the life of a perfect country gentleman. His superbly furnished house, with its thirty-two windows, was, with Mount Vernon, one of the handsomest in the United States. Every morning at seven o'clock, he roused himself in his second-floor apartments, which were made up of a bedroom, with magnificent mahogany furniture, bath, living room, library, and study. After a light breakfast, he read in the library, or reluctantly dictated his memoirs. In this task he was easily discouraged. "What's the use, after all? Whatever I may say has already been written." Guests and the staff occupied the third floor. Between ten and eleven o'clock host and guests met for lunch in the dining room, at a table large enough for twenty-four people. There they could admire two fine consoles saved from Egypt and enormous candelabras.

Between lunch and dinner, which was served between six and seven in the evening, there was no lack of distractions—long conversations on historical subjects with Napoleon's brother, reading in the fine library, hunting, fishing, horseback and carriage rides in the neighborhood. Guests enjoyed following the road around the artificial lake, peopled with swans and other aquatic birds. Joseph had imported pheasants, doves, hares, and rabbits from Europe and he promised a reward to anyone bringing him "any animal of this sort found outside his property."

Sometimes a group went in a rowboat to the far end of the lake, there to lunch near a summerhouse surrounded by tulip beds. After dinner they drove about in a carriage or listened to Prince Joseph's stories in the second-floor library, whence there was a fine view over the gardens. Often the evening wound up in the billiard room, one of the most attractive parts of the house, with its green-bordered white muslin curtains, mahogany furniture, and splendid paintings—including David's *Bonaparte au mont Saint-Bernard*, now at Malmaison, Rubens' *Two Lions and a Pheasant*, and Vernet's *Les Cascades de Tivoli*.

On Sunday, the comte de Survilliers held an open house for Philadelphians, who came up the river by steamboat. After admiring the marble statuary and the furniture of the spacious entrance hall, they were further impressed by the drawing room and the *"salon des bustes."*

The drawing room curtains were made of blue merino, and the furniture was of high quality, as were the pier glasses, the Gobelin carpets, the bronzes, and the candelabras. There were two monumental fireplaces, sent by Cardinal Fesch, which contrasted with the faience stoves to which Americans were accustomed. On the walls hung seascapes by Vernet, the Neapolitan streets of Denis, and a series of family portraits: a life-size painting of Napoleon in court robes, Joseph in the robe he wore as King of Spain,

Queen Julie and their two children, all by Gérard; two portraits of the Princesses Charlotte and Zénaïde, one by David, the other by Lefèvre.

In the "*salon des bustes,*" Joseph often lingered in front of the busts of his father, of his brothers Louis and Jérôme, of the Empress Marie-Louise and Catherine of Würtemberg, of his brothers-in-law Baciocchi and Borghese. Of particular artistic value were the busts of Elisa and Pauline Bonaparte and a statuette of the King of Rome by Canova. Joseph's art collection was of enormous value. Besides the works named above, it included paintings by Murillo, Titian, Velasquez, Van Dyck, Leonardo da Vinci, Raphael, and others.

In August, while he was taking the waters at Saratoga Springs, Joseph heard of the death of Napoleon. A letter from Bertrand told him of his brother's last months:

> He sat down during most of the day and did almost no writing. With the passing of each month, his health visibly deteriorated. Once in September and again in early October, after the doctor had told him to exercise, he wanted to ride his horse, but he was so weak that he had to come back in a carriage. His stomach could no longer digest, and he grew weaker and weaker. His feet trembled with cold and could be relieved only by the application of hot towels. Unable either to walk or ride, he drove out in a carriage, but without gaining any strength. Soon he stayed all day in his dressing gown.

Bertrand spoke again of Napoleon's disappointed hope of going to America: "We'd land at a place where we'd feel at home, we'd explore that vast country . . ."

After this, Joseph received a letter from General Montholon, with more details of his brother's illness. Both these companions of Napoleon's exile continually enjoined him to publish the Emperor's correspondence with the sovereigns of Europe. But Joseph did not have it in his possession.

Here is its story. At the time of his second abdication, Napoleon ordered the duc de Bassano (minister of foreign affairs during the Hundred Days) to make copies, immediately, of these letters. Bassano was to leave the copies at Joseph's house and the originals in the files of his ministry. Joseph, in his turn, asked his wife and secretary to distribute the copies among several trunks, which were to be entrusted to various faithful friends. As soon as he heard of Napoleon's wish to have them published, he requested his wife and his secretary, both of them in Europe, to forward the trunks to him. But when he opened the trunks, the precious papers were gone, and all attempts to retrace them were in vain. Meanwhile, the originals, deposited by the duc de Bassano in the Louvre, had been stolen. O'Meara tracked them down to London and ascertained that the Russian ambassador had bought the letters written by the Czar (except for a few reacquired by Bassano, which eventually found their way to the Bonaparte family archives) for the sum of ten thousand pounds sterling.

Joseph Bonaparte lived in the United States until 1832. His last years there were devoted to family matters and to the defense of his brother's memory. In December, 1821, he wrote to his friend Joseph Hopkinson that, were it not for the villainy of his enemies,

> Napoleon would have lived in this country as healthily as myself, who am two years older and less robust than he. . . . He would have been appreciated, not only by such enlightened men as yourself and Dr. Chapman, but also by everyday citizens, noteworthy for their reasoning ability.
> He was always greater than his fortune and superior to his glory. In his natural pride, he felt that he could win the esteem of the country of Locke and Newton and of that of Washington and Franklin. Like Julius Caesar, he did not suspect his enemies of committing a crime against him, and, like Caesar, victim of the party of Sulla, he was a victim of the European oligarchy.

Napoleon's brother Lucien never managed to join Joseph in the United States, although Jérôme Bonaparte, whose first wife was Elizabeth Patterson of Baltimore, wrote to him after the Emperor's death: "Don't you think, my dear Lucien, that the best thing your family could do would be to go to America?"

Even if his wife and brothers and sisters stayed in Europe, Joseph had the pleasure of welcoming his two daughters, one of his sons-in-law, and his nephews Achille and Lucien Murat, children of his sister Caroline, to his house in the New World. There he had years of happiness, surrounded by his children and grandchildren, as well as by his mistresses and illegitimate offspring. Two events cast shadows over this happy domestic scene: the death of a baby, born on the spot to his daughter Zénaïde, and that of a little girl borne to him by his mistress, Annette Savage, who was killed by the fall of a flowerpot.

CHAPTER 3

The American Refuge

"America was our true refuge, in every way."
—Las Cases, *Mémorial de Sainte-Hélène*

Since the very beginning of the Revolution, France had raised up generous-hearted idealists and greedy climbers; it had known uncompromising ideologies and flexible consciences, unconditional loyalty and despotism both intellectual and political, genuine enthusiasm and cynical opportunism.

Contradictory passions, truth and lies, victories and defeats had touched every faction. All Frenchmen had been affected, at one point or another, by overturned governments and fratricidal struggles. All, or many, had hoped; all had suffered from the collapse of a dream. Disappointment, insecurity, banishment, or proscription moved royalists, republicans, and Bonapartists alike to seek refuge outside France. They longed to leave commotion behind them and to find peace in a faraway, inaccessible, neutral place. America and, more precisely, the United States embodied a dream that Europeans had not fulfilled in Europe. They set out in search of the silence and solitude of great open spaces, the welcome of a happy and tolerant society, the security afforded by distance, and also, perhaps, the revival of a dead dream. Whatever their political sympathies, the French refugees did not envisage the United States as a place to which to immigrate permanently. They saw it as an inviolable sanctuary where they would sojourn for a limited time, a true refuge.

Only a month after the fall of the Bastille, a group of American land speculators advertised that the paradise of Jean-Jacques Rousseau lay in the virgin lands of Ohio. The political upheavals and violence shaking France offered nothing like the Eden of Rousseau's "natural man," so popular at the moment. And so Ohio became the goal of a certain number of emigrants. "We hope to arrive soon in our new territory," one of them wrote, "where we shall find things in their original state, as God made them, uncorrupted by the ungrateful hand of man." But because the promoters could not guarantee property rights, the colony was a failure. Some of the many Frenchmen who lost their dream of paradise amid the forests of Ohio founded the city of Gallipolis.

As the Terror grew, many royalist refugees made their way to the United States. Their most important colony was the "Asylum" on the Susquehanna River between Philadelphia and Baltimore. Two mansions, unusually large for the United States, were built for Louis XVI and Marie-Antoinette, in the hope that they could be spirited away from their prison. One was known as the "Big House" or "Queen's House," the other as the "Queen's Refuge."

Among the various groups of French refugees, the royalists were, obviously, the least sensitive to American democracy and the American dream. Rousseau's "natural man" had no counterpart in American society, which, far from embodying the virtues of a regenerated humanity, was patterned, pragmatically, on an English model. The most famous member of this group, Talleyrand, remarked: "The American's ways make him an Englishman, attached to England with bonds that no declaration or recognition of independence can sever." The royalist refugees taxed the United States with a lack of social graces, wit, distinction, luxuries—in short, refinement. As Talleyrand further wrote: "I admit that our luxuries often betray short-sightedness and frivolity, but their lack, in America, shows that no delicacy in either the conduct of life or its lighter side has penetrated American manners."

On Saturdays, in order to revive the pleasure of conversation as they had known them in Europe, the émigrés left their isolated farms and drove as far as sixty miles for a weekend of talk before hurrying home on Monday morning. Except for Jefferson, Hamilton, and a few others, prominent Americans ignored the French presence. In Philadelphia, the comte de Talon, the vicomte de Noailles, the duc de La Rochefoucauld, the comte de Rochambeau, and the duc d'Orléans (the future King Louis-Philippe) met in the bookshop kept by Moreau de Saint-Méry. Anthelme Brillat-Savarin played the violin in a theater, taught the French colony the art of making fancy desserts, and took down some American recipes that he later incorporated in *La Physiologie du goût*. Many aristocrats became dancing and fencing masters. According to Chateaubriand, even an Iroquois tribe had a French master of the dance! The marquise de La-Tour-du-Pin got up early in the morning to take care of her farm and to conduct her business affairs in a highly practical fashion, which she recognized as American. "Steamboats were not yet invented," she later wrote "although steam power was in use in various factories. We had a steam-driven spit [steam jack], which we used to cook our Sunday roast beef or big white and dark turkeys, of a breed superior to that of Europe."

Later on, during the reign of Napoleon, two famous exiles—General Moreau and Hyde de Neuville, future ambassador to Washington of Louis XVIII—arrived in the United States. Both were accused (Hyde de Neuville unjustly) of having taken part in the plot to overthrow Bonaparte organized by General Pichegru and Georges Cadoudal, a *chouan* or royalist insurgent from Brittany. Hyde de Neuville, who had an English father, was an idol of the royalists. Chateaubriand made him the executor of his will, and Lamartine portrayed him as follows: "His stature, noble bearing, and martial air, the dangers he incurred for the monarchy, and the subsequent persecution and exile, all these things gave him prestige among the royalists and, indeed, made Hyde de Neuville a sort of royal tribune."

As a very young man, at the Opéra, he tore the hat from the head of Ducos, a deputy to the Convention, who alone had not taken it off in the presence of the queen. During the trial of Louis XVI, he proposed a plan to spirit the king away, which the king turned down. Under the Directory, several royalist prisoners, thanks to him, won their liberty. Napoleon held two conversations with him in the hope of rallying him to his regime. Hyde, for his part, tried to persuade the First Consul to restore Louis XVIII to the throne. When he fell under suspicion and a price was put on his head, he hid until the Emperor allowed him to go into exile in the United States in 1807. Before his final departure he went there for a visit. Because of either his English antecedents or the admiration for British institutions cherished by the French royalists of the time, he praised the Americans' respect for law and the Constitution, a merit that they inherited from their Anglo-Saxon forebears. Although he decried Americans' excessive attachment to money, his observations were, in general, more clearsighted, objective, and kindly than those of most other royalist émigrés: "When we see America from close by, we feel that something new is astir for the future. The tyranny that weighs upon our unfortunate country is not the last word of the new century; a fresh breeze is playing over the world, the cause and at the same time the product of our revolution."

Hyde de Neuville had studied medicine and began to practice it in the New World. As "Dr. Neuville," he was elected a member of the medical society of New York and, in 1810, was the object of a public encomium. We note that it was through scientific, medical, or technical activities that French emigrants, whatever their origin, most successfully integrated themselves into American life and society.

Hyde de Neuville and his wife were close friends and neighbors of General and Madame Moreau. The two men frequently discussed their ideas and had an influence on each other. Hyde wrote to the king that Moreau had admitted to him: "I was a sincere republican, but today I realize that a monarchy is the form of government best suited to France and that only the Bourbons are suited to the role of monarch." And Hyde added: "The general made me more liberal than I should have been without him, and for my part I dispelled much of his prejudice against the Bourbons."

Among his various occupations in the United States, Hyde de Neuville set up a school for the children of the numerous penniless refugees from the black revolution in Santo Domingo (Haiti). On his farm between New York and Philadelphia, he raised merino sheep and entertained his many friends. He encouraged General Moreau to rally the French army to the support of the Bourbon monarchy. "You will play the intermediary between liberty and the throne, you will tell France and its armies that there is a rapid way to conciliate peace, glory, and true freedom." Moreau went off to join the forces of the Czar of Russia and to take part in a battle against his former rival, Bonaparte, in which he met his death.

The first fall of the Empire and its spectacular temporary return aroused brief hope and equally brief disappointment in the Bonapartist and royalist camps. Both the "Right" and the "Left" were exasperated and led into extremist positions. After his return from Elba, Napoleon detected, with dismay, the paradoxical nature of his popularity; people were not so much "for" him as they were "against" the Bourbons, the Church, and the nobility. One of the essential reasons for his second abdication was his refusal to wear a "red cap" and to take up a vaguely revolutionary stance in harmony with the shift to the left of the Bonapartists. The socialistic character of their opposition to the Bourbon government was inspired, in part, by the poverty of the proletariat, which the industrial revolution was bringing to light.

The "Eagle's flight"—that is, Napoleon's escape from Elba—and the Hundred Days had made the monarchist party aware of its weakness. The royalists who came into definitive power in 1815 had a violently defensive reaction and installed the "White Terror" and its train of banishments. Louis XVIII arrived in Paris, after Waterloo, on July 8; and on July 24 there appeared an ordinance of proscription, decreeing "the punishment of an unconscionable act of treason, to be effected in various degrees and upon a limited number of guilty persons, in order to combine the welfare of our people, the dignity of our crown, and the tranquillity of Europe with what is due to justice and to the security of all other citizens."

There were three lists of those guilty of treason, that is, of rallying to Napoleon in the course of the Hundred Days. The first list set forth the names of twelve generals and other officers who had betrayed the king before March 23, the date when the army had been disbanded, or who had borne arms against the monarchy. These men were to be tried before a court-martial. In the second list, there were thirty-eight persons who were enjoined to leave Paris within three days and to confine themselves to localities in the interior of the country designated by the minister of police. Here they would remain, under surveillance, until the Chambers decided whether they were to be tried in court or banished. Finally, there was an "administrative purge," making exclusions from the French Institute and the Academy, which, actually, was never applied.

Many of those cited in the July 24 edict were to meet up with one another in the United States, whether they were banished by the Chambers or had escaped thanks to the complicity of Fouché, now minister of the King's Police, or of Marshal MacDonald, who had replaced Marshal Devout as minister of war and had secretly warned them that it was urgent to get away. They were given a year in which to sell all their property and belongings and were authorized to export the proceeds and meanwhile to draw on any interest deriving from them until full payment had been effected.

A new edict, of January 12, 1816, announced another series of banishments inflicted upon the surviving deputies to the National Convention—the "regicides" guilty of having voted for the execution of Louis XVI—who had also signed Napoleon's Additional Act to his constitution or had taken high official positions during the Hundred Days. Many of them went to America.

Alongside the banished and the escapees, there was another category of emigrants, drawn from the legendary *demi-soldes* or half-pay officers, frustrated remnants of the Napoleonic armies. To them, Napoleon had been an infallible and invincible hero. As Talleyrand said to Hyde de Neuville about the First Consul: "He's a man who holds himself to be in control of his destiny, and his amazing self-confidence inspires his followers with a feeling of total security." Napoleon's downfall subjected them not only to political constraints and harassments, but also to psychological upheaval. Let us look at this category more closely. After the end of the Hundred Days, Louis XVIII's government excluded some 20,000 officers from the new royal army. First they were reduced to the pay of officers on six months' leave; then they were put on half-pay, which they were to collect, month by month, at the capital city not of a *département* but of one of its component units, the *arrondissement*. In order to prevent them from gathering together and pursuing any subversive activity, they had been sent back to their native towns whence, however, they could be called on short notice and even for only a few hours, to active duty. A *demi-solde*, however provisory his status, was still under the jurisdiction of the military and could not marry without his superiors' permission. Actually, numerous marriage permits were granted because, when the *demi-solde* married, he made closer contact with the civilian world from which he had so long been separated and was less tempted by the idea of subverting the army. In the beginning, he was not allowed to exercise a civilian profession, but there were many exceptions to this rule. In 1817 there were 15,639 such officers, in 1823 only 5,404.

At this time, France was a largely agricultural country and most of the officers of lower rank were of rural origin, many of them sons of well-to-do peasants, so that they quickly re-adapted themselves to the farms where they had grown up. This was the origin of the legend of the "soldier-farm worker." Jean Vidalenc, in his study of the *demi-soldes* as a social class, turns up the note of an examining commission on a certain lieutenant from near Pau: "He was taken from the plow; let him go back to his original station!"

Officers of high rank were often landowners and were allowed to return to their properties, because the supervision of agricultural production was not considered a profession. At the beginning of the Restoration, the countryside favored the monarchy; the Napoleonic wars and the enemy occupation had taken farmers' and peasants' sons and diminished the productivity of their land. Many of the *demi-soldes*, then, were happy to go back home and transferred their loyalty to the king. Members of a minority group, whose parents had belonged to local assemblies during the Revolution and had bought bonds issued by the republican government, were submitted to strict surveillance by the police and the local authorities.

In conclusion, out of approximately 20,000 *demi-solde* officers, there were some 10,000 peasants who returned to the land, 5,000 with miscellaneous occupations—a few industrialists, traveling salesmen, and shopkeepers whose wives had kept their businesses open—and 5,000 who had actively supported Napoleon during the Hundred Days. Out of the total number, no more than 1,000 could be called stubborn opponents of the monarchy. These last contributed to the legendary picture of the *demi-solde* as a hero incapable of adjusting himself to a life without glory and a hostile society. General Foy posed the rhetorical questions: "Which of us has not seen men formerly ennobled by a command post but now driven by hunger to the most menial type of work? Do we not meet every day men whose noble delicacy causes them to hide under their worn clothes a decoration reddened by their blood?"

The epic in which they had played a part had marked them to

the point where they could no longer conceive of a quiet, everyday existence. They were reluctant to abandon the military careers that had shaped them and often improved their social condition. Naturally enough, they were attracted by the revolutionaries of Latin America, who were searching for military instructors, or by the prospect of serving as mercenaries in Egypt and the Near East. Some led an idle, miserable life involved in gambling or in fruitless subversive plans excogitated by fellow veterans of the Napoleonic wars.

The largest and most boisterous group of *demi-soldes* was in Paris, and Balzac has portrayed the type in the pitiful and unattractive Colonel Bridau. The typical *demi-solde* lived in the Marais, where rents were low, and wandered from café to café, with military regularity, occupying the same seat in the same café at the same hour every day. He was immediately recognizable by his dress, a long blue frock coat buttoned up to the chin, a tie wound around a high collar, a broad-brimmed top hat cocked over one ear, and a malacca cane. His manner was aggressive, and a mere civilian was afraid to sit beside him. He frequented the cafés around the Place du Palais-Royal, the Univers and the Lemblin, where in 1815 there took place the brawls described by Véron in his *Mémoires d'un bourgeois de Paris*. Just after the Battle of Waterloo, the Lemblin was invaded by officers of Napoleon's army, "their helmets and shakos studded with bullet holes." When four Allied officers sat down at a table, the shout of *"Vive l'Empéreur!"* caused the windowpanes to rattle, and the foreigners fled by a side door. A short time later, the café owners placed a bust of Louis XVIII over the bar. The next day three hundred *demi-soldes* turned up to protest, and the bust was taken down.

These officers felt that they were rejected because of their republican ideas; they were guilty of having fought with a republican emperor against a legitimate king. At this point, the American dream supplemented the lost Napoleonic adventure. The desire to overturn the king harked back to the American Constitution and to that of the Year III of the French Revolution. Countering the restoration of the monarchy, laden with the weight of its thousand-year history, there was the new American republic, serene and inviolable.

From St. Helena, Napoleon clearsightedly analyzed the feelings of those who, after his fall, were impelled to immigrate to the United States. "There they have nothing to be ashamed of," he said to General Bertrand. "In the United States, they find a republic that was at peace with France at the time of the Revolution and the Directory."

In these early years of the nineteenth century, everyone, whether on the Right or the Left, was downcast by the loss of hope in universal happiness that had been so widespread in the century before. The Terror, military dictatorship, and interminable wars had favored the growth of conservative ideas: the theocracy of Joseph de Maistre, the "legitimism" of Talleyrand, the recall of a feudal world voiced in the romantic style of Chateaubriand and Lamartine. At the same time, the frustrations of workers, whose condition the Revolution did not have time to improve, and of soldiers returning to a world unappreciative of their useless heroism fostered the radicals' desire to overturn established society and build something else on a new basis. This trend, loosely falling under the heading of "Utopian Socialism," had for its theorists such philosophers and thinkers as Henri de Saint-Simon, Charles Fourier, and Robert Owen. America, at this juncture, called up the image of a virgin land, where civilization was not yet implanted. As René Rémond puts it, this condition "fitted the definition of the clean slate, the unconscious dream of all Utopias, where it was possible, at last, to make a fresh start."[1]

So it was that a number of officers of Napoleon's armies went to the United States, hoping to try out their theories of a collective endeavor. They were aware of the American myth but not acquainted with American reality. The first reason for their ignorance was the difficulty of communication. The Atlantic crossing was long—it took a month—and dangerous as well. Shipwrecks were frequent; that of the *Medusa*, one of the ships aboard which Napoleon might have escaped to America, which was lost off the coast of Africa in 1816, was long remembered. Before 1822, there was no scheduled transatlantic service, so that travelers embarked on the first ship available. There were few books about the United States at the beginning of the Restoration. Guillaume Thomas Raynal's *Histoire philosophique et politique des établissements et du commerce des Européens dans les deux Indes* (1770) confirmed Frenchmen's idea that America was the land of the noble savage and the honest and philanthropic Quaker. The most widely read writer on this subject was François René de Chateaubriand, who had little to teach about American society. Notions of the new continent's geography were based mostly on fantasy, the existence of an American literature was unsuspected, and the nation's brief history was not taught in the schools. The strongest link between the United States and French popular opinion was Benjamin Franklin's *Poor Richard's Almanack*, much read during the Restoration under the title of *La Science du bonhomme Richard*, consisting of a succession of moral and didactic principles that glorified the plain virtues and frugality of those who work the land. Tolerance, philanthropy, and bucolic peace of mind—the blessings of an agrarian society possessed of a certain archaic charm.

On pictures or medallions of George Washington, he was called "the modern Cincinnatus." This typified the image of the United States in France. And in the soldier-farmer of ancient Rome, an officer of Napoleon's Grande Armée saw a forerunner whose example he might follow.

A French emigrant could not leave his country without a passport in good order, and he was surprised when, upon his entry to the United States, he had to show no papers. His luggage was inspected, but there was no duty to pay on his clothing, books, furniture, or the tools of his trade. At once he drew in a breath of fresh air. The attitude of the American government remained the same as that which it had taken toward Napoleon's brother. As John Quincy Adams put it in 1818: no encouragement to would-be immigrants, no rejection of any who came, no special favors, and no discrimination.

And what help could a Bonapartist exile hope to find? Who would welcome him to America? First of all, Joseph Bonaparte. The poet Fitz-Greene Halleck was present at a restaurant dinner given in honor of a newly arrived exile at which the comte de Survilliers, Regnault de Saint-Jean d'Angély, Marshal Grouchy, and three generals—Vandamme, Lallemand and Lefebvre-Desnouettes—were present. Conversation was lively, and Napoleon's brother spoke eloquently of the past: "When I was king of Spain. . . . In the time of my prosperity. . . ." The guests became gayer and gayer, to the point where the startled Halleck saw Joseph Bonaparte blow into a paper trumpet, Grouchy sing songs with the other guests joining in on the chorus, Lallemand creep on all fours with a child on his back, and another general imitate a stuttering French soldier at the Battle of Waterloo. Joseph, it seems, gave many exiles financial aid, although not always as much as they had hoped for.

Many an army officer was helped by Masonic lodges. In 1816, a reception was held at the Philadelphia lodge in honor of General Clauzel, at which Grouchy, Lefebvre-Desnouettes, Regnault and his son, and some eighty other persons were guests. A toast was drunk to "the French citizens of Philadelphia, model members of a model community." In many people's minds, there was a definite relationship between Masonic ideals and American institutions. La Fayette, the accredited interpreter of the American mentality, cherished the idea of a transatlantic Masonic comradeship, and both Washington and Franklin were Masons. The two national Masonic organizations had few contacts, but their ideology and philanthropic practices made for an affinity between them. The combination of Masonic and American ideals was to be the basis of the electoral propaganda of the French Liberal party, of which La Fayette was the leader. And the adventures of Bonapartist officers in the United States illustrated, as we shall see, this Liberal legend.

Napoleon, unlike other members of his family—Joseph included —never belonged to a Masonic lodge. To Dr. O'Meara he said, in November, 1816, on the subject of Freemasons: "A set of imbeciles who meet to make good cheer and perform some ridiculous fooleries. They do some good actions. They assisted in the revolution and latterly to diminish the power of the pope and the influence of the clergy. When the sentiments of the people are against the government, every society has a tendency to do it mischief."

Masonry, to Napoleon, was only one of many elements in the world's political machinery, whereas *he* had been a darling of the gods from the start. But the dreams of his officers in exile were beginning to detach themselves from his.

When the exiles reached the United States, they quite naturally sought out the company of the Frenchmen already established there. From the beginning, French-speaking Louisiana was the state of their choice. According to Montulé, it numbered 40,000 French inhabitants. After crossing miles of fields of corn and sugarcane, the traveler caught sight of the entrance of New Orleans, which had a fort to defend it.

> We arrive [says Montulé] at a fine square planted with still young trees, which leave three sides of it visible; the fourth side gives onto the river. Opposite it the Church, with several fine houses, is a pleasant sight. The streets are straight, uniformly wide, and intersect one another at right angles. They have sidewalks and two gutters to draw off water, but they are not paved. Because this whole part of Louisiana is frequently flooded, there is little stone. . . . Along its course through the city, the river is bordered by a wooden pier, stacked up with goods and frequented by Frenchmen, Britons, Americans, and Indians, all of whom rarely get along together.

At this time, New Orleans numbered some 20,000 people, largely French-speaking and happy-go-lucky, although their southern vivacity often expressed itself in duels. The exiles had to adapt themselves to heat, humidity, and waters infested with alligators. Alongside the Frenchmen, there were a few Spaniards and many Americans. Black slaves worked the plantations, where the crops were sugar, indigo, corn, rice, cotton, wheat, and tobacco.

On the whole, the people of New Orleans gave the former officers of Napoleon a warm welcome. The exiles from Haiti demonstrated a fellow feeling for the exiles from France, and the local newspapers—*La Gazette, Le Courrier de la Louisiane,* and *L'Ami des lois*—were still sympathetic to the Bonapartist cause.

Among the new arrivals' friends in the North, there were two Frenchmen of note: Dupont de Nemours and Stephen Girard. Pierre Samuel Dupont, former representative of the Third Estate from the bailiwick of Nemours to the Estates General, was one of the most distinguished economists of his time. His career began when, as a pupil of Quesnay, doctor to Madame de Pompadour, he won this lady's favor ("She had a weakness for me," he later admitted). The king of Poland, Stanislas Poniatowski, made him his nephew's tutor. When his friend Turgot became inspector general of finances, Dupont left Warsaw in order to serve him. Then, when Turgot fell into disgrace, Dupont was exiled: his idea of economic freedom was displeasing. But, recalled not long after by Vergennes, he was responsible for part of the text of the treaty of 1783, which recognized the independence of the United States of America. During the early years of the Revolution, he cut a brilliant figure at the meetings of the Estates General but was rightly suspected of conservative views. On August 10, accompanied by his son, he went with a gun to the Tuileries to defend the king and escort him to the Assembly. Louis XVI caught sight of him and called out, "Monsieur Dupont, you're always there when you're needed!"

The tyranny of the mob and the bloody rage of the Terror left him indignant. "There must be an end to this chaotic horror and anarchy," he said. Robespierre had him jailed. Delivered by the coup d'état of 9 Thermidor, he was elected a deputy to the Council of Ancients. There he openly criticized the new regime. On 18 Fructidor of the Year V (1797), the Directory struck down the right-wing opposition. Just as he was about to be deported, Dupont exiled himself to the United States. He was not to see France again until 1814, after Napoleon's first abdication. When he learned of the Emperor's return, he went back to the United States and stayed there until his death in 1817. Musician, composer, naturalist, and reformer, Dupont first attracted notice with the publication, in 1767, of his *Physiocratie*, a word that he coined to define "the natural constitution of the form of government most advantageous to mankind."

Born a Huguenot, he believed that "a man of piety and common sense cannot be either Protestant or Catholic." He was a typical eighteenth-century *philosophe*, a deist who extolled nature, the land, and agriculture; "a natural society preceding any social contract"; and "universal education, the first and only social gain," whose function was to present man with "evidence" of the natural order. The United States, land of liberty and hope of mankind, was the ideal country of the *philosophes*. Dupont had a long-lasting relationship with Jefferson, who asked his advice on problems of education. He was elected to the Philosophical Society of Philadelphia, and Jefferson to the French Institute. Dupont had emigrated with high hopes of founding a community that would bear his name and function on the basis of his physiocratic theory, but insurmountable difficulties stood in the way. His ideas, as we shall see later on, did not fit into the American scheme; dogmatism collided with pragmatism. Franklin, who was a friend of Dupont, could boast that he had never uttered a dogmatic word, but dogmas and theories hampered many Frenchmen who tried to live out their dream in America. Dupont, who had an extraordinary capacity for work, was not discouraged and brought an observant eye to the American scene. "The distinct American trait," he wrote to Madame de Staël, "is enterprise. Almost everyone outdoes himself in taking chances." He himself became a banker, businessman, and shipbuilder, but wealth accrued to the family through his second son, Éleuthère Irénée, a pupil of Lavoisier, who took to the manufacture of gunpowder. He studied new manufacturing techniques in France and returned to America with machinery that Napoleon arranged for him to secure at a low price. A large part of the explosives used during World War I came from the factory of Dupont de Nemours, which had already attained worldwide importance.

In 1805, Dupont warned Jefferson of the possibility of a Napoleonic invasion of Florida. Years later, he interceded with Hyde de Neuville, with whom he was on good terms, on behalf of "a certain number of French refugees," complaining that "the severity practiced toward them and, above all, the obstinate refusal to listen to their grievances make it impossible for them to attend to their interests in France."

Stephen Girard, the wealthy French Protestant of Philadelphia, was impelled by his antimonarchist views to befriend the Bonapartist exiles. His niece eventually married the Napoleonic general Henri Lallemand.

As the Bonapartist exile faced up to American public opinion, *L'Abeille américaine*, the strongly Bonapartist paper published in Philadelphia by Simon Chaudron, former editor of *Le Nain jaune*, gave him advice as to "how to obtain the consideration" to which "an honorable foreigner" was entitled in the United States: "We venture to say that he need only rein in his haste to pass judgment on everything and a certain affectation in the display of gaiety and politeness. He should observe without criticizing and profit from the advantages offered by a country whose laws are more hospitable than its inhabitants, without allowing himself to complain of the latter."

Actually, Americans were well disposed toward the Bonapartists and sometimes enthusiastic about them. Their enthusiasm for the French Revolution had abated, but a majority of them belonged to Jefferson's Republican party and were thus opposed to the Bourbons and looked on the Bonapartists as victims. Their newspapers attacked the king and extolled the soldiers of Napoleon. Hyde de Neuville, for instance, was branded as a "slave of the French tyrant." And a Philadelphia paper informed its readers of the arrival of two generals of the Grande Armée in the following terms:

> We learn with pleasure that Generals Clauzel and Desnouettes have been warmly received in Washington, that they have been introduced to the President of the United States, that they have dined with the Secretary of War and that most of the enlightened and liberal residents of the city have called on them. We cannot believe that the French government will prolong the exile of men who are a credit not only to France but to the times in which we live. Until there is a general amnesty for men of their caliber, the Bourbon dynasty will appear to be a tool of the British Cabinet.

Hyde de Neuville informed Paris of the American welcome of the French refugees: "Democrats look on our rebel refugees as martyrs. Bonaparte, in spite of his despotism, remains in their eyes a man of the Revolution." And he went on to quote an American newspaper, which had called Napoleon "a man who asserted himself among the sons of democracy, who marched against the *status quo* of Europe and did not leave a single monarch by divine right on the throne."

The duc de Richelieu, French minister of foreign affairs, was further informed that "licence and delirium reign, at least in the party that claims to be friendly to France. Newspapers spew forth curses and insults directed at the august family of our kings, and refugees are welcomed by all ranks of society. Few doors are shut to them, and they are regarded not merely as unfortunate exiles but also as heroes and martyrs."

Indeed, there were noisy demonstrations of sympathy for the Napoleonic refugees. In New Orleans, in 1817, there was a play entitled *The Day of the Three Emperors, or The Eve of the Battle of Austerlitz*. Tricolor French flags were displayed, and many members of the audience had pinned a red-white-and-blue rosette to their hats. Between the acts, revolutionary songs were sung, and many of the verses were insulting to the king of France and his family.

The most serious event, the so-called "Skinner Affair," took place in Baltimore on July 4, 1816, at a banquet in celebration of Independence Day, Marshal Grouchy was hailed as a "marshal of France"—a title that was not accredited to him by the king—and Skinner, postmaster of Baltimore, proposed a toast, which provoked a diplomatic incident, to "the exiled generals of France and the glory of their native land—they should not be dishonored by the denunciations of an imbecile tyrant!"

Hyde de Neuville, understandably outraged, demanded that President Monroe remove Skinner from his post. Monroe replied that he was not responsible for the private opinions of government employees and that, since the French ambassador had lived so long in the United States, he must be familiar with its climate of free speech. At this point the French consul in Baltimore was recalled. In order to achieve reconciliation, Monroe recalled the American consul at Bordeaux, William Lee, whom Hyde accused of having mentioned "patriotic exiles" in a certificate that he had issued in that city.

Although they had no authority over the Bonapartist refugees, Hyde de Neuville and the French consuls in various American cities kept them under surveillance and could, by the reports they sent home about them, effect their return to grace or the extension of their banishment. The ambassador himself was generous-hearted. In November, 1815, he had opposed the banishment of the Bonaparte family. And in 1817 he wrote to the duc de Richelieu: "I treat the refugees as if they were ill. I disdain to react to what they dare say about the Bourbons, and I consider their insults to my person an honor. I have not denied my advice or services to those who have turned to me, either directly or through the intermediary of friends." Later he wrote in his *Mémoires*: "I may be allowed to say that I felt compassion for these Frenchmen, exiled as I had been before them when political vicissitudes cast me upon these shores. They were suffering on account of errors and crimes due to the ambition of a single man. Far from their families and their country, they were paying for mistakes into which they had been led by blind devotion."

His compassion did not prevent him, however, from sending to Paris stringent reports on exiles suspected of implication in the plots of Latin-American insurgents and in projects for the escape of Napoleon from St. Helena.

In spite of the support that the Bonapartist exiles found in America, life was not easy for them. Very few achieved anything like integration into American life. But perhaps it was impossible to reconcile the illusion that they had lived out during the Napoleonic epic and the American dream that they were striving to understand.

CHAPTER 4

Some Lives in Exile Outside the Agricultural Communities

Like the Roman legionaries who, after their days of military glory, set up agricultural enterprises, so most of the Bonapartist exiles in America turned into soldier-farmers. A few of them, however, do not fit into this picture. Among the faithful, three men achieved a status that places them in a category of their own: General Simon Bernard, Captain Guillaume-Tell Poussin, and Captain Pierre-Benjamin Buisson. These were the only officers whose technical or military abilities were put to use officially. The American army, obviously, did not have either the size or the training of the long-established armies of Europe. For one thing, the fear of military intrusion into political and administrative affairs had led to a defense system based on a militia rather than on professional armed forces. Many French officers, aware of their superior training, imagined that they would be promptly incorporated into the American army; but the notoriety of their past conquests and the insistence of their demands provoked mistrust, and the offer of their services was rejected.

However, the War of 1812 made Americans aware of the need for an efficient system of coastal defenses. The services of a skilled engineer from the army of Napoleon would be of obvious value. The choice fell upon General Simon Bernard, not only because of his technical and professional competence but also because of the modesty and tact with which he treated American staff officers of a rank superior to his own. He was compared to Vauban and entrusted with the task of building Fortress Monroe in Virginia.

Simon Bernard, son of an uneducated laborer, was born at Dôle in the Jura region in 1779. A priest gave him free instruction when he was a child and later arranged for him to go to a religious school. Young Bernard had a pronounced aptitude for science. In 1794, in order to enter the Central School for Public Works (now the École Polytechnique), he went on foot to Paris, where he lived a life of hardships. Two years later, he was a student-officer at the Army School of Applied Engineering at Metz—the beginning of a military career.

Bernard's first contact with Napoleon was stormy. The Emperor had looked for "a trained, able, and judicious young man to conduct a reconnaissance operation in regard to Vienna." But when Bernard, in presenting his report, went on to set forth a tactical plan for reaching the Austrian capital, Napoleon had a violent reaction: "What's that? A shavetail presuming to draw a campaign plan!" To the amazement of all those present, the twenty-six-year-old Bernard saluted and turned on his heels. But Napoleon appreciated his flair. "A young fellow of talent; I don't want to expose him to danger. . . . I may make use of him later on."

Assigned to the office of fortification projects, Bernard was invited, quite exceptionally, to voice his opinions at a meeting of the Council of State. In 1813, he was promoted to the rank of colonel and named aide-de-camp to the Emperor. He had already been twice wounded in the field and suffered a broken leg due to a fall from horseback. In 1814, Napoleon promoted him to the rank of brigadier general and gave him the title of Baron of the Empire. During the Hundred Days, Bernard followed his leader as his aide-de-camp and did not leave his side until Rochefort, where he proposed, unsuccessfully, to share Napoleon's exile.

The government of Louis XVIII enjoined him, discreetly, to retire to Dôle. Because the monarchy hoped eventually to utilize his talents, he was not sentenced to any punishment. It was of his own free will that, in 1818, at thirty-six years of age, he set out, armed with a letter from La Fayette, to the United States, where he arrived in the month of September. Two months later, he was named brigadier general in the Engineering Corps of the United States Army. Secretary of State James Monroe communicated this decision to Major General Andrew Jackson in the following terms:

> On the subject of fortifications, or works, for the defense of the coast and frontiers, an arrangement has lately been made by the President with which I wish you to be well acquainted. You

> have, I presume, been apprized that General Bernard of the French corps of engineers, under the recommendation of General La Fayette and many others of great distinction in France had offered his services to the United States. . . . We shall have four of our officers in every consultation against our foreigner, so that if the opinion of the latter becomes of any essential use it must be by his convincing his colleagues, where they differ, that he has reason on his side. . . . I have seen General Bernard, and find him a modest, unassuming man who preferred our country, in the present state of France, to any in Europe, in some of which he was offered employment and in any of which he might probably have found it. . . . He understands that he is never to have the command of the corps, but will always rank second in it.

And so General Bernard was given the task of inspecting fortifications and choosing the places where new ones should be built.

Soon he had as his assistant another voluntary exile, Guillaume-Tell Poussin, who had worked under the architects Charles Percier and J.-F. Fontaine and arrived in the United States with a letter of recommendation from the financier Jacques Laffitte to Stephen Girard. His first months were difficult, but in March, 1817, the Topographical Engineer Corps took him on with the rank of captain. Soon he became aide-de-camp to Simon Bernard, a post that he held until the latter went back to France in 1830. In 1827, he was made a major and an adjunct member of the Public Works Commission.

General Bernard's accomplishments in the United States were quite remarkable. To this day, the Atlantic Fleet has maintained the bases that figured in his strategic plan: Boston in the north, Hampton Roads in the south, and Narragansett Bay in a supplementary function. His masterpiece is Fortress Monroe, the magnificent military installation, familiar to Virginians, at the entrance to Chesapeake Bay, for which he drew up the plans. Its strategic location and the impregnability of its ten-foot-thick walls gave this fort, where Lincoln for a time made his headquarters, an important role in the Civil War. The immense heptagon, covering an area of some twelve square miles, with four sides looking out on the ocean and three on the shore, soon won the name of "the Gibraltar of Chesapeake Bay."

Bernard and Poussin more than once risked their lives in a

survey undertaken in order to open up a road between Washington and New Orleans. They made their way four times through wild and dangerous country from the one city to the other. A report delivered later to the Société de Géographie told how the two Frenchmen explored the wilderness, traversing ravines and crossing rivers "on improvised rafts or on crossed tree-trunks." Their object was to choose, among several possible itineraries, the one most advantageous from a military, political, and commercial point of view. The adventure lasted for fifteen months. Kentucky, Tennessee, Alabama, and Mississippi were, at this time, only partially settled by whites, and travelers could expect at any minute to run into Cherokees, Creeks, Seminoles, or other Indians. These were, for the most part, friendly; when Bernard fell ill, they treated him with herbs and with invocations delivered by their sachems to the Great Spirit. River navigation was often "aboard rafts made of buffalo skins, stretched and attached to crossed poles, with Indian oarsmen." The two French soldiers made use of a compass as they followed paths traced by the Indians through stretches of forest. General Bernard had brought along a few books and portable instruments and, when he could snatch the time, gathered material for geological and natural history studies.

Later, going by an idea originated by George Washington, he began the opening of a canal and towpath from the Potomac to the Ohio River. He left behind him the project of a whole network of canals along the coast of Florida.

In the course of one of his stays in New Orleans, he met Edouard de Montulé, who was still traveling through the United States and made note of the fact that Bernard's officially accepted services to America constituted a "political phenomenon." France and America had England as a common foe, but they had fought separately, not together. So the presence of one of Napoleon's officers in the American army was truly remarkable. Bernard, Montulé observed, was attached to the Emperor "by a kind of charm that knows no reason and that did, indeed, fascinate a large number of Frenchmen." Many other exiles had felt this same charm, but Bernard was set apart by the official position that he had acquired.

During a trip to New Jersey as a delegate of the federal government's Public Works Commission, Bernard passed the entrance to Joseph Bonaparte's estate at Point Breeze. The New Jersey engineer who was accompanying him asked whether he wouldn't stop to call on Napoleon's brother. At first Bernard demurred on the grounds of the delicacy imposed by his official position. But, his companion writes, "Just as we passed in front of the gate, we saw Joseph in the courtyard, getting into his carriage. At this sight, General Bernard could not resist his feelings. He entrusted his horse to our care and caught up with us an hour or two later, bringing with him an invitation to visit Point Breeze."

Bernard was enthusiastic about the United States, as we can see from a letter that he wrote to his friend, Lieutenant Colonel Huard:

> This country, my dear Huard, offers much food for thought to a man of quality, a statesman, or a philosopher. A man of quality sees that work is the only true source of domestic happiness and public wealth. Here there are none of those governmental parasites who shamelessly embrace the ideas and extravagances of anyone who will give them employment at the expense of the exploited working people. A statesman sees that public opinion is supreme, that it alone can determine the character of an administration good for both individuals and society. I say "administration" rather than "government" because here we have an administration subordinate to the individual's self-interest as determinant of his actions.

Bernard rejoiced in the fact that the founding fathers of the United States had put Europe's gothic and feudal notions behind them and had sown only "reasonable, generous, and philanthropic" ideas in a new country destined for "a great future marked by peace, happiness, and prosperity." He stands out among the Bonapartist exiles for, among other things, his dual fascination with both the Napoleonic and the American dream. He esteemed the absence of government, as set forth by Jefferson. But to Montulé, he spoke in the following terms of the man he had wanted to follow to St. Helena: "He had perhaps the best head of the century, the most highly organized mind moulded by the Creator. Nothing escaped him; he did everything by himself, thinking out his plan and reaching a decision without letting on to anyone until the moment came to carry it through."

Bernard stayed in the United States until the Revolution of 1830, by which time he had learned English well. His wife joined him and, in 1820, gave birth to a son. When he returned to France, King Louis-Philippe made him minister of war. On receiving news of Bernard's death in 1839, the U.S. Army observed thirty days of mourning.

A young Parisian, Artillery Captain Pierre-Benjamin Buisson, turned his voluntary exile into success in a somewhat similar manner. In 1812 he was at the École Polytechnique, and so he participated only in Napoleon's French campaign. The Emperor himself gave him a decoration at the Pont de Montreau. The Restoration left Buisson his army rank, but the boredom of garrison life and his Bonapartist yearnings made him decide to emigrate. He had relatives in New Orleans, where he arrived on Christmas Eve of 1817, eventually married one of his cousins, and died at a ripe old age. The city employed him as an architect and engineer, and he laid out and constructed many of its streets and buildings. In today's New Orleans, there are still streets named for Napoleon and for the battles of Marengo, Austerlitz, and Jena. City officials asked Buisson to create a corps of cannoneers and bombardiers. His recruits drilled on Sunday afternoons before a crowd that assembled on Congo Square, an open space that bore this name because in the evenings whites abandoned it to slaves who gathered there to shout and chant and to dance African dances.

At Point Breeze, Joseph Bonaparte often entertained exiles of note, such as Marshal Grouchy and General Vandamme. Both of these are listed as shareholders in an agricultural development that we shall consider in the next chapter, but they did not go there to live.

Marshal Emmanuel de Grouchy was a nobleman of the ancien régime who had fought in the army of La Fayette. In spite of his revolutionary views, the Convention put him out of the army because of his noble status; finally he was taken in again by a special decree. He protested publicly against the coup d'état of 18 Brumaire, then rallied, without too much difficulty, to the Empire. His fidelity to Moreau prevented him, for a time, from obtaining the advancement he so richly deserved, and the blame put upon him for the defeat at Waterloo darkened his last years. He was wounded nineteen times in the course of twelve major battles and sixty combats waged under his command. In the ordinance of proscription of July 24, 1815, Grouchy was on the list of those to be haled before a court-martial. He had recourse to a childhood friend, a royalist colonel whom he had saved from a death sentence after Napoleon's return from Elba. For forty days, he was hidden in the attic of a hovel. Subsequently he tried several times, in vain, to embark at Le Havre under the name of Monsieur Gauthier, a silk merchant of Lyons. Eventually a genuine merchant guessed at his identity and gave him passage on a ship leaving for Baltimore.

Upon his arrival in the United States, Grouchy received a somewhat cool and mistrustful welcome from his fellow exiles, who still held his behavior at Waterloo against him. During his stay, he wrote numerous letters to *L'Abeille américaine*, in which he maintained that he was not to blame for the defeat. He bought a house in Philadelphia, where his two sons, one of whom was a cavalry colonel, came to join him. La Fayette wrote a letter introducing Grouchy to former President Jefferson, and the marshal conceived a desire to visit Monticello. The correspondence between the two men runs as follows.[1] "I congratulate myself," Grouchy wrote to Jefferson on October 20, 1817, "on dwelling in your interesting country. How proud I am, and how thankful for the honorable hospitality which has been bestowed upon me here. If anything can lessen the bitterness with which a distant exile overwhelms me, and the state of servitude and degradation of my native land, it is to see yours happy, powerful, free and respected, and all through institutions founded upon the very same principles for the establishment of which I have so often needlessly shed my blood." And Jefferson replied on November 2, "Your name has been too well-known in the history of the times, and your merit too much acknowledged by all, not to promise me great pleasure in making your acquaintance."

Grouchy paid frequent visits to his friend Dupont de Nemours in Wilmington. On March 19, 1818, there was a tremendous explosion in the Dupont factory, which killed thirty people and injured ten. Grouchy and his two sons happened to be on the scene; they took part in the efforts to save Dupont's house, and the marshal displayed all the organizing ability of a military leader.

Grouchy's life in exile was an agreeable one. When he was not in Philadelphia, he went north to inspect the land on the Black River, not far from that of Joseph Bonaparte, which he had bought toward the end of 1818. The Grouchys made American friends, traveled, and, above all, hunted. In spite of these pleasures, Grouchy sought to obtain permission to return to France. At the beginning of 1817, he sent to Hyde de Neuville a signed declaration that "if I go back to France, it is with the firm will to live and die in the service of the government of my country." Hyde transmitted this message to the duc de Richelieu, who answered that, although for many refugees there could be no hope of return, "there is a certain distant prospect for Grouchy and Clauzel, depending on their conduct and the feelings that they express." In November of 1819, the king put an end to Grouchy's exile and restored all his rights and titles, excepting that of Marshal, which was later given back to him by Louis-Philippe.

Once upon a time, in the encampment of Boulogne set up to prepare an invasion of England, Joseph Bonaparte had commanded a regiment in the division of General Vandamme, and the two men must frequently have met during the two years of the general's exile. Dominique-René Vandamme had a violent and irascible character and hence stormy relationships with the other exiles, including Grouchy, under whose orders he had served at Waterloo. He was a brilliant soldier who had captured the plateau of Pratzen at Austerlitz and been decorated with the Grand Eagle of the Legion of Honor. When he was taken prisoner in 1813 by the Russians, he spoke up to the Czar in person: "At least I've not been reproached with the murder of my father!" He was held in Siberia until the peace of 1814. In 1815 his chateau and estates were ravaged by Cossacks, but he still had a fair amount of money. The ordinance of July 24 obliged him to make his domicile near Limoges, but on January 13, 1816, he was brusquely ordered to leave France within twenty-four hours. He went to Ghent and a year and a half later to the United States, where he landed in July, 1817, and soon rented an attractive house near Philadelphia, on the right bank of the Schuylkill River. In spite of his unsociable nature, he gave financial aid to some of his less fortunate companions in exile, who had turned to making furniture, by buying up their products at a high price and filling his house with them. He returned to Ghent in 1819, and soon after this he was authorized to return to France, where he was formally retired from the army.

The ordinance of July 24, 1815, exiled civilians as well as soldiers. Among the latter in the United States, we find the comte Regnault (also spelled Regnaud) de Saint-Jean-d'Angély. Born in 1760 to a deputy to the Convention who had voted for the death of Louis XVI, Michel Regnault had a good education and frequented the liberal partisans of La Fayette. As deputy from Saint-Jean-d'Angély, he held various administrative posts under the Directory. With the advent of the Consulate, he became a counselor of state and a member of the French Academy. The Empire made him head of a section of the Ministry of the Interior and prosecutor for the High Court. When, after Waterloo, he advised Napoleon to abdicate in favor of the King of Rome, he was minister of state to the legislative body.

Regnault landed in New York with his son, a squadron leader at Waterloo, in the autumn of 1815. He took a small house in the city where he settled down together with a lady named de Faussar and two servants. He entertained, went out, and, according to the French consul, Cazeaux, "drank grog with Americans, whose language he did not understand." Fellow exiles were shocked by his contradictory political affirmations; he spoke in one breath of his hopes for Napoleon's escape and in the next of the 12,000-franc income that he claimed to receive from Louis XVIII. Did he, we may wonder, recall to Dupont de Nemours the letter that the latter had written him in 1798, which so clearly foretells the contrast between the Napoleonic and the American dreams? At this time, Regnault was preparing to follow Bonaparte to Egypt, while Dupont, on account of his hostility to the Directory, was readying himself to leave for America and wrote to his friend as follows:

> Since we are faring one to the East and the other to the West, I can't resist telling you what I see on our respective itineraries. . . . You follow the chariot of military glory, I seek the temple of legislative wisdom. It is unlikely that our paths will cross, even if we go all the way around the world in different directions, and your success seems more assured than mine. . . . The empire of Alexander the Great will be reestablished. . . . But

while Asia once again becomes a center of power and light and America a peaceful refuge, an abode of calm and happiness, poor Europe will be lost and stripped of its resources. A hundred million men, women, and children will perish. However fair the face of the coin, my friend, it is marred by the reverse. But the die is upraised and the coin is struck.

In spite of a few disappointments, Dupont found an America that lived up to his expectations. Regnault, on the other hand, found neither peace of mind nor happiness in the New World. Montulé remarked that "Monsieur Regnault is affable and an eloquent speaker, but I suspect that, in spite of the efforts he makes to disguise his boredom, his thoughts are in France and he longs to return there." The sorrow of exile must have contributed to the upset of his mental balance, because eventually he lost his mind, after, as Montulé tells us, "having displayed his madness on the city streets [of New York] and in the many shops where he squandered money to his heart's desire."

Joseph Bonaparte made arrangements for his hospital care for two months. In times past, Joseph had courted Regnault's beautiful wife, of whom Napoleon wrote to Cambacérès: "Please call in Monsieur Regnault and inform him that his wife is behaving most unsuitably, that her boudoir is the scandal of Paris, and that she must change her ways at once, or else I shall have to bear public witness to my disapproval." The wife, probably unaware of the state of Regnault's health, wrote him, in March, 1817, a letter intercepted by the royalists in which she enjoined him to come back to Haarlem, where she was living. Forgetful of Napoleon's censure, she wrote, "There is talk in Paris of nothing but the Emperor's memoirs, printed in America. . . . He seems so great a man, so superior to anything else we have seen in history, that no one dares pronounce his name except with respect."

Regnault set sail for Antwerp on July 19, 1817. Hyde wrote to Richelieu that "some people think his madness is only a game." He went back to France in 1819 and died on the day of his arrival in Paris.

Other former deputies to the Convention or highly placed government officials were Quinette and Hentz. Nicholas-Marie Quinette was minister of the interior in 1799 and subsequently prefect of the Somme and counselor of state. In America he was entertained by Joseph Bonaparte. But America could not overcome his world-weariness and he went, in 1818, to live in Brussels. Hentz, from the Moselle region, lived in poverty in Philadelphia, where he died in 1824.

Of the exiles with no particular collective associations, Lieutenant Colonel Michel Combe was a happy example. He was one of the faithful on Elba and fought valiantly at Waterloo. In the United States, he found happiness in the person of Miss Elisa Walker, whom he married at West Point. His wife owned land near Utica, New York, which he managed until his return to France in 1830. He was a guest of Joseph Bonaparte at Point Breeze and displayed generosity toward comrades less fortunate than himself.

Madame de la Souchère-Deléry tells us that many Bonapartists who went to Louisiana had recourse to the traditional exile's trade of teaching. Cavalry Captain Porion became a riding master. Some *demi-soldes* were fencing-masters. Many were engaged as tutors to the children of rich planters, and some taught in public schools outside New Orleans. Brigadier Victor Charbonnier went in this capacity to Natchitoches. This foresighted young man, before leaving France, had his parents sign a letter authorizing him to marry. The space for the name of the bride was left blank, and nine years went by before Charbonnier filled it in.

Those who came with a small capital and a feminine companion often opened boarding schools, which supplemented those of the Jesuits and Ursulines. Colonel Cuvellier, for instance, started a school for young girls and had for a rival Monsieur de Perdreauville, who had trained pages for the court of Marie-Antoinette and later for that of Napoleon.

Sometimes an exile went into partnership with an American to teach French and English together. Others practiced the "Lancaster Method," introduced to the United States by an Englishman. Here children with two different mother tongues taught one another. In this case, young Creoles corrected the French of young Americans, and the Americans corrected the English of their French-speaking fellows. The Bonapartists left their mark on the educational system of Louisiana by their French training in the *lycées* and the École Polytechnique. The Collège d'Orléans was created on the model of a French *lycée*, and the Creoles welcomed the courses taught by exiled French *polytechniciens*. One of these, Jean-Baptiste Jeannin, advertised in the *Courrier* lessons in "all branches of pure mathematics and in geography, including the use of the globe."

Of course, many *demi-soldes* had no more than an elementary education and could not hope to enter the teaching profession. But their rough-and-ready military experience had fitted them to the exercise of trade under venturesome conditions. A huge quantity of merchandise held in storage in England during the blockade was suddenly dumped onto the piers of New Orleans. Veterans of the Grande Armée put together job lots and went off to sell them in the swamplands all the way to the Mexican border and beyond and up the Mississippi to Natchez, where rich planters were building their mansions. Many of them traded glass trinkets with the Indians for otter and muskrat skins.

The favorite meeting place of Bonapartists and other French exiles in New Orleans was the Hotel Trémoulet, where they were in obviously high spirits when they got together. "We French people are a bit vociferous," as Madame Trémoulet put it. Here the organizers of collective enterprises laid their plans, and political conspirators hatched their plots, built up their hopes, and staked out their utopias. Here, too, they wept over their dead dreams.

CHAPTER 5

Grapes and Olives in Alabama

The state of Alabama has much interesting pictorial documentation of the Napoleonic veterans who gathered there to plant grapevines and olive trees. We see soldiers of the Grande Armée cutting down trees, hauling away logs with which to build their houses, and hoeing the ground to ready it for planting, while a little group stands around talking to wives and daughters rigged out in the latest Paris styles.

Grapes and olives were products of ancient Rome, and in their minds the French soldiers associated the image of their Roman predecessors with that of George Washington, the soldier who went back to the plow and was known in France as the "American Cincinnatus." The homely virtues of ancient Rome, the century of the Enlightenment that admired them, the New World that imitated them, the myth of the soldier-farmer—all these things confusedly haunted the imaginations of the Napoleonic veterans who wanted to set up a colony or community on American soil where they could make for themselves a life and a living.

The first concern of the Frenchmen who founded such colonies was the building of a city and its legal structure. In April, 1818, *L'Abeille américaine* informed its readers of Aigleville, the second city to be built by French colonists (the first, Démopolis, having been, as we shall see, abandoned): "Aigleville is now a town of one hundred inhabitants. Carpenters, masons, blacksmiths, gunsmiths, and wheelwrights are needed. Every new arrival must bring with him a six-month stock of provisions. The town is on a bluff above the junction of two rivers. It has two wide streets which cross each other: the Rue de France and the Rue de la République."

The very names—Démopolis, Aigleville, République, France—

were nostalgic. The exiles did not want to be integrated into American life; they wanted to join forces in perpetuating memories and dreams of their own. Their lack of interest in the realities of America was doubtless one of the main reasons for the failures that dogged their attempts at colonizing.

Americans were colonizers, but their definition of the term was quite different from that of the Frenchmen. The latter had kept the psychology of a sedentary people, and their thrust did not go beyond the boundaries of the land that was conceded to them. American colonization, on the other hand, was based on notions of mobility and wide open spaces. The pioneer cleared the land, and the speculator bought and sold it; both were haunted by the immensity of the areas that lay before them, yet to be occupied. The existence of vast tracts available for preemption, of resources calling out for exploitation, made for an individualistic ideal at the same time liberal and capitalist, inspired by the liberalism of the English middle class of the eighteenth century. Individual liberty meant that every man was entitled to take advantage of the preemptive privileges offered him and to exploit them. Of course, the protection of the individual was a matter of concern to French as well as to English thinkers, but whereas the British school emphasized economic individualism in a competitive world, the French school laid stress on the individual's political rights, on social justice, and on reason. In the Frenchman's mind the organization of society held a preeminent place. The French settler-soldiers took immediate thought for the formation of a group, the establishment of a town, the organization of social relationships. The American settler was, on the contrary, a solitary pioneer, a disciple of Robinson Crusoe. Philarète Chasles quotes an explorer and settler on the bank of the Ohio River as follows:

> Often, after twenty months without seeing a human soul, with nothing but boiled barley for my daily bread, harassed by Indians and wild animals, forced to fight on foot against wild nature, I came back home in a state of exhaustion and, by the light of my reed candle dipped in beaver grease, I read this divine volume, which, with the Bible, has been my mainstay and consolation. I felt that what Robinson Crusoe had done I could do; the simplicity of his tale imparted conviction to my mind and courage to my heart. I went peacefully to sleep with my dog Friday at my

side, and, at four o'clock the next morning, after pressing this volume more precious than gold between my hands, I picked up my axe and went back to work, blessing the Lord for having given a man such power over others and such consoling strength.[1]

The pioneer and Robinson Crusoe were, indeed, kindred spirits. Robinson Crusoe, as a sailor, had crossed the sea and then fought alone against nature. The stylistic simplicity of Defoe's saga speaks to a public not given to intellectual speculation. To Jean-Jacques Rousseau, *Robinson Crusoe* is "the happiest treatise of natural education . . . the first book to be read by my Émile." Nevertheless, there is a world of differences between Rousseau and Defoe.

It would be a mistake to compare the experience of a solitary pioneer on a continent without history or any established community to that of Rousseau's "natural man," a stranger to society, living in harmony with nature. Frenchmen's identification of the American paradise, free of the Original Sin inherent in the vices of Old World society, with the paradise of Rousseau's "natural man" was the source of many misunderstandings and erroneous judgments.

In his *Discourse on the Origin of Inequality*, Rousseau describes his famous "natural man."

> Wandering in the woods without work, speech, home, war, attachments, with neither need of his fellows nor any wish to hurt them, without, perhaps, ever meeting one of their number, natural man, self-sufficient and subject to few passions, had only the feelings and intelligence of this estate. He felt only essential needs, looked only at that which was his advantage to see, and his intelligence made no more progress than his vanity. If he made a chance discovery he could not communicate it, since he did not know his own children. Art perished with the artist; there was neither education nor progress; generations multiplied uselessly each one from the same point of departure, so that centuries went by as grossly as in the beginning. The species was old, but the individual was still a child.

Rousseau meant that "perfectibility" and potential social virtues, without outside stimulus, might never develop, leaving man eternally primitive.

When Rousseau evoked the picture of a paradise existent before time, before history or knowledge, he unconsciously took up one of man's oldest dreams. The originality of his idea was the connection between "perfectibility" and social virtue, between the origin of history and the origin of sociability. With him, historical sociology was born. Biblical man lost paradise by tasting the fruit of the tree of knowledge. God cast him into time and condemned him eventually to die. Rousseau's natural man lost his goodness and condemned himself, becoming at the same time a historical and a social being.

The Bible's notion of atonement was likewise taken up by Rousseau. How could the lost paradise be recovered? Certainly not by becoming once more a natural man. This contradiction of his idea rightly drove Rousseau to exasperation. "What's this? Must we destroy societies, obliterate the difference between what is yours and what is mine, and go back to living with wolves and bears in the forest? A conclusion on the part of my adversaries, which I prefer to forestall rather than to leave to them to discover."

Historical, or modern, man is fated to stay within history; he cannot go back. But since man's fall (in a manner of speaking) into history is linked to the beginning of social life, his only hope of even partial recovery of the lost paradise is in the reform of society. Social relationships were, from the beginning, at the origin of power relationships. It was necessary to found a State that should guarantee the freedom and equality of individuals, because Law had become the expression of the "general will." By virtue of a pact that Rousseau called the "social contract," man ceded all his rights to the "general will"—that is, to the interest of the community.

In most cases, this reform demanded a clean slate in order to set up a new form of association between man and society. "There were constant false starts, because we should have begun by cleaning the entire area and throwing out all the extant materials, as Lycurgus did in Sparta, in order, subsequently, to raise a good building." The temptation to set up an ideal state in a virgin continent with no history behind it was particularly evident among the founders of the curious colony known as the "Champ d'asile," which we shall consider later on. Because the new state set forth by Rousseau was situated in history, it had a tendency to evolve and degenerate, so that institutions had to be continually readapted to circumstances.

Can we say that Rousseau's ideas had any concrete influence on America? According to Rousseau's hypothesis, ever since man became a historical being he has been obliged to conquer natural wealth. The American pioneer, setting out to conquer nature, was certainly not a "natural man"; the antihistorical character of America derives from the continent and not from its inhabitants. American Robinson Crusoes, like Defoe's hero, demonstrated their "perfectibility" by their unlimited power over nature. But the increasingly victorious war that they waged against nature was linked less to the condition of social man than to the condition of a man belonging to a technologically superior society whose superiority he was proud to prove.

Rousseau called for a "Legislator"—a sort of modern sage, a successor to Lycurgus—who should define the Law most expressive of the "general will." But American man, at this time a pure Anglo-Saxon, was satisfied with his own laws, which were mostly unwritten. The all-powerful role attributed by Rousseau to the State, which, however regenerated and just, is still the State, runs up against Americans' mistrust of any abuse of governmental power. Americans had no need to do away with their political and social institutions and to create new ones based on a spelled-out project of social reform. They were content with their individual liberties and social setup, which had been attained by a succession of gradual and empiric reforms whose beginning dated back to the Magna Carta. There was no reason for a continual readaptation of institutions considered to be very nearly ideal.

Americans, as heirs to the Anglo-Saxon mentality, had, so to speak, "deproblematized" the social question. In their view, the social instinct did not necessarily have bad consequences. Anglo-Saxons were by nature community-conscious, and there was no need for a social contract that already had a tacit existence confirmed by unwritten law.

Even the individualistic and crude solitary American pioneer was, to some extent, conscious of belonging to society. He sold the land that he had cleared and begun to cultivate to other immigrants, who cultivated it further and then sold it, in their turn, to speculators and middle-class city-builders. There was the implicit creation of a chain action, in which every participant achieved some personal advantage.

It was when London denied them economic and financial independence that Americans fought a war in order to sever their political ties. Their egalitarian ideas did not imply so much a social leveling as the right to individual economic independence and profit-taking. Most Frenchmen were of peasant origin, whereas Americans came from an English city-based middle class, concerned with business efficiency and technological progress.

The Frenchmen who won a concession for a Society for the Cultivation of the Grape and Olive were not psychologically equipped to face the problems of colonization in America. Their attachment to a dream now engulfed by history was, more than they realized, a ball and chain that they had dragged behind them to this virgin land, where the need was for manual and mechanical abilities and a mentality suited to an empirical and technically efficient society.

Grapes and olives, as we have said, called up a remote historical context akin to theirs, that of the veterans of ancient Rome. But neither grapevines nor olive trees could be successfully grown in Alabama. How did it happen, then, that these amateur colonists placed their project in a region of swamps and gigantic trees?

Many of them were unemployed and destitute. The curiosity and enthusiasm that they had provoked upon their arrival was beginning to fade away. The American government and a certain sector of public opinion looked with mistrust and a certain annoyance at the verbal violence and inactivity of these exiles, who hashed and rehashed their memories and resentments in the taverns of the Eastern Seaboard cities.

When, toward the end of 1816, Louis XVIII's ambassador, Hyde de Neuville, learned that some leading Bonapartists in Philadelphia were planning to set up a colonial establishment at the point where the Ohio River flows into the Mississippi, his first reaction was to be glad that a number of troublemakers would be removed from the East Coast. But the duc de Richelieu advised him "not to seem to have lent support to any such establishment." The minister of foreign affairs feared that these colonists, in moving closer to

Spanish-held lands, might become mercenaries in the service of the insurgents who had their base there.

But the attempt to obtain the concession of land on the Ohio River must have been unsuccessful, because the project fell through. A little later, the Colonial Society of French Émigrés, determined to found a colony whose center was to be called Démopolis, did get the grant of an area bordering the Tombigbee, a tributary of the Alabama River. William Lee, former American consul in Bordeaux, was named vice-president of the association and charged with writing a letter to Jefferson "asking him to outline the basis of a social pact governing the local regulations of the association." The reply of the former American president, dated January 16, 1817, deserves to be quoted at length:

> No one can be more sensible than I am of the honor of their confidence in me, so flatteringly manifested in this resolution; and certainly no one can feel stronger dispositions than myself to be useful to them, as well in return for this great mark of respect, as from feelings for the situation of strangers, forced by the misfortunes of their native country to seek another by adoption, so distant, and so different from that in all its circumstances. I commiserate the hardships they have to encounter, and equally applaud the resolution with which they meet them, as well as the principles proposed for their government. That their emigration may be for the happiness of their descendants, I can but believe; but from the knowledge I have of the country they have left, and its state of social intercourse and comfort, their own personal happiness will undergo severe trial. The laws however which are to effect this must flow from their own habits, their own feelings, and the resources of their own minds. No stranger to these could possibly propose regulations adapted to them. Every people have their own particular habits, ways of thinking, manners, etc., which have grown up with them from their infancy, are become a part of their nature, and to which the regulations which are to make them happy must be accommodated. No member of a foreign country can have a sufficient sympathy with these. The institutions of Lycurgus, for example, would not have suited Athens, nor those of Solon Lacedaemon. The organizations of Locke were impracticable for Carolina, and those of Rousseau and Mably for Poland.
>
> Turning inwardly on myself from these eminent illustrations of the truth of my observations, I feel all the presumption it

would manifest should I undertake to do what this respectable society is alone qualified to do suitably for itself. There are some preliminary questions too which are particularly for their own consideration. Is it proposed that this shall be a separate state? Or a county of a state? Or a mere voluntary association, as those of the Quakers, Dunkards, Mennonites? A separate state it cannot be, because from the tract it asks, it would not be of more than 20 miles square, and in establishing new states, regard is had to a certain degree of equality in size. If it is to be a county of a state, it cannot be governed by its own laws, but must be subject to those of the state of which it is a part. If merely a voluntary association, the submission of its members will be merely voluntary also; as no act of coercion would be permitted by the general law. These considerations must control the society, and themselves alone can modify their own intentions and wishes. With this apology for declining a task to which I am so unequal. I pray them to be assured of my sincere wishes for their success and happiness.[2]

There was a world of difference, as Jefferson states quite strongly at the beginning of his letter, between French and American cultures, social traditions, and psychologies. The Bonapartist exiles hoped to find in America a land uncorrupted by man where they could create a community based on a new social contract, such as that set forth by Rousseau. This writer thought that certain states, by the extent of their corruption, their power, and the injustices of a long-established order, were beyond saving. It was in order to save at least some of their citizens that he wrote *Émile*, which, in his mind, was a complement and not just a continuation of the *Social Contract*, which had been addressed to salvageable states. To the French exiles, the United States was salvageable and, indeed, was a country that allowed Europeans to achieve a social ideal that Europe was bound to stifle.

The exiles' fidelity to Rousseau was evident not only in the wording of their request—"association" and "social pact"—but also in their appeal to a "Legislator." For it was of Rousseau's "Legislator" that the exiles were thinking when they asked William Lee to seek a definition of the basis of a social pact from "the sage of Montebello" (a name out of their own military past that they erroneously applied to Jefferson's residence, Monticello).

Jefferson, as a reader of Rousseau, recognized their frame of reference, and his reply brought up Rousseau's ideas. When he says that Rousseau's organizational theories as applied to Poland (which had asked the philosopher for a constitution) were not fitted to Poles and that he himself could not draw up the laws for a French community because "no stranger could possibly propose regulations adapted to them," it is because he is arguing against the whole principle of a "Legislator." And, beyond his refusal of this personage, to whom Rousseau gave capital importance, he denies the whole principle of an organization founded on universal, abstract reason as alone capable of rediscovering the lost secret of the harmony of nature.

Jefferson wanted to adapt laws to the "particular habits" and "ways of thinking" that accompany all people from their birth and become "part of their nature." Rousseau condemned this second nature and insisted that, if it could not be done away with, it should be reformed by regulations inspired by nature. For the American Jefferson, it was a question of understanding another people's behavior; sympathetic feeling seemed to him superior to reason: "No member of a foreign country can have a sufficient sympathy."

In December, 1817, a first contingent of about a hundred and fifty colonists left Philadelphia, having had the good news that William Lee had been elected governor of Alabama. In April of the following year, the main body of colonists set out on an especially chartered schooner, the *McDonough*, taking with them an assortment of olive and vine shoots. A promise to specialize in these two crops was part of the contract between the colonists and the American government. In order to forestall any temptation to speculation, the secretary of the treasury, who was in charge of the concession, had imposed hard terms, which caused much uncertainty and misunderstanding. First, titles to the land were granted not individually but to a group supposedly versed in agriculture. Moreover, the titles were not definitely attributed until the total payment had been made and the colonists had settled down and begun to clear the land. Indeed, the colonists left for Alabama before the signing of a contract, summarized below, which did not take place until 1819.

The contract stipulated that: (1) settlements on the allotted tracts were to be made within three years; (2) within fourteen years, 10 acres out of every 160 had to be cleared and under cultivation; (3) within seven years, 1 acre out of every 160 had to be cultivated in vines; (4) within seven years, no less than 500 olive trees had to be planted in the whole area, unless it were proved that they could not successfully be cultivated. The entire arrangement represents a curious example of economic planning in a country that supposedly went in for free enterprise!

Some of the first concessionaires never came at all to the Tombigbee River and consequently lost their titles. These included Marshal Grouchy and his sons, General Charles Lallemand, Colonels Galabert and Fournier, and Comte Réal. Others, such as Generals Lefebvre-Desnouettes and Clauzel, Colonel de Cluis, Georges Garnier, a former delegate to the Convention from Saintes, and Simon Chaudron, did actually go to Alabama and were later joined by a few refugees from Santo Domingo.

Troubles beset them from the start. The *McDonough* was shipwrecked in Mobile Bay. However, the lieutenant in command of Fort Bowyer, near which the disaster occurred, organized a lifesaving operation. A dinner was given in Mobile in honor of the French colonists, and they were offered help for their journey up the Tombigbee River. But this was not the end of their misadventures. They failed to find the land allotted to them on the map, and there had been no surveying. In July, they decided to stake out a town to be called Démopolis in a locality known as White Bluffs. They had already thrown up a few huts when they were told that they were out of bounds. Undiscouraged they withdrew to the banks of the Tombigbee, where they founded Aigleville. In Marengo County in west-central Alabama, there is still a Demopolis, whose name perpetuates the French exiles' venture.

Alabama is a southern state, suited to the cultivation of rice and cotton and, the Frenchmen had thought, to that of their familiar grapes and olives as well. But the swampiness of the uncleared land and their ignorance of agricultural techniques caused their efforts to fail. They hired some German farm workers who managed to plant a certain number of olive trees. Several thousand grapevines were, with difficulty, put in the ground as well. But frost, floods, yellow fever, and other maladies defeated their hopes.

The colonists of Aigleville left behind them the memory of a brilliant society where the few women wore silk gowns and tried to entertain in the way to which they were accustomed in Paris. General Charles Lallemand, third president of the French "company," never set foot in Alabama. Indeed, he dissuaded other officers from investing their funds there because he hoped to enlist them for his own colonial project in Texas, to which he tried also to attract disaffected settlers from the Tombigbee River.

Colonel Nicolas Raoul operated a ferry at Démopolis. His wife, the former Marchesa Sinibaldi, lady-in-waiting to Queen Caroline of Naples, made pancakes for the passengers. Later, the Raouls went to Mexico, where the colonel served in the revolutionary army. In 1833, after returning to France, he became governor of Toulon. Colonel de Cluis, formerly commander of the fortress where Ferdinand VII was imprisoned, kept an inn at Greensborough, Alabama.

Soldiers were not the only ones to make a poor show as settlers in the New World. Former members of the Convention were equally inept. Small wonder that politicians, theorists of government, and revolutionaries were unable to prove their notion of the perfectibility of man when it came to struggling with the forces of nature! Georges Garnier, known as Garnier de Saintes, was a former *conventionnel* who lived in a not too well-kept house near the Ohio River. He was one of those who had voted for the execution of Louis XVI. Before this he had demonstrated his energetic nature in the organization of the Committee of Public Safety. Various missions to the Napoleonic armies were entrusted to him, and, under the Empire, he presided over the criminal court of Saintes, his birthplace. After the ordinance of July 24, 1815, he was arrested in Paris, then released on condition that he leave the kingdom with the shortest possible delay. Banished from Belgium on account of the anti-Bourbon writings that he published in his paper, *Le Surveillant*, he took refuge in the United States. After living for some time in Philadelphia, he became the first president of the Alabama company. It was in the village of New Albany that Montulé found him:

> A log cabin, in rather poor condition, was the dwelling of the former representative of the people. We knocked at the door of a sort of shop, for he sells whiskey, rum, and cigars for a

living. A little boy opened and led us into the kitchen—that is, the bedroom, livingroom, and in short the only room of the house. Monsieur Garnier came to greet us with a spoon in one hand and a notebook in the other. He does his own cooking and, at the same time, he is writing a book. He received us with a cordiality that hardly exists nowadays outside a novel, and which, in view of his situation, we especially appreciated. Because I come from the army, he welcomed me with particular grace. Without any formal invitation to dinner, he killed and plucked two chickens and made them into a stew, doubled the beans, already on the stove, made a salad, and then asked us to sit down at his table. We ate with a good appetite, and I can assure you that our conversation was gayer than could have been hoped under the humble roof of an exile's log cabin. After dinner, I asked Monsieur Garnier to read a few pages from his book. The title is *Emerides, or Evenings with Socrates*, and it is of a strictly philosophical character.

In his report to Paris of August 29, 1818, the French consul in Philadelphia wrote: "Monsieur Garnier de Saintes and his son drowned in the Mississippi River during a voyage from Louisville to New Orleans. The capsized boat, which has been discovered, is the only trace of their passage."

Jean-Augustin Pénières, a former member of the National Assembly, was another member of the French colony in Alabama and had been charged with informing the settlers about the local soil and what could best be grown in it. In 1818, the consul in Philadelphia noted: "Monsieur Pénières was admitted to the bar in Natchez even before he had learned English." He died in 1823 in Florida, where he was living as a government-appointed commissioner for the Seminole Indians.

Like Garnier de Saintes, Simon Chaudron had to leave Belgium on account of the Bonapartist views aired in the paper of which he was the editor, *Le Nain jaune*. In Philadelphia he set up another paper, *L'Abeille américaine*, which came out for four years, from 1816 to 1819. The poverty of the exiles' community and the lack of American readers prevented its survival. In desperate need of money, Chaudron went with his numerous family to Aigleville. Before leaving, he wrote to Jefferson, informing him of his financial troubles, asking for letters of introduction to influential citizens of Alabama, and adding: "I should be grateful, sir, if I could obtain from you some sesame seeds to be planted in Alabama. Our colonists are anxious to try them out."

The two most noteworthy figures of the French colony in Alabama were Generals Lefebvre-Desnouettes and Clauzel, who were often seen together on the porch of the Hotel Trémoulet in New Orleans, where they came in search of supplies and the latest news. From this porch, Lefebvre-Desnouettes could see the arrival and departure of ocean steamers. For the whole length of his exile, he hoped in vain that his wife would manage to join him. Stéphanie Rollier, the future comtesse Lefebvre-Desnouettes, was the daughter of Marie Benielli, a first cousin of Napoleon's mother and of Cardinal Fesch. For her marriage in 1805, Napoleon gave her, as a dowry, the Hôtel Bonaparte on the Rue des Victoires, where, in 1815, she bore her daughter and only child, whom the father was never to know.

Charles Lefebvre-Desnouettes had an amiable nature and considerable charm; he was quick to win everyone's esteem, including that of the French ambassador. In 1817, Hyde de Neuville wrote to the duc de Richelieu: "Lefebvre-Desnouettes is, I believe, in New Orleans. I have heard nothing against him; indeed, I am told that his frank talk goes to prove that he was not so much a conspirator as he was a tool in the hands of others. What will he do in Louisiana? Some think that, in despair, he will cast his lot with the Spaniards. But I doubt that so intelligent an officer will play such miserable cards."

Later Hyde de Neuville came to know the exiled general personally, and his memoirs say: "His character was admirable, whatever cause he was serving. He was both gentle and firm, and devoted, without any display of words, to the man he had followed." Obviously his name was on the first of the lists included in the ordinance of July 24, 1815, as one of the twelve officers to be called up before a court-martial. Here he was sentenced, *in absentia*, to death.

Lefebvre-Desnouettes was born in Paris on December 15, 1775, to a family of prosperous drapers. Three times he ran away from school to join the army, and before he was seventeen he enlisted, in 1792, and found himself under the command of General Dumouriez. His military career was brilliant. As Bonaparte's aide-decamp during the Italian campaign, he was favorably noted at the

Battle of Marengo. After Austerlitz, he was made a commander of the Legion of Honor, and during the Russian campaign he was promoted to the rank of brigadier general. Throughout the Napoleonic wars he continually gave proof of his courage and military talent. After making him a commander of the Order of the Lion of Bavaria, Napoleon bestowed upon him, in 1808, the most enviable command post in the army, that of the cavalry of the Imperial Guard, and, not long after, the title of count. During the Spanish campaign, he was made general of a division. Wounded by a pistol shot, with his horse shot down from under him, he was taken prisoner by the English but escaped in 1811 and resumed the cavalry command that the Emperor had kept in his name. He fought in Russia and Saxony, and, on January 29, 1814, at Brienne, another horse was killed under him and two bayonet wounds in the left side put him *hors de combat*. Before the end of February, he was back in the field and, in March, at Arcis-sur-Aube, for the third time he lost his horse.

After the Emperor's first abdication, Louis XVIII named Lefebvre-Desnouettes a *chevalier de Saint-Louis* and renewed his command in the section of the Guard that had been renamed the Royal Light Cavalry. But as soon as Desnouettes heard that Napoleon had landed in the south of France, he hurried to La Fère, where he hoped, with the support of the Lallemand brothers, to seize the arsenal and persuade the garrison troops to march with him on Paris and imprison the royal family in the Tuileries Palace. When the resistance of the royal forces brought this plan to naught, he tried in vain to raise up a regiment from the Berri region, garrisoned at Compiègne, against the king. Abandoned by these shaky followers, he took refuge, in disguise, with General Rigaud. During the Hundred Days, Napoleon raised him to the rank of Peer of France, and he went on fighting until the second abdication. Little wonder that he was a "wanted" man! Upon arriving in the United States, he was received by Joseph Bonaparte and made friends with one of Joseph's intimates, General (and Comte) Bertrand de Clauzel.

Listed, like Lefebvre-Desnouettes, in the ordinance of July 24, 1815, Clauzel was likewise sentenced to death *in absentia*. The French consul in New York, Cazeaux, called him "a soldier and nothing more. He talks very little, disavows any personal loyalty to Napoleon, and attributes his misfortune to circumstances over which he had no control." In New York and other cities, Clauzel met refugees from Haiti, where he had served under General Leclerc in 1801. "Refugees from Santo Domingo, who never gave up their loyalty to the Bourbons," the consul went on, "call on and receive General Clauzel because of the benefits he conferred upon them in the island. Everyone agrees that his conduct as both a soldier and an administrator were beyond reproach. I'm told that he proposes to go live in obscurity on the Ohio River."

Clauzel was born at Mirepoix in the Ariège region on December 1, 1772. At twenty-two years of age, he was a colonel, and he took part in the turn-of-the-century military conquests from beginning to end: the Italian campaign, the expedition to Santo Domingo, the campaigns of 1806, 1807, and 1808, the Spanish campaign, where he commanded an army corps, and the battles of 1813 and 1814 in the south of France, where he fought against the English.

His threatening appearance during the Hundred Days with three hundred men at Bordeaux, where Louis XVI's daughter, the duchesse d'Angoulême had taken refuge, was the cause of the death sentence passed upon him by the ordinance of July 24, 1815. He protested the sentence and denied having in any way favored Napoleon's return. Philadelphia gave him a warm welcome, but his wife remained on their property near Tarbes. After 1817, the duc de Richelieu told Hyde de Neuville that there was some hope for Clauzel's return to France if he conducted and expressed himself circumspectly. In 1820, he was one of those who benefited from an amnesty, and he went home that same year.

As fellow exiles and soon fast friends, Clauzel and Lefebvre-Desnouettes shared agricultural adventures and experiments of the kind we have described above. Like all their fellows, they were suspected by royalist agents of two dangerous activities: aid to the insurgents of the Spanish-American colonies and plots for an escape of Napoleon from St. Helena. However, Hyde de Neuville was convinced early on that Lefebvre-Desnouettes was not involved in any Latin-American adventure. A private letter on this subject from the general, intercepted by the royalists in 1817, confirmed the ambassador's intuition: "The leadership of the Independents in Mexico lacks funds," Lefebvre-Desnouettes noted. "There are more than four hundred French officers in the United States who ask nothing better than to serve this cause. But the need is not for a general staff but for well-trained European common soldiers in such numbers as to count in military operations. There is no shortage of arms or gunpowder; in fact there are, in New Orleans, twenty thousand unsalable rifles. In short, the project is useless because impracticable."

As for Clauzel, he had considered, for a time, a purely agricultural project in Cuba, but obviously this had no subversive design. He wrote, in a letter of December, 1818: "The governments of France and Spain know that I have nothing to do with plans or expeditions intended to raise up the Spanish colonies against the mother country."

More alarming were the rumors about plots to abet Napoleon's escape from captivity. A certain Colonel Roul[3] convinced royalist agents of the truth of a highly romanticized account of a supposed plot, involving Lefebvre-Desnouettes, to free not only Napoleon but his young son, the King of Rome, as well. The royalists were convinced that Roul had suspicious connections with Mademoiselle Desportes, a former chambermaid of the comtesse Lefebvre-Desnouettes, who had recently arrived in the United States.

In 1816, Stéphanie Lefebvre-Desnouettes had attempted to join her exiled husband, and he had gone to New York in the expectation of meeting her. But the ship on which she had set out went first to England, and she was so upset by the roughness of the English Channel that she gave up the idea of going on to America and returned to France. Her chambermaid, after a quarrel with her mistress, decided to go alone to the United States; she settled down in Philadelphia with a fisherman. Actually, it is uncertain why Mademoiselle Desportes undertook the long sea voyage in the midwinter season. She refused the aid offered by her former master and earned her own living. It is unlikely that she brought money from France to Lefebvre-Desnouettes; one of his sisters had married a brother of the banker Jacques Laffitte, and letters of credit circulated freely between the United States and France. Mademoiselle Desportes was forty years old and not particularly pretty, which makes it unlikely that her voluntary emigration was determined by sentimental motives. But at this point Roul made some surprising statements to the effect that Napoleon had conceived a plan for an attack on St. Helena that would lead to his liberation, and that he, Roul, was involved in its execution. Hyde de Neuville had one of his secret agents follow Roul and, since it seemed as if he were seeing Mademoiselle Desportes, she was subjected to interrogation and declared that she had brought letters from Napoleon and that Roul was, effectively, charged with a mission of liberation.

These events took place at a time when refugee activities caused the French ambassador and consuls considerable preoccupation. Only a short time before Roul's statements, Hyde de Neuville had informed the duc de Richelieu of his concern over the refugee conspirators "who come and go from New York to Philadelphia and Baltimore, who recruit followers, spend money, and are financing two secret expeditions, one with a ship that has small arms, munitions, and twelve cannons aboard. Are these being sent to the Spanish colonies? I devoutly hope so." And he went on to voice his suspicions of Frégomain, a navy officer "presently sojourning with Joseph Bonaparte," of General Jordan, "an aide-de-camp to Napoleon," who had recently arrived, and of Colonel Galabert. "Refugees who, a month ago, seemed to live in the direst poverty now ostensibly spend money. Last month, when imbibing together, they drank a toast to 'November,' as if they expected something to happen during this month."

As for Roul, a protracted inquiry about his personal history and the validity of his supposed revelations showed that the royalists had no reason to worry about him. First, the former colonel had asked for money before making his statements to the consul; then when the consul tried to follow up on them, he discovered that they had no substance whatsoever. No weapons had been stored in Baltimore, and no armed schooner financed by Stephen Girard was waiting in the harbor of Philadelphia to set sail for St. Helena.

As for Roul's past, it came out that he had been a colonel during the Hundred Days and then had offered his services to the Independents of Buenos Aires, who made him a general but subsequently sent him away. Joseph Bonaparte had sent him away, also, and he was persona non grata to the exiled French generals of whom we have spoken above.

Lefebvre-Desnouettes must have heard the rumors about plans for the Emperor's escape, but he was never suspected of participating in them. Plans, of course, there were. In October, 1818, on St. Helena, Bertrand noted: "The Grand Marshal met young M., bearer of a letter from *D.*, who is still busy with escape projects." Does "*D.*" stand for Desnouettes? It is tempting to build a romantic story on this initial. There may be another clue in the fact that, in his will, Napoléon left a hundred thousand francs each to Desnouettes and Clauzel, "although," he said to Bertrand, "probably they are above such things." The two generals had had entirely different careers, and if the Emperor linked their names it must have been because he knew about their lives in exile.

Royalist agents watched closely every move of these two men. In May, 1817, in Philadelphia, Clauzel bought a schooner, intended to transport some German families and also some plows that he and Desnouettes had purchased for the cultivation of the land they had bought on the Tombigbee River. The French consul, at first suspicious, soon learned to his relief that "the ship had been rented, not bought, and that it was fit only for navigation in coastal waters."

In Alabama, Desnouettes and Clauzel, in spite of the considerable amount of money that, according to Marshal Grouchy, they had invested, ran up against the same difficulties as their fellows. Let it be said to their credit that, in spite of the shortage of labor, they both refused to buy slaves. Besides their agricultural ventures, they jointly opened a general store, which Dr. Lucien Guillot's biographical thesis tells us, carried everything from liquor, flour, and salted fish to hats. Whiskey and ordinary rum were for sale, but not gin and rum from Jamaica, which Lefebvre-Desnouettes thought were "too good for the country."

In September, 1818, the partners went to Washington in the hope of obtaining a revision of their contracts. They were welcomed by the capital's most prominent citizens; the president received them and the secretary of war invited them to dinner. Lefebvre-Desnouettes, accompanied by an American senator, called on Hyde de Neuville in order to ask for the king's pardon and a return from exile. The French ambassador was charmed by the petitioner's personality but said that the gravity of his actions during the Hundred Days made abrogation of his sentence difficult to obtain. In the years that followed, however, Hyde de Neuville, himself, as we may recall, a royalist exile under Napoleon, persistently advanced a plea for the pardon of Desnouettes, the Bonapartist general.

In January, 1819, the two men returned to Aigleville. Desnouettes' farmlands were doing well, but Clauzel's less so, to the point that he ceded his rights and bought other property near Mobile. The general store was on the verge of failure and invaded by rats. Desnouettes wrote to his partner, warning him against "getting involved in things with which neither of them was well acquainted." The partnership continued, but Desnouettes, who had more capital, often called for repayment of a sum he had lent to Clauzel. Accounts were confused, and many goods were unsold or lost.

Lefebvre-Desnouettes had 480 acres of land and, as he himself wrote, "a commodious house and a good life." Alongside the house, he built an annex that he called the "sanctuary," whose walls were papered in red, white, and blue, and where he kept a bust of the Emperor and his own sword and pistols.

On his farm near Mobile, Clauzel grew vegetables and conveyed his own products to market. When Desnouettes invited him to Aigleville for the summer, he chose to stay at home with his mulatto mistress, who was about to bear him a child. Desnouettes sent his congratulations. In July, 1819, the general store was permanently closed down. The final inventory made for some differences of opinion, but the two men's friendship did not suffer.

Clauzel went back to France in 1820 and picked up his army career. Lefebvre-Desnouettes remained a melancholy exile, always hoping for the arrival of his wife, together with the daughter whom he had never seen. Meanwhile, the wife had given his estate, Les Noëttes, to his parents who, in 1821, sold it to the famous comtesse de Ségur, née Rostopchin, who wrote there most of her children's books. In 1822, Hyde de Neuville thought that his efforts on behalf of Lefebvre-Desnouettes were about to be crowned with success. The general grew a beard and embarked under a false name on the *Albion*, bound for Belgium via Liverpool. On April 22, this ship was wrecked off the Irish coast, and Desnouettes was drowned at the age of only forty-seven years. His widow dedicated a beacon light near Le Havre to his memory, and here he was buried. His name is engraved on the west side of the Arc de Triomphe in Paris.

To this writer, the most noteworthy feature of these two generals' colonial life is their refusal to buy slaves. They had been soldiers of Napoleon, and they lived in the United States. Now Napoleon came out of the French Revolution, which had proclaimed the rights of man, especially his right to liberty. And the United States was the country of liberty by definition. Yet both the United States and Napoleon departed from their ideals and took a pragmatic attitude toward slaves and slavery.

Paradoxically enough, machines and technology brought about a sudden increase in the number and price of slaves in the United States. Before 1793, slavery made little contribution to the profits of the plantations of the American South. Tobacco and indigo did not sell well, much land was uncleared, slaves stood about idle, and there were proposals for the abolition of slavery. At this point, there came along the idea of growing cotton, a product easily exportable to England, where highly efficient mills wove it. The planters had, however, one apparently insurmountable problem to overcome, that of ginning, the long and expensive process of separating the cotton fiber from seeds and waste material, which a slave could carry out at the rate of only a pound per day. At this juncture, the Deep South vacation trip of a young student from Massachusetts, Eli Whitney, changed the course of the economy, politics, and history of the United States. After he had seen how it was for his hosts, the Greene family, to make their plantation pay, he invented a machine for cleaning cotton, operated by one man alone and doing the work of fifty slaves. The first consequence of this invention was to make cotton-raising profitable. The second was to release slaves from ginning and put them to work at sowing and tending ever greater quantities of cotton plants. In 1720 there were 690,000 slaves; by 1860 there were 4,000,000. Before the cotton gin, a slave cost three hundred dollars; immediately after, the price went up to eight hundred and continued to go even higher. From the beginning, the northern states condemned slavery, but their representatives sat alongside those of the South in Congress, thereby explicitly recognizing it as an institution.

In France the Constituent Assembly, in 1791, accorded equal rights to the free blacks of the colonies. The protests of white slaveowners, followed by black revolts and civil wars, led to the

Convention's vote for the abolition of slavery in 1794. Toussaint L'Ouverture, a former slave, became a general in the French army. And thousands of white refugees from the Antilles, particularly Santo Domingo, sought refuge in the United States.

These events increased the conservatism of certain Americans, particularly in the South. The abolition of slavery in an area close to the United States and the dictatorship of a former slave in Haiti struck fear into the hearts of southern planters, surrounded as they were by slave labor. Moreover, the alien body of French refugees (some 20,000 in 1797), although most of them were victims of the Reign of Terror, called up memories of the Jacobins and substantiated Americans' mistrust of the French Revolution.

In 1811, a young southern congressman, John C. Calhoun, future vice-president and a fierce isolationist, gave the following opinion of the black people of the United States: "Even in our Revolution no attempts were made by this portion of our population; and however the gentleman may frighten himself with the disorganizing effects of French principles, I cannot think our ignorant blacks have felt much of their baneful influence. I dare say no more than one half of them never heard of the French Revolution." The problem of the blacks and its consequences must have caused a certain number of American liberals to rate their Revolution as less complete than that of France.

Near where he lived on St. Helena, Napoleon often met a poor black slave called Tobie, to whom he enjoyed talking. After one of their meetings, the Emperor communicated to Las Cases the following reflections on slavery:

> Poor Tobie has been taken from his family, his country, and himself and sold. Could anything be more of a torment to him, more of a crime committed by others? If the crime were of the English captain alone, he would surely be one of the wickedest of men, but if it was committed by an entire crew then it was committed by men no less wicked than is generally believed, for wickedness is always individual, seldom collective. Joseph's brothers, in the Old Testament, could not make up their minds to kill; Judas, in the New, quite calculatedly betrayed his Master. Imagine Tobie as Brutus: he would have killed himself; as Aesop, he might be, today, a counselor to the government; as an ardent and zealous Christian, he would bear his chains in the sight of

God and bless them. As for poor Tobie, he is less analytical; he innocently bends over and works.... Of course, there is a great gap between poor Tobie and King Richard, but the crime is no less atrocious for all that. After all, this man had his family, his enjoyments, his own life, and it was a horrible crime to bring him to die here under the yoke of slavery.

It is difficult, of course, to systematize Napoleon's thinking, and on the black question his sentiments and policies were inconsistent and, in any case, pragmatic. At heart he was favorable to the French Revolution, and we may believe that his feeling for Tobie was sincere. It is revealing that Tobie's plight did not inspire him with any idea of "collective sin" (which, indeed, he belittled) or with any anathema directed at slavery in general, although he condemned the trade in blacks. With Tobie, as with all events and situations, he was taken up with the obsessive presence of Destiny as the determining factor of individual fates and of history. Tobie in the guise of Brutus, Aesop, a Christian martyr—Revolution may tread the path of Destiny, but Destiny has the upper hand. Revolution is a moment, a passing aspect of history, but Destiny watches over the human epic from the start. Destiny is not an equation; it does not proclaim clear formulas or decree permanent and universal laws. Its domain is that of caprice, of darkness illuminated by occasional flashes of light. There is no way of doing without pragmatism if a man is riding out the gallop of history, and history is volatile, disturbing, and enigmatic. In fact, Napoleon's pragmatic attitude toward blacks and their enslavement distressed many of his contemporaries. "I never ordered slavery," Napoleon said on St. Helena to General Bertrand. "But where it already existed, as on Martinique and Mauritius, I did not abolish it. Probably it still exists."

As First Consul, Napoleon had to face, first of all, the conflict with England. The French colonies in which slavery was the rule were in the Caribbean, an area of strategic and commercial importance of the first degree. It was essential to subordinate the governments of these colonies to the policy of France. If liberation of the blacks were to constitute an obstacle to this subordination, then slavery had to be maintained or even reestablished. And, on the other hand, if liberation of the blacks were supportive of French policy, then it had to be confirmed. Thus at the meeting of the

Council of State on 28 Thermidor in the Year VIII, called to discuss the matter of the colonies, the First Consul declared:

> The question is not whether it's good to abolish slavery, but whether it's good to abolish freedom in the free part of Santo Domingo. I'm convinced that this island would go over to England were the blacks not attached to us on account of their liberty.
>
> They'll produce less sugar, perhaps, but they'll produce it for us and serve us, in case of need, as soldiers. Even if we have one less sugar refinery, we'll have one more citadel occupied by soldiers who are our friends.
>
> My policy is to govern men as the majority of them want to be governed. That, I believe, is the way of recognizing the sovereignty of the people. It was by turning Catholic that I won the war in the Vendée, in turning Moslem that I set myself up in Egypt, in turning papist that I won minds in Italy. If I were to rule a people of Jews, I'd rebuild Solomon's temple. So I shall speak of freedom in the free part of Santo Domingo, and I shall maintain slavery on Mauritius and even in the slave part of Santo Domingo. I reserve the right to limit and soften slavery where I maintain it and to reestablish order and introduce discipline where I maintain liberty.

During the Revolution, the freedom given to blacks seemed to favor France. Martinique had gone over to England in order to keep slavery, whereas Toussaint L'Ouverture, the master of Haiti, had declared himself England's enemy. As soon as Bonaparte came to power, he confirmed the authority of Toussaint; after all, on Haiti there were 450,000 blacks and only 40,000 whites and 30,000 mulattos. Toussaint L'Ouverture, who had an extraordinary talent for organization, tried to slip out of the political and economic control of France, while Bonaparte alternately restrained and conciliated him. In 1801, Toussaint was offended when Bonaparte sent a proclamation (which was actually flattering in his regard) to the representative of the central government instead of to himself. He took over the Spanish part of the island and expelled the French representative, while still calling Santo Domingo a French colony. This was what provoked the Leclerc expedition. After Toussaint L'Ouverture was brought as a captive to France, he suffered under an unduly harsh prison regime that hastened his death. Along with yellow fever, the order to disarm the black population was one of the main causes of the French expedition's failure, for to the black his gun was the last guarantee of freedom. After this, Bonaparte's attitude toward slavery hardened. He kept it going on Martinique when this island was returned to France and reestablished it on Guadeloupe in order to encourage the return of the former colonists, who were better able than the blacks to defend French interests against those of the British in this area of rivalry.

Still, as we have said, Napoleon's feelings about slavery were complex, and we may legitimately believe that he hoped for an eventual solution to the black problem and even saw it in a fusion of races to match the fusion of ideas and civilizations to which he vaguely aspired. The generals who went with him to St. Helena took down his remarks on the subject, which, we may note, were in harmony with the principles of Portuguese colonization.

> The question of freedom for the blacks is difficult and complicated. It has been answered in Africa and Asia by polygamy. Whites and blacks belong to one big family. Since the head of the house has white, black, and mulatto wives, the children, white, black, and mulatto, are siblings, raised in the same cradle and at the same table, and bearing the same name. Mightn't it be possible to authorize polygamy on our island possessions, with a limit of two wives, one white and the other black? . . .
>
> In the early centuries of Christianity, the patriarchs had more than one wife. The Church allowed a sort of concubinage that, effectually, gave a man several wives. The Pope and the Council have the power to authorize such an institution, since its purpose is the reconciliation and harmony of society rather than the spread of carnal pleasure. Such marriages would be limited to the colonies; care would be taken that they did not bring disorder into the present social order.

If Napoleon's pragmatism in regard to the black question was of a political and historical nature, that of the Americans was essentially capitalistic.

The attitude of Generals Lefebvre-Desnouettes and Clauzel recalls that of the American abolitionists and also of the Masonic lodges, to which La Fayette had formerly announced his intention of buying up land in the West Indies in order to give it to freed slaves. Indeed, the Liberal party, of which La Fayette was the leader, was beginning to exploit the disappointment of the Bonapartists. And, in spite of differences and misunderstandings between

French exiles and Americans, a concern for new ideas and for philanthropy—including that promoted by the Freemasons—made for an ideological bond between them.

Did Napoleon have any real idea of the life led by his veterans in their role as colonists? When he imagined himself in the service of an American agricultural enterprise, the classical myth of the soldier-farmer, devoid of sociological or philosophical preoccupations and associated, rather, with the idea of simple happiness and prosperity, filled his mind.

The *Mémoires* of his valet and secretary, Marchand, tell of Dr. O'Meara's astonishment when he heard that the townspeople on St. Helena were saying that the Emperor "knew how to handle a plow just as well as a sword." The origin of the story was the following. One day when he was out riding his horse, Napoleon saw a farmer tracing a furrow with his plow, preparatory to sowing wheat. The former Emperor got down from his horse and made a try at tracing a furrow himself. The farmer, according to the story, was amazed by the "precision of his operation." When Dr. O'Meara repeated the story to Napoleon, the latter said: "If I'd gone to America, I'd have been a farmer. I'd have cared for my garden; I'd have welcomed some stray remnants of my army who would have come to join me, and we'd have lived together. Are you laughing, Doctor? My tastes are simple. I have few needs. In fact, I've always envied the solid bourgeois of Paris with an income of 12,000 pounds a year, which makes it possible for him to cultivate arts and letters. I may add domestic harmony, without which no happiness can exist, to whatever class one may belong."

CHAPTER 6

The "Field of Refuge"

In 1815, after learning of his expulsion from the French Institute, a curious individual set sail for the United States. A former priest and deputy to the Convention, who had voted for the execution of Louis XVI, Jacques Lakanal was a swarthy man with a volitive expression and piercing eyes set under bushy brows with two vertical lines between them. The plans he hatched were to draw the attention not only of French diplomatic representatives in the United States, but of the chancelleries of Europe and the headquarters of Sir Hudson Lowe on St. Helena as well.

He was born, as Lacanal, in 1762 to a middle-class family in the Pyrénées region. He had three royalist brothers and changed the spelling of his name in order to underline the difference between their opinions and his. In 1792, he was a deputy to the National Convention from Ariège, and he was charged with the administration of the region of Dordogne, upon which occasion he stated, "This representative declares that the sublime and moving mission of a civic apostle to the rural areas is the greatest that anyone can accomplish."

Lakanal's name has come down to posterity on account of his importance in the field of education. As a member of the Committee of Public Instruction he virtually organized a whole educational system. He made a particular effort to obliterate the memory of the monarchy from young people's minds and enjoined them "to visit the cottages of the poor, imparting to them instruction and love of country."

He was one of the first members of the Institut de France and a friend of numerous professors and scholars and was elected to the Council of Five Hundred. Refusing to go along with the coup d'état of 18 Brumaire, he lost the chance to accede to the influential positions that the new government might have offered him and remained a teacher of ancient languages at the École Centrale of the Rue Saint-Antoine in Paris. Nevertheless, in 1809 the Emperor named him Inspector General of Weights and Measures, in which capacity he enforced compliance with the new metric system.

When the return of the Bourbons caused him to lose this post and also his membership in the Institute, he decided, as we said above, to go into exile in the United States, where he arrived in February of 1816. As early as the following month, this man who had opted for poverty and independence in order to be true to his republican convictions wrote from New York an incredibly obsequious letter to Joseph Bonaparte, former king of Spain.

> It would be utterly reprehensible, to my mind, to disclose what is said in Your Majesty's presence. Nevertheless, I am not, I believe, indiscreet in confiding to my correspondence with the Institute, entrusted to a sea captain who sailed yesterday for Le Havre, the admirable achievements of your Spanish reign. The prestigious wise men of France will relive the glorious Age of Saturn and Astraea. The Institute members, imagining themselves among the clergy and inquisitioners of Cordova, will rediscover in Your Majesty the benevolence of Titus and the philosophical mind of Marcus Aurelius. . . . I salute the fair land of France, which I shall never see again but which I congratulate because it will soon enjoy the happiness of being ruled by Your Majesty. . . . As I set out for the West, I fear that I should importune Your Majesty by presenting my respects in person and feel that a letter is the shortest and most suitable way of expressing my gratitude for your kindness.

As we shall see, the tone of the letters sent by Lakanal during his American exile to the Emperor's brother was to become more and more bizarre.

He settled in Kentucky, on a plantation across the Ohio River from the village of Vevey, seat of an old French-Swiss colony. In 1817, with Pénières, another former deputy to the National Convention, he went down the Ohio in search of land where French colonists might grow grapes and olives. Although a stockholder in the French Agricultural and Manufacturing Society, Lakanal did not personally take part in the Alabama experiment.

On August 27, 1817, there was a moment of excitement at the

French embassy in Washington as Hyde de Neuville opened a packet of letters sent to Joseph Bonaparte and intercepted by a royalist agent. The packet was addressed "To the comte de Survilliers: personal," and the seal reproduced the insignia of the National Convention: a Phrygian cap mounted on a pike, with around it, in the form of a garland, the words: "Lakanal, deputy to the National Convention." Inside, Hyde de Neuville found an envelope; inside this a second, then a third, a total of six altogether, all of them containing letters written and signed by Lakanal. The French envoy had in his possession other documents from the same source and recognized the handwriting immediately. "Sire," Lakanal wrote, "I am charged with conveying the enclosed papers to Your Majesty, requesting him to examine them in the order in which they are presented. I was asked to convey this important communication to you directly. But because I am about to start on a long and tiring journey, I am forced to hoard both my energy and my money."

He went on to explain that, unwilling for reasons of secrecy to entrust so important a communication to the mails, he had arranged for it to be delivered by a person unknown to him but recommended by reliable acquaintances.

His aim was to persuade Joseph Bonaparte to assert his claim to the throne of Spain and hence to that country's American colonies. The theory that Lakanal set forth in support of this proposal was hazy and quite contradictory to the ideas of his revolutionary past, although he asserted that its proponents "had logical principles and wanted to see free nations with legitimate rulers, in these terms' reasonable interpretation." Joseph, he said, was the legitimate leader of the Mexican insurgents. And, as king of Spain, he had a right to bestow Spanish decorations. Had not Louis XVIII ("the imposter now imposed upon us") made use of this right during his years of exile? Coming, then, to a more direct and personal point, he continued:

> In the position where Your Majesty's interests place me, I respectfully request him to confer upon me a Spanish decoration such as to link me to a country with which I have been familiar since childhood, since I was born in the former county of Foix, today the department of Ariège, where part of my family still lives.

> This new sign of your gracious favor will give me, in the eyes of your Mexican subjects, a political importance, which, I can confidently assure you, will be of great advantage to the interests of Your Majesty.

What, then, was the crux of the matter? It was the establishment of a "Napoleonic Confederation," which, as the project's first proposition defined it, "would entail the recruitment of nine hundred armed and equipped men as auxiliaries to the independent troops of Mexico." In order to assure "rapid enlistment" of westerners in this body,

> A hundred and fifty men will be appointed recruiting commissioners and go immediately to different parts of the District of Columbia, Michigan, Tennessee, Kentucky, and Ohio. . . . Sire: If it pleases Your Majesty to welcome our latest and definitive proposals, then he will set up a fund of a hundred thousand francs for their realization. Thus Your Majesty can be sure of rewinning one of the great thrones of the Universe and of reestablishing his illustrious dynasty.
> Among those of us who are sincerely devoted to Your Majesty's august cause and who have, moreover, exact knowledge of the situation, there is no doubt as to the success of the enterprise.

According to Lakanal, the settlers of the West went in exclusively for raising corn, and during the long periods of the year when they were not engaged in sowing or reaping they were free to indulge in "hunting, fishing, and adventurous undertakings." Thus they would gladly give over their free time to reconquering the throne of Mexico for King Joseph!

Hyde de Neuville wrote immediately to the duc de Richelieu to convey his double concern over, first, an uprising stemming from the American West, "for the secret purpose of making Joseph Bonaparte king of Mexico" and, second, a plan to achieve the escape of Napoleon.

> Watchfulness is called for [he wrote in alarm]. According to the latest news from St. Helena, Bonaparte is well but refuses to see anybody. Is he trying to get away without immediate notice of his absence? If so, and if he has a fishing craft at his disposal and also the services of a naval officer, he might well arrange to be met, at a prearranged time and latitude, by swift sailing vessels

from South American ports. I have no knowledge of the sea, but I have consulted with navy men, and I say that, unless unparalleled care is taken, we may fear the worst.

Where should we be if this extraordinary man were to land in a reconquered Mexico?

Several events provided a basis for Hyde de Neuville's concern. Two months before the discovery of Lakanal's project, two members of Napoleon's suite—Rousseau and Archambault—expelled by the English from St. Helena had arrived in the United States. Were they to communicate orally to Joseph Bonaparte an escape plan conceived by his brother? And when the Emperor first heard of Joseph's arrival in the States, he had said to General Montholon: "In his place, within a year I'd put together a great empire of all the Spanish Americas."

In the course of his detention on St. Helena, more than one escape plan was proposed to the Emperor. In May, 1816, he refused a project of Las Cases. In August of the same year, a proposal was made, through Montholon, to effect a rescue for the sum of a million francs, payable, on his word, when he actually set foot on American soil. "The Emperor," Montholon tells us, "listened with an apparently meditative air. He walked up and down the room, turned to ask the opinion of Gourgaud and myself, then, without any discussion, said to me: 'Turn it down!' . . . . On October 12, another escape plan was submitted. He listened to it without interest and merely asked to see the historical dictionary."

In this same year, the celebrated American freebooter, Carpenter, was said to have proposed to Joseph Bonaparte a plan for the rescue of his brother at the price of 100,000 piasters. The various escape proposals made in 1817 and Napoleon's furtive dallying with them further aroused Hyde de Neuville's fears. Indeed, a plan conceived by Napoleon himself and set forth to Montholon in July was in line with what Hyde de Neuville imagined just a month later. An officer of the St. Helena garrison had made what seemed like serious suggestions. The Emperor was to go secretly to a point opposite Jamestown, where the soldiers of an infantry post would shut their eyes to his presence. Thence a launch manned by powerful oarsmen (just what Hyde de Neuville imagined) would take him to a waiting sailing vessel. Napoleon refused without hesitation. But, in July, as we have indicated, in Montholon's presence, he studied a map of the island, pointing out "the ways and means of getting out of Longwood, reaching the coast, and secretly sailing away." Here, too, the Emperor's ideas were matched by Hyde de Neuville's deductions: "It could be thought that I was sticking to my bedroom. The governor is used to my habit of staying shut up there for several days in succession. We should send one or both of our ladies to pay a call, that day, at Plantation House. O'Meara would go to town, and, while in her Plantation House drawing room Lady Lowe was conducting a fine conversation about me, we should get out of this cursed place." Then, with a laugh, the Emperor added: "I have fifteen years of life ahead of me, and the idea of escape is attractive. But it's sheer madness. I must die here unless France comes to fetch me. If Jesus Christ hadn't died on the Cross, he wouldn't be God."

Martyrdom, transfiguration, a living legend, impregnating France and impregnated by her—such was what Napoleon wanted, at this point, to make of his destiny. The dreams of his exiled followers did not haunt the general who had once said, "I draw up my battle plans from the dreams of my sleeping soldiers." And his final resignation to the estate of prisoner was not understood by the veterans who sought to free him and restore his empire.

All the while the governor of St. Helena, Sir Hudson Lowe, had every reason to fear that his prisoner might escape. Napoleon, he knew, had a particular score to settle, for Hudson Lowe had commanded a Corsican battalion that chose to side with England against him. The interviews between Napoleon and his jailer on St. Helena were notoriously stormy. In complaining of the way Hudson Lowe spoke to his aide, General Bertrand, Napoleon shouted, "You write and talk to him as if he were a corporal, not in a troop of brave soldiers, but in the battalion of deserters and traitors that you commanded." Later the Emperor said to Mr. Ricketts, nephew of Lord Liverpool, when he stopped at St. Helena: "As colonel of the Corsican battalion, Sir Hudson Lowe is the last man whom your uncle should have assigned to this post. He is a horrible fellow and no true Englishman. Crime is written on his face."

In Napoleon's animosity there was plainly an element of

Corsican vendetta. Sir Hudson could expect a repetition of the humiliating experience that he underwent at Capri with the Corsican soldiers under his command. Capri had fallen into English hands, and, with its steep cliffs, not unlike those of St. Helena, it seemed impervious to attack. Lieutenant Colonel Hudson Lowe was appointed governor, with five companies of the regiment of Royal Corsican Rangers under his command. In 1808, Napoleon's brother-in-law, Joachim Murat, became king of Naples and immediately organized an expeditionary force, led by General Lamarque, to conquer the island. Thanks to the resourcefulness, endurance, and audacity of the French soldiers, Hudson Lowe had to cede it to the Kingdom of Naples in return for a safe-conduct for himself and his men. Later he was to say: "More than once, on Saint Helena, Napoleon made fun of my defeat and called me 'the hero of Capri.' As if I could have won out against betrayal, the cowardice of my soldiers, and the terrible audacity of the French who, at this time, recognized no resistance or obstacle."

Actually, the precautions with which the London government surrounded the defense of St. Helena made escape virtually impossible. In August, 1817, while Hyde de Neuville was worrying about an escape plot, the king of France's commissioner to St. Helena, the marquis de Montchenu, wrote reassuringly to a friend in Angoulême on this very subject, explaining the measures taken by the British for the surveillance of their prisoner:

> Have no fear, good people of Angoulême; you will never see the fellow again, I promise you, as long as I am here! The garrison numbers around 2500 men, some 500 pieces of artillery and 20 mortars. He [Napoleon] lives in the lieutenant-governor's country house, situated in the only flat area of the island, a pleateau called Longwood, which is surrounded by terrifyingly steep cliffs and accessible by a single road. Here there is a camp occupied by the 58th Regiment and an artillery depot, and rimmed with guard posts. Within this area he can walk, accompanied by a high-ranking uniformed officer who is lodged in his house and keeps track of his every movement during the day. The persons of his suite are similarly watched by a lieutenant and his servants by a sergeant. A sort of telegraphic system covers the island and gives out news every hour of what is going on. Inside one or, at the most, two minutes, an alarm can be registered and within no more than four minutes the whole

place would be under arms. So much for the land arrangements. At sea they are even more systematic. At least two frigates are always at anchor and two brigs sail around the island day and night, while from six in the evening to six in the morning armed launches patrol the inlets of the mountainous shores. At night no other boat, whether publicly or privately owned, is allowed to navigate; after nine P.M. it may be gunned on sight. There is no passage without a watchword, and constant fear of arrest. No foreign vessels are allowed to land. Their approach is immediately signaled, and a reward of a piaster is given to whoever first detects them, which is when they are as far as sixty miles away. This distance cannot be covered in a single night. The coast is dangerously rocky and the sea is so rough that days sometimes go by when it is impossible to make a landing. You see, dear friend, that escape seems to be materially out of the question.

Nevertheless, the British government considered every hypothesis, no matter how far-fetched. Although it seemed as if no ship could approach St. Helena without authorization, what about the disquieting rumors from America about the construction of an undersea vessel? Napoleon's soldiers had so often been unbelievably intrepid—might they make daring use of this new and fearful invention?

French royalists were particularly disquieted by the arrival in the United States in April, 1817, of General Charles Lallemand. On St. Helena, Napoleon spoke of him to Dr. O'Meara as follows: "Lallemand was employed by me at Acre as a negotiator with Sidney Smith, during which he displayed considerable address and ability. After my return from Elba he . . . declared for me in a moment of the greatest danger. . . . *Lallemand a beaucoup de décision, est capable de faire les combinaisons*, and there are few men more qualified to lead a hazardous enterprise. He has the *feu sacré*. He commanded the *chasseurs de la garde* at Waterloo, and *enfonça* some of your battalions."

Lallemand had tears in his eyes when he witnessed Napoleon's embarkation on the *Bellerophon* in 1815. Later, he wrote, "They were the tears of courage reduced to impotence." Before the Emperor's final decision, he had gone aboard the ship with Las Cases in order to see Captain Maitland. He stood out alone, against Bertrand, Savary, Montholon, Las Cases, and Gourgaud, in the conviction that "there is no liberty for the Emperor except in the United States of America." In 1817, Lakanal's project and the idea of freeing Napoleon gave him an opportunity to plunge into what his former chief had called a "hazardous enterprise."

General (and Baron) Charles Lallemand was born in Metz in 1774, so that when he came to the United States he was forty-three years old. After taking part in the Italian and Egyptian campaigns, he was sent to Santo Domingo with General Leclerc. His conduct during the campaigns in Prussia, Poland, and Spain won him the rank of brigadier general in 1811. Under the first Restoration, he remained loyal to the army rather than to the Emperor and, as a consequence, was decorated with the Cross of Saint Louis and given military command of the department of the Aisne. But when he heard that Napoleon had disembarked in France, he began to conspire—along with his brother Henri and General Lefebvre-Desnouettes—in his favor. Under suspicion, Desnouettes hid in the house of General Rigaud, but both Lallemands were arrested at La Fère. Napoleon, back in power, made Charles a lieutenant general and member of the Chamber of Peers; he fought at Fleurus and Waterloo, where he was wounded. The English would not heed his plea to accompany his adored Emperor to St. Helena but held him prisoner on Malta, while the government of Louis XVIII put him on the first list of the Ordinance of July 24, 1815, and a court-martial sentenced him to death *in absentia*. After being freed by the English, he went to Smyrna and Constantinople, where he asked the sultan to appoint him as a military instructor to the Turkish army. Reluctant to offend the king of France, the sultan turned him down, and so did the shah of Persia. Back in Constantinople, he got a letter from his younger brother, Henri-Dominique, telling him of the arrival of himself, Joseph Bonaparte, and other exiles on American soil. Without hesitation, Charles embarked on the first vessel sailing to the United States.

His brother, born in Paris in 1777, was of a quieter nature. He, too, entered the artillery: he was made general of a division during the Hundred Days and commanded the artillery of the Guard at Waterloo. As a refugee in London, under a false name, he heard of the death sentence passed upon him and set sail for the United States. Charles rejoined him just in time to attend his marriage to a niece of the millionaire Stephen Girard on October 26, 1817. Other guests included Joseph Bonaparte, Marshal

Grouchy and his son, and General Vandamme. The wedding dinner, according to witnesses, was exceedingly gay. Henri settled in Bordentown, near Joseph Bonaparte, and edited a treatise on artillery, little known in France but highly appreciated in the United States.

Charles Lallemand was tall and broad-shouldered, with an excitable manner and persuasive and authoritarian ways. He exercised an immediate influence on the other Bonapartist exiles. In the United States, he soon met the future partner in his adventures, General Rigaud, now sixty years old, whom Napoleon had called a "martyr to glory." Among his many battle wounds were those caused by a bullet that broke his jaw, mutilated his tongue, and perforated his palate.

Born at Agen in 1758, at the age of thirty Rigaud was a captain in the Belgian cavalry. When Belgium was joined to France, he found himself a French officer. He took part in the campaigns of Napoleon, who in 1807 made him a brigadier general. After Waterloo, he was captured by the Russians while defending the town where he lived, Châlons-sur-Marne, with a garrison of only 150 men. Like Lallemand, he was sentenced to death *in absentia*. Escaping from his captors, he made for Ghent and Antwerp, whence he sailed to the United States; he disembarked at Philadelphia with his son Narcisse and his daughter Aimée in 1817.

The commanding and decisive personality of Charles Lallemand quite naturally won him the presidency of the company formed to introduce the cultivation of grapes and olives in Alabama. But he soon wrote to his brother: "I have more ambition than that which is gratified by the colony upon the Tombigbee." Indeed, he bent his efforts to winning over officers of the company to the pursuit of mysterious interests of his own. Instead of going to join General Lefebvre-Desnouettes on the Tombigbee, he frequented the docks of New Orleans, questioning the captains of newly arrived ships and looking over the merchandise that they had unloaded. What, people wondered, could be the reason for his varied purchases? He collected glass trinkets of the kind used to gain the friendship of the Indians and tried to obtain 1500 Bibles printed in "the language of the natives of Texas." But what about the cases of guns and ammunition and the rumor that he was after cannons as well? What was the subject of his discussions with rough seamen in the back-street taverns of the city? Where did he get the money to buy what he did? For, as the traveler Edouard de Montulé tells us, Lallemand had left the Hotel Trémoulet and taken lodging in the country "for economic reasons. Like most of the Frenchmen forced by recent events to take refuge abroad, he is not rich, a fact that Americans find surprising."

A Napoleonic confederation, insurrection in Mexico, preparations for an armed expedition to Texas (a territory of Spain), and the presence of Charles Lallemand who, according to Napoleon, possessed the "sacred fire"—all these things combined to disquiet French diplomatic representatives and, to a lesser degree, the United States government. After Hyde de Neuville had examined the documents signed by Lakanal, he sent copies to the State Department, in the hope that they would be published. To Secretary of State John Quincy Adams he wrote: "I thought that, in the case of documents so authentic, there would be no obstacle to a juridical enquiry and perhaps even to the arrest of that conspirator whose writing and signature have been recognized and verified. But Lakanal had, on this score, nothing to fear, for Adams replied: "From the nature of the institutions and laws of this country you must be aware that the repressive powers of the government, in their application to the freedom of individuals, are limited to cases of actual transgression and do not extend to projects which, however exceptionable in their character, have not been matured at least into an attempt or a commencement of execution." He gave assurance, nevertheless, that the American government would take into account any "designs illegal in their character."

Although this reply to the French envoy was evasive in its wording, the American government sought on its own account for further information. President Monroe asked William Lee, governor of Alabama, to inform him of the activities of French officers. In a letter of September 27, 1817, Lee wrote:

> It appears from all I can learn that an expedition is contemplated against Mexico, at the head of which is General l'Allemand, his brother, Col. Galabert and many other French officers of inferior grade. They have engaged eighty French officers and one thousand men. A mercantile house at Charleston S.C. has offered

to assist them with money and two brigs well armed. Some merchants in Philadelphia, among whom is a Mr. Curcier—some at New York and two in Boston, Stackpole and Adams, are also connected in the enterprise.

I learn that the younger Gen'l L'Allemand, returned from New Orleans but a short time since and while there, sent a French officer of talents to Mexico, to obtain information and sound the patriots. This officer has lately returned . . . and is in Philadelphia. He represents that two of the most opulent and influential men in Mexico—Valencias and Cordovo (if I have their names correct) are ready with all their means, being proprietors of the largest mines and having at their disposal ten thousand raw troops who only wait for French officers to discipline them.

Gen'l L'Allemand intends to go up the Red River with his officers and about 400 men, there to form a *noyau* for collecting together all his forces and means.

Joseph Bonaparte and the high-ranking officers close to him disapproved of Lallemand's project. The irascible General Vandamme called Lallemand and Galabert "boys, fools, and madmen," and Joseph Bonaparte refused to guarantee financing of the expedition. Meanwhile, when Lee explained to Lallemand "in as strong terms as I am master of . . . the mischiefs his projects were calculated to heap upon his countrymen and their friends," the French general promised "not to prosecute his plan of attacking Mexico until next winter," because he thought that, before then, the American Congress would come out in favor of the Mexican insurgents.

Adams held that the government should put a speedy end to all such schemes, but he was reluctant to publish the Lakanal papers even if, as he wrote to President Monroe in October, "the representatives of a Bourbon sovereign may fairly claim to be indulged in an extraordinary degree of solicitude with regard to any project in which the Bonaparte family are concerned." First, publication would involve Joseph Bonaparte in a matter of which he actually disapproved and, also, it would give the European governments another excuse for refusing to allow his brother, Lucien, to come to the United States. It was uncertain, moreover, to whom the documents were meant to be useful and for what exact purpose they had been drawn up.

In November, Adams had a visit from Charles Lallemand, who "entered into a long explanation of his views and intentions, with a strong denial of his having ever contemplated engaging in any project contrary to the laws of the United States." Lallemand claimed to have turned down an invitation to take part in ongoing insurrections. Moreover, "he did not know Lakanal, had never seen him, knew nothing whether he had written these letters, whether they were forgeries or what they were."

Adams was not convinced by Lallemand's explanations. The matter seemed to him even more complex when he learned, in January, 1818, that the general's second-in-command, Colonel Galabert, had called on Don Luis de Onís, minister of the king of Spain. Then, too, there were the secret contacts between the French officers and certain British agents sent out to favor upheaval in Latin America in order to strip Spain of its colonial trade. Lallemand's project aroused interest or suspicion among many of the major powers.

France wanted to play the role of mediator between Spain and the United States in connection with the contested boundaries between these two countries in Florida and Texas, for which it had, as we have seen, a historical responsibility. Charles Lallemand's presence in Texas did not simplify the task. Clearly, Spain did not want to cede an inch of its colonies for the benefit of another country. Perhaps the Spanish minister in Washington had proposed to make it financially advantageous to the French officers to desist from aid to the Mexican insurgents. As for England, at the time of the continental blockade it had owed the maintenance of its economy in part to its trade with Spanish America, which was cut off from the mother country and half independent. Now that the contact between Spain and its colonies was reestablished, it behooved London to reconquer and broaden its Latin-American markets. So soon after the War of 1812 any armed English intervention in a region close to the United States was inadvisable, but England might be tempted to stir up trouble through French officers of proven military ability. The United States, for its part, did not hide the urge for expansion to the detriment of Spain. But the shrinking of the Spanish frontier must not occur for the benefit of some other power. And the question was on whose behalf Lallemand was acting.

The tension of the various governments was heightened by the explosive nature of the Latin-American situation. While Joseph Bonaparte reigned over Spain, the Spanish colonies were virtually autonomous. Their leaders, refusing to recognize the legitimacy of the Bonaparte rule and severed from the motherland, governed in the name of Ferdinand VII, an absentee king who could exercise no authority over them. After Waterloo, Ferdinand returned to the throne of Spain but the autocratic rule that he tried to impose on the colonies turned the leaders who had formerly governed in his name against him. Wars of independence sprang up all over Spanish America, led by General Bolívar in the north and General San Martín in the south. These two insurgent generals had recourse to the military skill of the French officers exiled after Waterloo. At the time when Charles Lallemand came to the United States, Mexico, Peru, Colombia, and Venezuela were under the iron rod of Madrid. But, from Jamaica, Bolívar was hatching his revenge.

The Chilean insurgents had taken refuge, after their defeat, with San Martín in Argentina; "liberated" Buenos Aires and Montevideo proclaimed their independence. Mexico had fallen back into Spanish hands. In 1813, a priest called José Maria Morelos had caused a "congress" to ratify a declaration of independence and a constitution; but Spanish troops of the *reconquista* won the last battle, and Morelos was shot in 1815. The "congress" moved from town to town, evading the conquering army, and armed insurgents took to the mountains to pursue the struggle. In 1816, Francisco Javier Mina, with a group of fifteen Spanish, Italian, and English officers, left London to participate in the Mexican insurrection. Like Lallemand, Mina gathered men and munitions and traveled to New Orleans, Galveston, and Port-au-Prince to organize an expedition. It was justifiably worrisome that Lallemand, too, was readying his expedition in New Orleans and leading his men, as we shall see, to Galveston, near the Mexican border. Mina, in any case, recruited no more than 250 men. He was defeated and executed by the Spaniards on October 11, 1818, not far from the site chosen by Lallemand for his colony. However, no formal proof of connivance between the two men has been found.

Portuguese Brazil, too, was swept by the wind of independence. The insurrection in the province of Pernambuco was particularly

The "Field of Refuge" 115

disquieting to the courts of Europe and to Hyde de Neuville, inasmuch as this was the base for an expedition—one considered particularly threatening—to rescue Napoleon from St. Helena.

Since the end of 1815, Brazil had been a kingdom ruled by the house of Bragança. King João VI of Portugal, driven out by the armies of Napoleon's General Junot, disembarked at Rio de Janeiro in 1808. But liberal and revolutionary ideas, triggered chiefly by Masonic lodges favorable to independence, ran through the country.

On March 6, 1817, the province of Pernambuco rose up in arms. At Recife, the provincial capital, the governor capitulated and was conveyed to Rio in a revolutionary vessel. A republic was proclaimed, privileges abolished, and liberties accorded. The new government was rapidly set up, in order to obtain recognition on the part of other countries and also material and military aid as soon as possible. Without delay, the citizens of Pernambuco sent a representative to the United States. "I am convinced," Hyde de Neuville wrote to the duc de Richelieu, "that the self-syled minister of this self-styled government, who, Your Excellency tells me, has arrived in Boston, will not be received in Washington."

Hyde de Neuville was very nearly correct. The envoy of Pernambuco was received only privately and unofficially by the secretary of state. He did, however, assemble men, ships, arms, and ammunition, and exiled French officers were among the first volunteers. The reason for their alacrity was the location of Pernambuco and, in particular, of an island called Fernando do Noronha, off the coast, the point of land from which St. Helena was most accessible.

Colonel Latapie, a refugee in the United States since 1816, went to Philadelphia to expose the plan of attack on St. Helena to Joseph Bonaparte. It seems that Joseph took the plan seriously and encouraged the young colonel to group men and ships in Brazil.

Paul de Latapie was a cavalry officer, born at Cahors in 1786, and was thus only thirty years old when, after several spectacular escapes from captivity, he reached the United States. After the Hundred Days, he was on the list of those to be tried before a court-martial. Disguised, alternately, as a peasant and a British captain, he managed to set sail from Antwerp.

Toward the end of 1817, an American ship, the *Paragon*, with

Latapie, the comte de Pontécoulant, and seventy other volunteers aboard, approached the coast of Brazil. According to royalist agents, General Brayer, exiled by the Restoration and in the service of General San Martín in Buenos Aires, and Admiral Cochrane, a British renegade who was in command of the fleet of Chile, were to join Latapie at the island of Fernando do Noronha.

General Brayer was forty-six years old. His energetic manner and enterprising character attested to his taste for adventure. Lord Cochrane had been a brilliant officer of the British navy, famous for his destruction of a French squadron in 1809. But, from his seat in Parliament, he was an enemy to Lord Liverpool's government. Accused of having provoked a panic in the Stock Exchange by announcing false news of a victory of Napoleon, he was sentenced to payment of a fine and to an hour in the pillory, which latter punishment, however, was spared him. Cochrane left England and offered his abilities and the prestige of his name to the revolutionaries of South America.

Reports on the undertaking of Latapie, Brayer, and Cochrane came to the desk of the duc de Richelieu. He was informed that "the expeditionary force consisted of two 300-ton schooners, mounted with cannons, and a vessel armed by Lord Cochrane, carrying, all together, eighty French officers and seven hundred men recruited in the United States."

Events conspired to frustrate Latapie's dream. Although the Portuguese ambassador to Washington was unsuccessful in his demand that the American government seize the men and arms on their way to Pernambuco, the colonial governor general in Rio de Janeiro dispatched a large contingent of troops to the provincial capital and the young republic's army was quickly destroyed. When Latapie and his companions disembarked on the Brazilian coast, the Republic of Pernambuco was no more, and the local authorities, acting now in the name of Rio and the Bragianças, arrested and jailed the French officers. But when they were brought up for trial, the court at Recife declared itself incompetent to pass judgment upon them. Latapie stated to the governor general that "he and the other Frenchmen were in Philadelphia when they heard news of the revolution in Pernambuco, that Joseph Bonaparte, with whom he had connections, had urged him to go down there, investigate the actual state of affairs and report on it, that, according to what Joseph Bonaparte had said, he was looking for an opportunity to set up a small fleet and free the former Emperor."

When Latapie was sent for questioning to Rio, he told the truth about his enterprise to Minister of State Bezerra, who had promised, in exchange, to set him free. When Bezerra expostulated that it was sheer madness, Latapie said he had counted on embarking Napoleon on a steamboat. How ironical this would have been, in view of the fact that Napoleon had not been farsighted enough to favor the development of this invention in France when Robert Fulton had offered it to him! In any case, the court at Rio, in March, 1818, decreed that the prisoners should be taken to Europe and liberated at the Portuguese border.

From the very beginning of 1818, European governments and also St. Helena were acquainted with Latapie's project. Longwood was in a state of subdued excitement. Count Balmain, the Russian commissioner, whispered to Gourgaud, while they were riding horseback together, the names of Brayer and Latapie. Rumor had it that the French officers arrested in Pernambuco had intended to attack St. Helena with a "Sommariva" submarine vessel. An alarmed Sir Hudson Lowe doubled and tripled the number of sentries ringing Longwood.

No connection between Lallemand and Latapie was ever discovered. According to the reports of various French consuls, the two men had not even met. It is not inconceivable, however, that, while Latapie planned for Napoleon's escape, Lallemand sought to set up in Texas a base from which the liberated Emperor could launch the conquest of Mexico.

Did Napoleon himself, as certain historians maintain, lay the plans for an attack on St. Helena? This theory is based, chiefly, on the extravagant revelations made by Colonel Roul, of which we have made earlier mention. According to Roul, when Rousseau was expelled from St. Helena he brought with him a plan of the island, bearing the signatures of "Bonaparte" and of "Napoleon." And it is true that Rousseau came to the United States in order to see Joseph Bonaparte. Roul further claimed that Generals Lefebvre-Desnouettes and Clauzel were involved in the plot. The royalists, as we have seen, came to the conclusion that Roul was totally untrustworthy. The only element of plausibility lies in the coincidental fact that his revelations closely preceded the discovery of Lakanal's papers and of Lapatie's undertaking.

It has been said, likewise, that Napoleon corresponded from St. Helena with a former aide-de-camp, the Dutch general Dirk van Hogendorp, who was living a hermit's existence on the peak of Corcovado near Rio de Janeiro. Is it possible that, in spite of this isolation and the surveillance of a British agent, the Dutchman served as a connecting link between Napoleon and the French officers who were plotting to free him? No proof of such linkage has been found. Latapie's venture did, however, make a widespread impression. Chateaubriand writes in his memoirs: "There were rescue projects. A certain Colonel Latapie, at the head of a band of American adventurers, had the idea of descending upon St. Helena. A rough-and-ready smuggler called Johnston said that he could spirit Bonaparte away on an underwater vessel. Young lords had a part in his plans. . . . But Bonaparte himself laid his hopes in political events in Europe."

The testimony of Napoleon's companions in exile confirms Chateaubriand's last assertion. Napoleon was looking to a change of government in either London or Paris. In France, the Liberal opposition party was gaining strength, and its newspapers spoke of the "heroic Bolívar" and of the Independents' struggle for "liberty." Hyde de Neuville, as a conservative, thought that "two Bourbon monarchies in the Southern Hemisphere would be useful not to Spain alone but to all the governments of Europe. . . . For this ultraliberal spirit, if it fires the New World, may eventually devour the Old." Indeed, the gains of the "ultraliberal spirit" in both France and South America threw royalist and conservative spirits into disarray. Richelieu confided to his ambassador in Washington that he had lost hope of resolving "the important matter of the Spanish colonies" by means of a European meeting. And Chateaubriand, Hyde de Neuville's personal friend, wrote to him: "Mine is the voice of the prophet announcing its fall to Jerusalem."

Great Britain could brook a worldwide influence of the Bourbons no more than that of Napoleon. No man or government or country must be strong enough to cut off Britain's trade routes, a vast network encircling the globe. Hyde de Neuville perspicaciously evaluated the importance to the British economy of the Isthmus of Panama. "What does it matter," he wrote to the foreign minister, "if the Floridas fall into the hands of the United States as long as, one day, the British flag flies over the inland sea of Nicaragua, and England is mistress of this spit of land called Panama, which brings China three thousand leagues closer and gives exclusive access to invaluable exchanges with the Far East? I return frequently to the subject of this Isthmus, because I am convinced that, more than ever, the British have designs upon it."

The Gulf of Mexico and the waters near the Isthmus of Panama were overrun by numerous privateers and adventurers who, in the opinion of Hyde de Neuville and his colleague, the ambassador of Spain, were in the pay of Great Britain. Hyde said insistently to the duc de Richelieu that, if the Isthmus were to be pierced, "all countries wishing to route their freight-carrying ships through the canal would be dependent on the nation that owned it." And he added: "Your Excellency tells me that a great buildup of arms is under way in England. Might not the purpose be the one I have indicated above? MacGregor is certainly a British agent."

Gregor MacGregor, the handsome son of a Scottish laird, had taken part in the revolutionary movement in South America by offering his services to the Venezuelan Francisco de Miranda. The expedition that he was to organize, with the support of English traders, against the province of Panama confirmed Hyde de Neuville's suspicion. The year before, he had been named a general in the insurgent forces of Venezuela. In late 1817, when Lallemand was preparing his expedition to Texas, the American government used MacGregor in its project to conquer the Spanish province of the Floridas (East and West). MacGregor, at the head of a group of adventurers from various countries, seized Amelia Island, proclaimed the independence of the Floridas, and then, in connivance with Washington, ceded his place to an envoy from the American capital. At this point, a French privateer, Louis Aury, in his turn conquered the island, drove the Americans away, and declared himself president of the Republic of the Floridas. Finally, threatened by Washington, Aury withdrew, and, in December, 1817, the Americans took possession. Half a year later, in July, 1818, General Andrew Jackson, under the pretext of a punitive expedition against the Seminole Indians, took over the Floridas. Faced with this state of affairs, Spain later officially ceded the province to the United States.

Among Aury's followers was a Captain Maurice Persat, decorated with the Legion of Honor by Napoleon's own hand and undyingly devoted to him. When he heard, in Paris, a rumor that Joseph Bonaparte was readying an expedition to free his brother, he set sail immediately for the United States and went straight to the comte de Survilliers.

> The Prince [he says in his *Mémoires*] welcomed me with the amenity that Frenchmen have always found him to possess. He said, in a touching manner, that he was ready to sacrifice his life and fortune for the deliverance of the Emperor, but that news of certain barbarous threats on the part of the English government had forced him to give up any such plans. London had sent orders to St. Helena that the Emperor would be put to death in the event of any serious attack on the four thousand jailers who were watching over him as gloatingly as cannibals over a human prey.

Because he had "no vocation for business," Persat resolved to go serve the insurgents of Colombia. In September, 1817, he embarked on the *Libre Américain*, along with "250 other passengers, white and black." Overtaken by a violent storm, they fought off seasickness by drinking cognac and singing the *Marseillaise*. At Charleston they ordered from a certain Citizen Picault "a regal dinner, that is, copious, refined, and accompanied by good wine." When dessert came, it was proposed that they drink to the health of the Emperor. As Persat tells it:

> Frenchmen, Englishmen, Americans, Italians, and mulattoes rose spontaneously to their feet and responded to the toast. Only one man remained seated and said, in a voice as frail as his body: "I do not drink to the health of tyrants." The speaker was Citizen Picault, whom we had invited to dine with us. The poor fellow had hardly come out with his inopportune observation when he was seized by Captain Bernard, who wanted unceremoniously to throw him overboard. And such would have been his fate had I not snatched his trembling body from Bernard's hand, for the captain had grabbed his throat so roughly that he had fainted away. "Scoundrel!" said Bernard, "I served

the Republic better than you did, but I serve the Emperor as well, and I shall never allow either one to be insulted."

At Charleston, also, Persat heard of the presence of Aury on Amelia Island and resolved to join him. Aury made him major general of an army of Frenchmen, Italians, and Creoles from the islands.

Secretary of State John Quincy Adams suspected General Lallemand of complicity with Aury. In the course of their interview, Lallemand denied having anything to do with either Aury or MacGregor. But, as we know, Adams remained skeptical and asked William Lee to pursue his inquiry. In his report, received by Adams on January 20, 1818, Lee wrote:

> It appears the Generals L'Allemand are seriously engaged in an expedition destined for some part of Spanish America.
> They are purchasing arms and ammunition in New York.
> They have agents in Louisiana and the Mississippi enlisting frenchmen and others.
> They have, it is said, engaged in the United States about three hundred men.
> Aury's forces, it is said, is to join them and I am told they have acted from the beginning with them.
> They are going to the Danish Island of St. Thomas where a rendezvous is established it is said under indulgence of the Governor of the Island who served as Colonel with General L'Allemand and is much attached to him.
> They calculated on about 1500 men besides officers—with this force they are to leave . . . for some port in the Gulf of Darien to cross the Isthmus for Panama, there embark for Guayaquil and throw themselves into the mountains of Quito in the Province of Peru. . . . They expect to conquer that province and intend to organize it in such a manner as to afford protection to all who chose to join their standard.

From the start, the story of the Field of Refuge was enveloped in mystery and uncertainty, the mystery surrounding the succession of events and uncertainty, which has prevailed until this day, as to the colony's true purposes. A first contingent of Lallemand's recruits sailed from Philadelphia on an American schooner, the *Huntress*, on December 17, 1817. The leader was Rigaud, the only other general to participate since, according to Captain Just Girard, the remaining French officers of this rank found the project "impractical, perhaps mad, and, at the very least, dangerous and untimely." With him were fifteen colonels, fifteen staff officers, seven doctors, and about a hundred men, all of them squeezed into "very close quarters."

Charles Lallemand must have had tremendous powers of persuasion to involve this many men in a voyage to an unknown destination and one whose purpose few of them, except for General Rigaud, knew. The voyage, as far as New Orleans, was fraught with hardships, a violent storm when they had been only three days at sea, insufficient food, and passage from the severe winter of Philadelphia to the stifling heat of the Gulf of Mexico. According to Captain Just Girard, they had aboard six cannons, six hundred rifles, and four hundred swords.[1] After a stop at New Orleans, where the French population, largely Bonapartist in its sympathies, gave them a warm welcome, the voyagers finally learned their final destination: the island of Galveston in Texas, where General Lallemand and a second convoy were to join them.

The island of Galveston had been the point of departure for more than one ambitious expedition. A narrow, sandy piece of land off the coast of Texas, it was in a region where the boundary between the United States and the colonial empire of Spain was still disputed. For some years, it had been a hideout for pirates, privateers, mercenaries, and other adventurers operating in the Gulf of Mexico. In 1816, the representative in the United States of the Mexican insurgents had set up on the island a base for marauders whose aim was to harass Spanish shipping in the Gulf and to mount expeditions against King Ferdinand's army in Mexico. The Frenchman Louis Aury, whom we mentioned in connection with Captain Persat, was charged with occupying the island; on September 12, he was named commodore of the fleet of the Republic of Mexico as well as civil and military governor of Texas and Galveston. In November, Aury and his men were surprised to see come over the horizon the sails of the ships commanded by another revolutionary in the service of the Mexicans, General Francisco Javier Mina. The two men did not hit it off, but for fear of an American raid they joined forces in minor marauding excursions against the Spaniards. In April, 1817, about a year before Lallemand's arrival, Aury left the island, after setting fire to the few buildings he had erected, and withdrew all but one of his ships from the harbor. Mina was soon captured and executed by the Spanish. As for Aury, he prepared to return to the island, but, when he got there, he was amazed to find that it had a new master, the picturesque and celebrated privateer or pirate Jean Laffite.

It was Jean Laffite, a figure still legendary in America today, who greeted General Rigaud and his companions at Galveston. Laffite was born at Port-au-Prince, Haiti, around 1782 to a French father, probably from Bayonne, and a Spanish Jewess mother. His maternal grandfather had been accused of practicing alchemy and died in the prisons of the Inquisition. Jean wrote on the frontispiece of his Bible: "I owe all my ingenuity to the intuition of my grandmother, a Spanish Jewess who bore witness at the time of the Inquisition." He was a physically impressive man with a dark Creole complexion, black hair and beard, and a usually courteous manner, although at times he displayed violent anger. He spoke most often in French but was almost equally fluent in English, Spanish, and Italian.

Jean Laffite and his brother Pierre came in the early years of the century to New Orleans, where they held jobs for a while in the city's custom office. They were responsible for the arrest of a number of smugglers, but, at the same time, they had relations themselves with freebooters and adventurers from a variety of places, whom they met in taverns such as the Maspero, the Hôtel Trémoulet, Le Veau Qui Tète, and, above all, the Café des Réfugiés, where the host, Jean-Baptiste Thiot, served a special alcoholic drink based on the root of the century plant.

In 1811, a delegation of freebooters, set up in Barataria Bay, at the mouth of the Mississippi, came to ask Jean Laffite, with whose strong personality they were acquainted, to take on their leadership. The task was not easy because of the group's heterogeneous and volatile character.

Jean Laffite accepted without hesitation and soon managed to attach his followers to the Latin-American revolutionaries. Laffite's men, flying the flag of Cartagena in Colombia, attacked Spanish shipping and brought their booty back to Barataria. Jean Laffite himself often stayed ashore and sent out his brother, Pierre, and his young lieutenants: Dominique You from Santo Domingo, known as "Tiger"; Renato Beluche, the future Venezuelan admiral; and two Italians, Gambio and Chigizola ("Slit Nose"). The Laffite brothers opened a store on the Rue Royale in New Orleans, where they sold the great quantities of merchandise on which they had laid hands. This happy turn of affairs was spoiled, however, by the arrival of a new governor of Louisiana in 1813. The pirates beat up his customs guards; the sheriff offered $500 for the capture of Jean Laffite, and the latter, in his turn, offered $30,000 for the kidnapping of the governor! Pierre Laffite was the one to be captured, but he soon escaped and hurried to warn his brother that armed forces were about to swoop down on Barataria. Foreseeing an unequal combat, Jean Laffite beat a retreat with his men to the interior. The American army laid waste to Barataria and confiscated half a million dollars' worth of goods.

At this point, the War of 1812 between Britain and America gave Jean Laffite and his followers a chance to enter history and legend. During the first days of 1815, an army of 14,000 Englishmen was preparing to attack New Orleans, and General Andrew Jackson had only four companies of regulars, 600 militiamen, and no artillery with which to oppose them. Neither side, as we remember, knew that the war was over. Jean Laffite emerged from his retreat and offered Jackson reinforcements. On January 8, the pirate battery commanded by Dominique You and Renato Beluche effected a massacre among the English. New Orleans was saved, and President Madison offered an amnesty and American citizenship to Jean Laffite and his men.

Laffite put together another fleet and occupied the island of Galveston during Aury's absence. He rebuilt the settlement of Campêche (Campeachy) where, in memory of the Commune of Paris, he installed forty "citizens," whose numbers were soon increased by an influx of freebooters eager to serve under the celebrated pirate's command. In 1817, Galveston had more than a thousand inhabitants. Laffite maintained iron discipline; anyone who attempted violence against a woman was hanged on the spot. He himself lived in what, by reason of its color, was called the "Red House." Under his leadership, a motley crowd of Frenchmen, Spaniards, Portuguese, Maltese, blacks, and half-breeds from the West Indies infested the Gulf, sailing now under the flag of Venezuela.

Laffite made no secret of his admiration for Napoleon. Earlier on, as we know, the Mexican insurgents had given him a formal commission to run down the merchant ships of Spain. So the welcome that he gave to General Rigaud and the first contingent of Lallemand's Napoleonic veterans was not surprising. After all, Lallemand was suspected of plotting to rescue Napoleon and set up a base from which he could move to conquer Mexico.

This was the theory voiced in a report to Paris from Guillemin, the French consul at New Orleans: "The secret purpose of this undertaking seems to be known only to those who have planned it. I am almost certain that their agents, both here and at Galveston, do not know the object of the preparations to which they are devoting such hard work or the purpose of the expedition of which they are the instruments. We may, nevertheless, fix our gaze on two localities in particular: St. Helena and Mexico."

St. Helena was in Guillemin's mind because of the expedition leaders' personal attachment to Napoleon, the fact that the members—both officers and men—were exclusively French and, finally, that the command of an armed sailing vessel and a considerable sum of money in case of success had been offered to a former officer of the imperial navy. "Once saved, Bonaparte was to be taken to New York." As for Mexico, the consul alleged: "The nature and extent of the preparations under way in more than one place simultaneously; the meeting-place (Galveston on the coast of New Mexico); the journey of the elder Lallemand to Opelousas and in the direction of the border between Texas and the colony of Spain; the reported conversations of his followers, and his purchase of objects considered suitable gifts for savages." Hence the consul's conclusion that both St. Helena and Mexico were involved in General Lallemand's plans.

This reasoning had a historical and political basis. These men who had participated so actively in Napoleon's great designs quite naturally sought to deliver their chief, to give him another chance to leave his mark on history, and to take part themselves in his future conquests. Hyde de Neuville accepted an offer from the chevalier de Mun, a royalist living in the Mississippi Valley and a lieutenant colonel in the American militia, to mount a sort of counterguerrilla action against Lallemand and his followers. Louis de Mun alarmed the ambassador by his description of the region that was Lallemand's destination: "I consider New Mexico, under present circumstances, as one of the most vulnerable of the Spanish provinces that do not border on the sea. There are direct communications with the United States and conditions favorable to the insurgents if they choose to dig in and fortify themselves."

The story of Lallemand's colony and of the legend that grew up around it deserves more than a simplistic explanation and contains elements of true pathos, as we shall see in the pages to follow. Laffite put supplies and three boats at General Rigaud's disposal, but two months went by before General Lallemand's arrival. The veterans of the Grande Armée, suffering from the heat, mosquitoes, and forced idleness, endured with impatience their stay on the sandy, desertlike island of Galveston. Rigaud had to deal with frayed tempers, violent quarrels, and duels.

Finally, on March 20, Charles Lallemand, with a hundred followers, arrived on the scene and settled the date of departure for the site of the new colony for four days later. Embarkation was on the boats acquired from Laffite, and pirates and veterans bade one another farewell with cheers for liberty. At once a violent wind dispersed the boats, and one of them sank, bearing with it, among others, Colonel Vorster, and leaving Lieutenant Chenet as the sole survivor. Another boat, carrying Hartmann, one of the most important historians of the Field of Refuge, was grounded on a sandbank and stuck there until midnight, when some of Laffite's men, alerted by gunshots, came to the rescue. Four days later, the little fleet came to the Trinity River. Here the veterans split into two groups. Generals Lallemand and Rigaud, with a hundred men, proceeded up one bank on foot in order to reconnoiter the site chosen for the colony, while Colonel Sarrazin commanded the group charged with transporting arms, munitions, and supplies up the river by boat. The foot contingent beat its way with difficulty through a swampland and tropical vegetation, with no path or track to follow. Stragglers went astray, and, when food fell short, some of the marchers ate the leaves of something that looked like lettuce, which produced the effects of poison. Indians, watching their advance from behind the heavy foliage, emerged from hiding and offered them other leaves, which had an immediately curative effect. On the sixth day, they reached their destination and soon after had the joy of greeting Colonel Sarrazin and his men who had navigated the river. At last the Promised Land! "A broad, uninhabited plain, stretching out for several miles in semicircular shape like that of a bow, with woods all around and the Trinity River running in a straight line at one end like a bowstring." So Captain Gerard describes it. "Soil rich in plants and flowers, a river as wide as the Seine but infested with alligators, pure blue sky, and a temperature as mild as that of Naples—such was the place chosen for us to settle, to which we gave the name of Field of Refuge."

A pamphlet about Lallemand's colony published by L'Héritier in Paris, where there was passionate interest in the venture, explained the choice of its name as follows: "Greece, when it was still semibarbarous, had a number of preserves variously known as 'places,' 'fields,' or 'lands' of 'refuge' or 'asylum,' where a man could not be touched by the forces of the law or the political establishment."

Here we have another aspect of Lallemand's project, a haven from legal and political reprisal for soldiers victimized because they had fought on history's losing side. Texas was, at the time, a disputed territory of uncertain ownership. Small wonder that Owen, Cabet, and Considérant thought to set up their utopian colonies in this lonely, remote expanse, where they could hope to live out dreams stifled by civilization. Lallemand's vigorous denial of the political plotting attributed to him and the legend that at once grew up and around the Field of Refuge seem to point in a utopian direction.

The Field of Refuge, joining the idea of living in peace and benefiting from the resources of a land free of the demons of history to the idea of participating again in the epic of a leader who had seemed to his followers a man of destiny, seemed to combine the American and the Napoleonic dreams. The geographical location contained both elements: it was a no-man's-land, lending itself to utopias, and, at the same time, near an area where diplomats and strategists were engaged in the historical process of ideological and economic conflict.

Ever since they entered recorded time, men have expressed, alternately or together, their fascination with the lightning flashes of fate and the metamorphoses of history, and their fear of the sweeping sequence of events with all the cruelties that follow in its train. Gilles Lapouge, in *Utopies et Civilization*, gives a graphic picture of men's attempts, through the ages, to escape from history and "appease the precipitation of time." There are two ways to break the chains of time: either by seeking a paradise where time and its companion, death, no longer exist and a generous, frontierless earth gives forth its bounty, or else by submitting time to mastery.

> The utopian [says Lapouge] detests time and imprisons it. He saves himself from the horrors of history by elaborating a political "countersystem." A utopian city is a world in chains, a cruel state, an algebraic systematization of social life.... Utopians have fallen prey to a curious misfortune. Morality has taken them over and disfigured them. We have been persuaded that a utopian is an anarchist when, on the contrary, he dreams of constraint and organization. Men seek refuge from history in either the closed system of the utopians or the original anarchy of the counterutopians.

The discovery of America momentarily dispelled the ghosts haunting European men, so long steeped in history. America was the land unsoiled by history, where the Indian was a descendant of Abel, eating the fruit given him by a loving God. John Eliot, in his 1659 treatise on the Indians, tells how some colonists took the Indians for remnants of the lost tribes of Israel. And the Pilgrim Fathers, who went through life as if it were a long purgatory with a glimpse of paradise at its far end, unconsciously, little by little, identified their journey across the ocean and into the new continent as a march to the Promised Land.

Everyone who dreamed of an imaginary government capable of organizing life in a system closed and regulated like the mechanism of a watch looked expectantly at the New World. Here, at last, was a land where the imaginary could come true, where utopia was possible. The study of Aztec society confirmed this impression. In a city laid out on geometrical lines, with mathematically sublime architecture, thousands of uniformly accoutered individuals had their being. A perfected decimal system, city planning, the symmetry of pyramids: what a boon to utopians!

Thomas More, lord chancellor to Henry VIII and inventor of the word *utopia*, was fascinated by Indian societies. Under the gaze of his parrot, Sir Thomas wrote the story of a Portuguese sailor returning from "Utopia," where reigned "King Utopus I." Utopia meant "nowhere"; the capital, "Amaurote," meant "city of fog"; the inhabitants were "Achorians," "men without a country," or "Apolites," "citizens without a city." By virtue of this terminology, Utopia seemed to be the direct opposite of a country with a history. It did not appear on any map of the known world, and King Utopus had cut the isthmus that joined it to terra firma. Isolated from worldly tumult, his subjects led an ideally organized existence, marked by health, comfort, and simple happiness. Although the collective form of government did not call up the United States, the rectangular layout of the streets, the diet based on fruit, and the love of moralistic aphorisms (like those of *Poor Richard's Almanack*) had something American about them. Above all, the concept of a simple, comfortable, happy existence, linked to a condition of isolation or isolationism, foretold the American dream or the "American way of life."

The idea of going beyond countries ravaged and occupied by history and civilization and reaching a land of abundance where tyranny could never take root was central to the way both Europeans and colonists thought of America. When Jefferson was ambassador to France, he wrote to his friend Madison that civic virtue would endure only "as long as . . . there remains vacant lands in any part of America. When we get piled upon one another in large cities, as in Europe, we shall become corrupted as in Europe."

Equally important was the myth of the frontier. As they pushed their way into the continent, the pioneers were, of course, seeking their fortune, but at the same time they were creating a mythology that deeply reflects the American soul. Beyond the history and civilization that had borne down upon them, the colonists advanced into virgin lands where law and divine justice were to hold absolute sway. The avenging cowboy took the place of the righteous Puritan.

The virgin lands were also to be fertile, like paradise; the dream of an incorruptible world was linked to that of a world of abundance. As Ray Billington puts it: "In the West, according to the frontier myth, a veritable garden of the world waited to transform newcomers into superior beings. There, where nature's abundance stifled the competitive instinct, men lived together in peace and contentment, freed of the jealousies and meanness inevitable in the crowded East."

After the War of 1812, which seemed to have cut the last bonds between Europe and America—just as King Utopus had severed the isthmus connecting his country to the rest of the world—Americans discovered the extent of their natural resources and the possibilities for their industrial exploitation. The dream came true; Utopia was all around them. It is not by chance that Vernon L. Parrington spells Utopia with a capital *u* when explaining how every major region of the United States in turn discovered a Utopia of its own. It was a question no longer of an imaginary form of government but of a flesh-and-blood country. The foundations of these Utopias were economic, and so the dream came true in the form of triumphant capitalism and economic imperialism. By degrees, economic well-being undermined the simple serenity of the early, religious-minded colonists and led to a romantic concept of prosperity. "Unfortunately," Parrington writes, "economic romance is more imperious in its demands than literary romance. Its dreams follow objective desires, and in the American of those days of new beginnings the desires of diverse economic groups conducted straight to economic imperialism."

While the Northeast found its Utopia in industrialization, the South romanticized cotton. Just as King Utopus relegated demeaning, menial tasks to slaves, so the Utopians of the American Northeast and South exploited Irish immigrants and African slaves. Western frontiersmen and settlers were more equalitarian and respectful of the liberty of their fellow-men, but they interpreted this liberty as everyone's right to exploit the resources of the newly opened lands. Observing how acreage prices went up with every wave of the westward advance, they found their Utopia in real estate speculation. In short, when the Americans' dream became reality, their country departed from the image that, in the centuries of early colonization, Europeans had had of it.

If ever there was a group dominated by a dream, it was that of the veterans of the Field of Refuge. They set out in search of an America such as Europeans had dreamed of since its discovery, and, at the same time, of the riches which, it was beginning to be known, could be found in its far reaches. (And, we must not forget, the memory of great European battles and the aura of their lost leader were still with them.) At first they thought they had turned back the years and found a golden-age land inhabited by "noble savages." Had not the Indian inhabitants of this new paradise followed and watched over them like guardian angels, saving them from poison? The goodwill shown them by "the wild Choctaws" after they had reached their destination bore out this opinion. So did the fertility of the land. Because it was springtime, Hartmann writes, "there was already rich vegetation, and the ground was soon overrun by plants and fruit. Melons, particularly, were of extraordinary size and rare beauty." There is an equally idyllic picture of the colonists, who were like "the shepherd peoples of remote antiquity." Hunting and fishing were their favorite occupations. "Sitting quietly on the banks of Trinity River, we threw out perfidious hooks to lure the denizens of the deep waters." The almost baptismal qualities of the new land seemed to purify and sanctify the bodies, souls, and customs of the newcomers.

> There were acts of thoughtfulness and friendship, demonstrations of interest and attachment that constantly strengthened the bonds among us. Such things are characteristic of new societies; what a pity that they cannot always live in this light of dawn, with no dissension, born of passion, to trouble their harmony! We were living on untrodden ground and drew something fresh and new from it. The pure air we breathed acted not only on our lungs but also on our inner selves. Certain ideas that permeate big city society had left us. Like the surrounding nature, we thought we had returned to the age when all the weaknesses and vices that afflict men and make them unhappy were as yet undeveloped.

But let us not be mistaken. In spite of the dreamlike atmosphere of its beginnings, the Field of Refuge did not enjoy the pure anarchism that we are wont to associate with the earliest societies. By its rules, regulations, and rigid discipline it drew, rather, upon the immobile, constrictive order of a utopia.

Lallemand's first decision was to give the colony a military character. The colonists were divided into three cohorts, of which the first was commanded by Colonels Douarche and Vasquez, the second by Colonel Sarrazin, and the third by Colonel Fournier. Each one included one or more medical officers. The veterans' first task was to build a fortified encampment, under the direction of four artillery officers: Mauvais, Guillot, Arlot, and Mancheski. With tree trunks from the nearby forest, they threw up four solid forts—on the west side Fort Charles and on the east Fort Henri, each armed with two cannons; between them a redoubt called the Fort du Milieu or Middle Fort, with one cannon; on the riverbank the Fort de la Palanque or Stockade, which served as a depot for ammunition and supplies and, with its three cannons, defended the rest of the colony. "The dwellings were built in a widely spaced circle," we learn from Hartmann. "They were made of large logs joined together, impervious to cannon fire. The rooftops were crenellated, so that none could be taken except by siege."

In the center of the encampment, a tricolor flag hung from a great tree. Protected from Indians, snakes, and forest animals, the veterans imagined that they were "safe from all setbacks and misfortunes." Cut off from a world that had mocked their ideals and cut short their careers, they wanted to impress on an unstoried land the best image they had of themselves, the image of a soldier. Soldiers they were, and soldiers of the Revolution. The communistic aspect of the colony's organization harked back to the period when Napoleon had pervaded Europe with the Revolutionary ideal. The Field of Refuge represented what was to be called in Europe "utopian socialism." Only soldiers of the Grand Army belonged. At the beginning they were four hundred, with only four women: two veterans' wives; Aimée Rigaud, daughter of the general; and Adrienne Viol, daughter of one of the doctors. Later the colonists came to number six hundred.

The day began with a bugle call, and every colonist had to render six hours of service, three in the morning and three between four and seven in the afternoon. "Service was meticulously performed and discipline strictly observed; due respect for superiors the basic factor." In their free time the colonists hunted, fished, or worked on their own houses and gardens. Every veteran was to be fed and supplied with agricultural tools at the general expense but was not entitled to vote until after he had gathered in his first harvest. He was allotted twenty acres of land, with five more, if he was married, for every member of his household under eighteen years of age. Marriage was obligatory for anyone aspiring to public office. Three directors, elected for a five-year term and responsible to a community council, were to serve as administrators. If a colonist married, the community helped him to build his house and cultivate his land and provided him with food for a year. Education, of course, was to be a community affair. Beggary, gambling, and slaveholding were forbidden; there were no taverns or tavern keepers and no lawyers. Questions of conflicting interests or opinions were to be settled by relatives and friends.

In order to dispel any suspicion of his colony's political basis, Lallemand drew up a proclamation that was published, in part in American papers and in its entirety by *L'Abeille américaine* of May 11, 1818:

> Brought together by the consequences of untoward events that took us away from our homes and scattered us abroad, we are determined to find a place of refuge where we can remember our misfortunes and learn a lesson from them.
>
> A vast stretch of country lay before us, abandoned by civilized men and occupied by scattered Indian peoples that content themselves with hunting and leave unproductive an area as fertile as it is farflung. Putting our honorable misfortunes behind us, we claim the first right that the Author of nature gave to man. That is, we are settling on this land in order to cultivate it with the work of our own hands and to gather from it the fruits that perseverance has always won.
>
> We war against no one and harbor no hostile intentions. We ask peace and friendship of all those who live around us and shall be grateful for their goodwill. We respect the religion, laws, and customs of civilized countries, and we shall respect, in equal measure, the independence and ways of the Indian nations, with whose hunting and other activities we shall not interfere.
>
> We shall maintain neighborly relations and trade with all those who may find advantage therein. We want to live in freedom, hard work, and peace. We shall make ourselves useful where we can and return good for good.
>
> But, if our situation is not respected and persecution dogs our steps to these deserts where we have sought refuge, then, we

ask all reasonable men what self-defense can be more legitimate than ours? This defense will be wholehearted; such is our resolve. The instinct of self-preservation, in our case, as in others similar to it, dictated that we should acquire arms for this purpose. The land to which we have come will see us endure and prosper, or perish like men. Here we shall live in freedom and honor or else find a grave that just men will remember and honor. But we have the right to expect a happy future, and one of our first concerns is to merit general approval by drawing up the simple rules and regulations that will vouch for our purposes.

We shall call the site of our colony Field of Refuge. This name, while recalling our reverses, will also remind us of the necessity of creating a future, of settling our household gods—in a word, of finding a new country.

The colony is to carry on agriculture and trade; the military aspect will serve only for its preservation. It will keep a register of its members. A general register, inclusive of those of all the cohorts, will be kept by the overall leadership. The cohorts will all live in the same place, for safety from attack, each one in peace and quiet, under the protection of all. A charter will be drawn up in order to guarantee personal and property rights, forestall injustice, assure tranquillity, and defeat malcontents' machinations.

The place where we have settled offers multiple resources; here Nature sets out its most precious riches. Fish and game are so abundant that most of the men we meet look for no other means of subsistence. But we shall not follow their example. Although aware of these advantages, we shall not take up the nomad life of people and individuals who live by hunting and fishing. Such a life makes for rude and rough ways; it isolates man, makes him selfish, sacrifices his social side to brute instinct, and leaves no room for his natural gifts to develop. Man is led, on the contrary, by reasons of security and self-interest, to live in society. In this estate, by mutual aid and the exercise of his intellectual faculties, he multiplies his advantages and attains full dignity through the process of perfecting his moral qualities.

Let us imitate the Spartans, whose devotion to the common good and persistence make them enduring examples; let us follow the three hundred Thebans, forever famous for the comradeship that made them into heroes, the Romans of the Republic, whose first duty and virtue was to save another Roman. The Roman who saved one of his fellows won the supremely prestigious civic crown, which was even more of an honor than the crown awarded to him who had scaled an enemy wall or captured an enemy banner. . . .

Far from us those who would subvert society, false braves whom to know is to disdain! We wish to live in peace. We shall set such an example that unhappy men will be moved to embrace our ideas. Our arms will be used only against such as hatred and injustice may move to attack us!

With his disdain for subverters of society and his admiration for the soldier who lays down his arms and goes back to the plow, General Lallemand evoked the legend of Washington. A vague reference to the "Author of nature" and the cult of the civic virtues of the ancient world pointed up the secular nature of this colony, quite different from that of most other American utopias. Indeed, socialist and communistic utopias never really took root in American soil and were generally inspired by foreigners. The Scottish industrialist, Robert Owen, came in 1825 to explain to the president of the United States and to other interested, highly placed persons how man could be changed by a change of environment. It was in Texas that he founded his communistic utopia, which, although in some ways prophetic, lasted for only two years. The Frenchman, Étienne Cabet, in the same general period, set up his utopian community of "Icaria" in America and, indeed, in Texas. It also failed.

The only lasting American utopias had a religious character. First, the early settlers belonged to religious groups, like that of the Puritans, who brought to the New World the utopian ideals that they had not been able to pursue in the Old. Subsequently, various sects were subject to spectacular emotional explosions and partook of the specifically American phenomenon called the "Great Awakening." This was a reaction to the skeptical rationalism of the eighteenth-century Enlightenment and also to the indifference to religion that had insinuated itself into American tolerance. Philanthropy came to replace theology and dogma, and Protestants took their faith from an individual "inner light." Unintellectual and with little dogmatic content or ecclesiastical structure, the sects channeled their religious aspirations into emotional rebirths. Shakers and Ephratans, among others, held meetings marked by collective hysteria, where the participants shouted out psalms until they fainted from exhaustion and, in certain cases, fell into an orgy. The "Great Awakening," inseparable from a certain religious laxity of which it was both the consequence and the counterweight, inspired numerous American utopias. A passage from Gilles Lapouge about the creator of the original Utopia suggests an explanation of the particular forms assumed by religion in America.

> Thomas More, the lord chancellor, was a rabid persecutor of heretics, and proud of it. Yet this *Utopia* describes a religion so tolerant as to seem like a cult of virtue. This tolerance is generally attributed to the influence of his humanist friends, Erasmus, Guillaume Budé, and others. But *Utopia* was written in 1516, and he held the post of chancellor until 1532. The truth of the matter is more subtle. Thomas More acted as a double personality. As a minister in the king's government, he obeyed the precepts of the historical religion of Christ; as the author of *Utopia*, he was unwilling to embrace a dated religion. This dichotomy had a logic of its own. The tragic and sorrowful God of the Garden of Olives can be attuned to temporal convulsions. But the bland happiness of Utopia, the harmony that presides over the unrolling of its days, its character of timelessness and anonymity, these do not accord with the obscure, personal, complex, historical God incarnate in Christ.

Tolerance and smiling benevolence could take root only in a land that had escaped temporal convulsions. Exaggeratedly emotional outpourings could issue only from people who had no historical direction.

Tolerance and the cult of virtue were set forth, as we have seen, in Lallemand's proclamation. But his followers, although most of them were not religiously minded, had been brought up in the historical religion of Catholicism, and they had fought for a man who was vitally concerned with leaving his imprint on history. It was to be difficult for them to isolate themselves from the tumultuous events of the great world.

The thought given to the charter of the Field of Refuge owed its inspiration to Rousseau's *Social Contract*. It was too late to recover paradise, where there was no need for law; there was, instead, a hope of applying a charter based on social justice in a country as yet uncorrupted. The day of the "noble savage" was gone, and man was definitely committed to a social structure. Lallemand said clearly that it was impossible to take up the nomad life of the Indians who, as in the primeval days imagined by Rousseau, hunted, fished, and "looked for no other means of subsistence." On the contrary, "man was led to live in society" and under the rod of a purposefully articulated charter.

To take an extreme example, let us compare Lallemand's utopia, where marriage was a prerequisite for public office, and the utopias of the "Great Awakening," which allowed sexual relationships outside of marriage on the premise that Original Sin had been vanquished and man had been morally regenerated and born again. If the Bible says that in heaven there is no marriage, then why marry?

The substantial differences between the native American utopias and that of Lallemand derived from the fact that the Field of Refuge represented an image of America seen by European and, more particularly, French eyes. One essential point, however, they had in common. Lallemand, like the Americans, believed that civilized man (the white man) had a right to cultivate fertile, empty land, in spite of the presence of Indian peoples. The land, according to this theory, was not truly theirs because "they contented themselves with hunting and left unproductive an area as fertile as it was farflung."

Once this claim was stated, however, Lallemand took pains (in a way unusual for the times) to justify his presence and to solemnly promise "to respect the independence and ways of the Indian nation" and not to interfere with their "hunting and fishing activities." In so doing, did he mean to affirm his regard for the universal rights of man or to recall that Napoleon and his soldiers had been friends to oppressed and underdeveloped peoples? Captain Just Girard tells the following episode from his Texas days. While hunting on horseback, he ran into some galloping wild horses, which his own mount instinctively and uncontrollably followed. Girard was thrown to the ground, lost consciousness, and, when he came to, found himself in the middle of a circle of Indians. He remembered what a pioneer had told him—if he had a run-in with the Comanches, who hated the Spaniards, he should make it clear that he was French. Now, he opened his jacket, displaying the Legion of Honor, and said: "Napoleon!" The Indians admiringly repeated the Emperor's name, took Just under their protection, and made him a cult object, so that it was only by stealth that he ever got away. Whether or not this story is true, the veterans chose to think of Napoleon as the Indians' friend. Apaches, Tonkawas, Pawnees, and Comanches were the tribes that they most probably encountered.

The Apaches and Tonkawas captured and trained wild horses; the Tonkawas knew poisonous plants and their antidotes. The Pawnees were great hunters and left agricultural pursuits to their wives. The Comanches had some happy memories of French Louisiana and, perhaps for this reason, were better disposed toward Frenchmen than toward the hated Spaniards. Of the tribes named above, they seemed to be most developed.

One day, in order to distract his followers, Lallemand organized a ceremony for ratification of a treaty with the Indians, most likely the Comanches, according to Girard's description. Before the delighted soldiers, the Indians offered General Lallemand the peacepipe, placed a crown of feathers on his head, and declared him a chief. Here is how the veterans of the Grand Army saw their Indian allies: "To the woolen blanket that they always wore around their shoulders, they had added a headpiece decorated with long feathers, a belt made of shells, a copper necklace and breastplate, rings in the ears and nose, and scalps—disgusting trophies of their warring exploits—hanging from bracelets on their wrists."

A violent and bloody episode spoiled the relationship between the Indians and the Field of Refuge. Two officers—Albert and Fallot—were lost in the woods while out hunting. There they came across some Karankawa Indians who were torturing two Spanish missionaries. The Frenchmen set them free, but while they were looking for the way to go home the whole tribe attacked them. General Lallemand sent two hundred men to the rescue, but they found only the bare remains of their comrades, who had been strangled, torn apart, and eaten.

After the euphoria of the early days, Lallemand's colony fell prey to boredom and melancholy. The early attempts at agriculture were fraught with difficulties because of the colonists' lack of experience. During the rainy season, floods destroyed the first planting of tobacco. The "consoling angels," Madame Jeannet and

Mesdemoiselles Viol and Rigaud, were subjected to unwelcome advances. As General Vaudoncourt tells it, there was an attempt to ruin their lives by "branding them with an unerasable stigma."

The image of a certain America was gradually blurred, and the veterans' dreams were haunted by the Napoleonic epic. "We resumed practicing the use of our weapons, we recalled battlefield maneuvers and celebrated the anniversaries of our triumphs; the solitude of America echoed our patriotic songs."

Strategical theories, maneuvers, camping trips with rations eaten out of a mess-tin—the colonists were no longer taking Cincinnatus for a model; they were miserable *demi-soldes* trying to reenact their former glory. Like their companions who had stayed in Paris, they had their "Palais-Royal," the name that they gave to a great fire built to scare off beasts of prey, where they sat in a circle, exchanging tales of days gone by.

> Sometimes, [says Just Girard] General Lallemand came in person to the Palais-Royal to tell stories of his own and to reveal scraps of his last conversations with the Emperor to the brave men who had hitched their fortunes to his star. Under the influence of his stirring words, his hearers would indulge in strange dreams and fantastic projects. The idea of colonizing Texas was far from their thoughts. They dreamed, rather, of serving under the flag of the Mexican Revolution. After they had contributed to the Revolution's success, Mexico would give them a fine sailing vessel with which they would waft the Emperor away from St. Helena. He would be emperor of Mexico and then . . . then their imaginations ran riot, and I cannot tell you all the fantasies to which they gave birth.

In the veterans' dreams, history had swept utopia away.

Without their realizing it, the veterans of the Field of Refuge, by their very presence, participated in the history of Texas and of Spanish-American relations. Both Louisiana and Texas were borderline areas. Texas had belonged for over three centuries to Spain; Louisiana had been American since 1803, when Napoleon, as First Consul, sold it to the United States. The uncertain boundaries were due to the ambiguities of the treaty between the United States and Napoleon, in which the boundaries were considered the same as when the French first occupied the territory.

Actually, France had taken possession four times, the first in 1682. As for the boundary of Spanish Texas, it was to the Americans' advantage to push it back to the farthest point reached by the French. It was the famous sieur de La Salle, acting for Louis XIV, who gave French Louisiana its maximum size. In 1685, near the Spanish border in Texas, he disembarked by sheer mistake on the shores of Matagorda Bay. At once Spain voiced its indignation: the installation of French troops in this place was "a thorn in the flank of Spain, which must be eradicated." Secretary of State Adams took pains to follow the traces of La Salle's exploratory expeditions and to make note of all the eighteenth-century French outposts in Louisiana and Texas in order to justify American claims in these regions. Almost 130 years after his installation in Texas, the sieur de La Salle played an important part in Spanish-American relations. Don Luis de Onís, Spanish ambassador to the United States, wrote to the Washington government that La Salle's presence in Texas was only a "passing adventure" and something like a "raid" on the territory of another nation. In reply to which, on March 12, 1818, Adams defended the Frenchman and compared him to Christopher Columbus. "La Salle's undertaking has every characteristic of sublime genius, magnanimous enterprise and heroic execution. To him and to him alone the people of this continent are indebted for the discovery, from its source to the ocean, of the Mississippi, the father of floods; and of the numberless millions of freemen destined in this and future ages to sail on his bosom and dwell along his banks, and those of his tributary streams, there is no-one but will be deeply indebted, for a large portion of the comforts and enjoyments of life, to the genius and energy of La Salle."

If it was granted that Matagorda Bay, where La Salle landed, was one of the boundaries of French Louisiana, then the Field of Refuge could be considered, geographically, to belong to the former French province and hence, since 1803, to the United States. We can see why the American government encouraged or at least permitted the veterans of the Grande Armée to settle in an area which, by virtue of its former French ownership, the United States claimed for its own.

In a report from Ambassador Hyde de Neuville to the duc de Richelieu, dated July 2, 1818, we find a sentence that confirms this attitude. Speaking of the Field of Refuge, Hyde wrote: "Let us not forget the last words of Mr. Clay on the day when he took leave of me: 'It's a trick on the Don' " ("Don" being the nickname pinned upon the Spanish ambassador, Luis de Onís). We may wonder if General Lallemand was aware of the role that Washington assigned to him in the boundary line quarrel with Spain. In any case, when leaving Galveston for the site of his colony, he issued a message directed to the Spanish king:

> Since an official proclamation has invited colonists of all classes and countries to settle in the Spanish-American provinces, His Most Christian Majesty will doubtless welcome the establishment of a colony in desert land that awaits only hardworking settlers to become one of the fairest and most fertile regions on earth. The members of the Field of Refuge are, in any case, willing to recognize the government of Spain, to act toward it with good faith, and to pay whatever taxes it feels must be imposed. In return, the colonists ask to be ruled by their own laws, without obedience to the Spanish government, but in accord with their old military habits. Come what may, they are determined to settle in Texas and to stay there in the face of any and all opposition.

A text as open to various interpretations as the boundary between the two provinces! Lallemand admitted that he was settling on Spanish ground but, although accepting taxation, he refused compliance with Spanish law and stated, threateningly, that no one should dislodge him.

At this time, Texas counted only some seven thousand inhabitants of the most varied origins: Spanish, Indian, American, Creole, Irish, and French. The Spanish soldiery was made up, for the most part, of cavalrymen armed with carbines and lances and protected by shields against Indian arrows. There were a few scattered military posts, chief among them Nacogdoches on the Trinity River, where there were no more than five hundred men. The government representative lived in the provincial capital, San Antonio de Béjar, a town of 2500 inhabitants, whose houses were roofed with grass.

For the birthday of General Rigaud's daughter, the Field of Refuge staged a ball to which notables from San Antonio were invited. "The strangest assortment of white men, half-breeds, and

Indians attended," Captain Just Girard tells us. General Lallemand wanted to establish his political neutrality and his peaceful intentions toward the Spanish community. But the provincial authorities did not go along: soon contact between Spaniards and veterans was forbidden. Just Girard continues: "Here we are, once more thrown back on ourselves, with no distractions and no news of our friends in either Europe or the States. To cap our misfortunes, many of us have fallen ill, either of nostalgia or as a result of working too hard in a torrid climate."

The refugees from Santo Domingo who had come to join the colony were soon discouraged and went away. Finally, after a month of isolation, a boat arrived from Laffite, charged with supplies, bundles of newspapers, and the letters for which there had been so much longing.

Did General Lallemand know that the famous pirates, Jean Laffite and his brother, who plundered Spanish shipping, were at the same time spies in the service of the king of Spain? Proof is now available that Jean and Pierre Laffite were agents 13-A and 13-B of the Spanish secret service. The confidence Spain had in these two marauders was not due simply to the ineptitude of an empire well on the road to decay. The Laffites played, at Galveston, a role, on Spanish behalf, not dissimilar to that which Lallemand was, even if unconsciously, playing on behalf of the Americans. Galveston was disputed between Spain and the United States, but, meanwhile, Laffite had possession. If he were ousted by American troops, Galveston would be lost to Spain. And so Spain chose to convert the pirates.

The boundary agreement finally reached between Spain and the United States led to the simultaneous expulsion of both Lallemand and Laffite from the Texas region. There was no more need for the two powers to play tricks on each other. Negotiations, in which Hyde de Neuville had a not unimportant part, began as early as December, 1817. Spain was having trouble keeping its colonies under control and felt powerless to contain American encroachments. Moreover, it owed Washington money. In order to pay off its debt, it proposed, through Hyde de Neuville, to cede Florida. How galling it must have been to give up a province that had been Spanish since the time of the conquistadors! In any case, since the Spaniards considered Lallemand's trespassing on their territory an indirect American needling, Washington decided that, in order to facilitate the cession of Florida, it would do away with the Field of Refuge.

No sooner had they heard of this intention than the Spaniards began to press Lallemand to withdraw. Troops from the garrisons of San Antonio de Béjar and La Bahía pitched camp near the French colony and notified Lallemand in no uncertain terms that he must quit a territory belonging exclusively to the king of Spain. Some of the veterans wanted to resist, but the Spanish emissary declared that there were large forces behind him. A majority pointed out the uselessness of waging an unequal combat, and Charles Lallemand, with his men, went sadly back down the Trinity River, with their arms and paraphernalia, until they reached their point of departure, Galveston Island. The life of the Field of Refuge was of only a few months' duration.

At Galveston, Hartmann says, there were at first "preparations for military resistance." But provisions were lacking, and the Frenchmen were soon reduced to two biscuits and a small glass of spirits per day. Toward the end of September, Lallemand decided to go with a United States commissioner, Mason Graham, to New Orleans "where he hoped to find help and put an end to our misery." The veterans waited in vain, under the command of General Rigaud, for Lallemand's return. They did not know that Graham had been sent by President Monroe to disband their group and to expel Jean Laffite. On August 26, from Galveston, Graham had sent letters to both men in which he set forth the government's intentions. To Laffite he said that the United States government, in claiming the territory between the Sabine River and the Rio Bravo del Norte, could no longer tolerate any outsiders' establishment at Galveston, particularly one "of such a dubious nature." The pirate chose to ignore Washington's intimation. He evacuated the island only in 1821, when summoned by an American warship to do so.

To Lallemand Graham wrote:

> Though convinced from what has passed in the interviews which I have had the honor to have with you, that you have no interest in the privateering establishment, which has been made at this place, and that there is no connection between yourself and the persons interested in that establishment, except such

as has been imposed upon you by circumstances, it is nevertheless a duty imposed upon me by the instructions of my Government to call upon you for an explicit avowal of the national authority, if any, by which you, with the persons under your immediate command, have taken possession of this place, and also to make known to you that the Government of the United States, claiming under the treaty with France by which the Colony of Louisiana was ceded with all the country between the Sabine and the Rio Bravo del Norte, will permit no permanent establishment whatsoever to be made within these limits under any authority other than its own.

Paradoxically enough, French soldiers were politely bidden to leave an area that other French soldiers had conquered before them.

The last episode of the story of the Field of Refuge is truly pathetic. After Lallemand's departure, old General Rigaud imposed iron discipline, setting up a court-martial and a death sentence for anyone who tried to escape from the reign of hunger and terror. Toward the end of September, a seasonal hurricane dealt the last blow. A tidal wave destroyed the veterans' camp and a large part of Laffite's fleet. Several men were killed. The pirate gave shelter to the ill and injured, and when the veterans unanimously decided to leave he offered the most sorely tried among them a schooner, which after a stormy, twenty-day voyage brought them to New Orleans. Those who couldn't be taken aboard made their way to the mainland. Some enrolled in the army of the viceroy of Mexico, Apodaca; others joined General Lefebvre-Desnouettes in Alabama, while still others petitioned hospitality from the Natchitoch Indians in order to cultivate their fertile land. A final group proceeded along the coast, under General Rigaud, in an effort to reach New Orleans by foot. They marched for five weeks, subsisting on what game they could shoot along the way. Six died of exhaustion. Forty-seven ragged, hungry men arrived in New Orleans, the last remnants of the Field of Refuge.

In our day the story of Lallemand's colony is largely forgotten, but between 1818 and 1820 it aroused considerable repercussions in France—where it was heard enthusiastically—and also in the rest of Europe. To Bonapartists, the Field of Refuge was a defiant answer to the humiliating measures that the Bourbon regime had taken against the followers of Napoleon. The Liberal opposition party took it up for propaganda purposes and joined the Bonapartists in glorifying the participants.

Among other things, the legend of the Field of Refuge, as René Rémond points out, confirmed the traditional image of America seen from a European point of view. "The 'deeds of the soldier-farm workers' rejuvenated the image of an America devoted to the working of the land, of a society close to nature that preserved 'the amiable simplicity of a newborn world'; it revived the picture of the American farmer and substantiated the mirage of a primitive and virtuous Arcadia."[2] The American farmer and the soldier of Napoleon were momentarily linked by the same aspiration, although the American dream was very different from Napoleon's vision of the world and of history.

This paradoxical association was exploited by the Liberal party, whose most conspicious leader was General de La Fayette. The image of the soldier-farm worker permeated literature, painting, and decoration. The great composition of Horace Vernet on this subject is well known. An impressive proliferation of etchings and statuettes representing the new Cincinnatus spread through markets and mansions. In *La Rabouilleuse*, Balzac wrote: "You can still see soldier-farm workers on the wallpaper in distant provinces."

The Field of Refuge was celebrated in cafés and on street corners, by lyrics set to familiar tunes. One of them ran:

> Ah! si la France tributaire
> Poursuit encore ses fils meurtris,
> Que chaque exilé solitaire
> Vienne s'unir aux vieux proscrits.
> Au lieu d'une plaine inutile
> Forgeons le fer agriculteur,
> Nobles débris du champ d'honneur
> Fertilisons le Champ d'Asile!

> If a tyrant king enslaves you,
> Persecutes a wounded son,
> Other exiles bid you follow
> To a refuge newly won.
> Where the land is sere and fallow
> Let us till a fertile farm,

Field of Honor, now of Refuge,
Where we shall be safe from harm.

Most popular of all was the song by the famous Béranger, to the tune of *La Romance de Bélisaire*:

Un chef de bannis courageux
Implorant un lointain asile
À des sauvages ombrageux
Disait: l'Europe nous exile,

Heureux enfants de ces forêts
De nos maux écoutez l'histoire.
Sauvages, nous sommes français
Prenez pitié de notre gloire.

Le Champ d'Asile est consacré.
Élevez-vous cité nouvelle,
Soyez-nous un fort assuré
Contre la Fortune infidèle.

Peut-être aussi des plus hauts faits
Nos fils vous racontant l'histoire
Vous diront: "Nous sommes français
Prenez pitié de notre gloire!"

The exiles' leader seeks
A refuge, a new day.
"Fear not, you Indian braves,
Europe sent us away.

"Happy in these your woods,
Hear out our woeful story;
Frenchmen we call ourselves;
Take pity on our glory!

"Our Field of Refuge holy
To a new city rises;
May it protect us hence
From fickle fate's surprises.

"Our children in their time
Will tell our epic story,
Will echo: We are Frenchmen;
Take pity on our glory!"

The glorious soldiers, wounded by history, were safe in the

deep woods of the land of the noble savage, where cruel fate could not strike them. But when Béranger wrote *Au Champ d'Asile*, he did not know that nature had run wild and almost wiped out the unfortunate colony.

For some time, Texas inspired the Liberals' imaginations. One of their papers, *La Minerve*, founded by Benjamin Constant, said that the region was "so fertile that a single grain of wheat, in one year, sprouts a hundred and fifty others. Sugar and cotton abound, and there are hopes for coffee. The forests are filled with animals of every kind, especially wild horses, as swift and strong as those of Arabia." At the beginning of October, 1818, when news of the colony's tragic fate had not yet reached France, *La Minerve* launched a drive to raise funds on its behalf. In every issue there was an accounting of the sums turned over to Gros and Davilliers, Bonapartist bankers, who were to transmit them to their correspondents in Charleston, South Carolina, who would, in turn, distribute them among the veterans. The drive ended only on July 1, 1819, nearly a year after the colony had gone under, and contributions were still coming in. The total amount raised was 95,018 francs and 16 centimes. This drive aroused royalist suspicions of the Liberals, whom they accused of wanting to bring down the monarchy. The royalist paper *Le Conservateur* spoke of "philanthropic phantasmagoria."

In *La Rabouilleuse*, Balzac judges the Field of Refuge and the Liberal party with equal severity. One of the novel's chief characters, Colonel Philippe Bridau, a *demi-solde* who is portrayed unsympathetically, has "the magnificent idea of joining General Lallemand in the United States and taking part in the foundation of the Field of Refuge, one of the worst hoaxes ever presented in a fund-raising campaign." The colonel, "gulled, like so many others, lost everything." When he came home with a "bronzed" face and in a state of abject poverty, his poor mother welcomed him as a hero and "couldn't deny him the right to eat, drink, and amuse himself, to which any escapee from the Field of Refuge was entitled." The writer heaps blame on the Liberal party. "The behavior of this party under the Restoration goes to show that its interests were not patriotic but strictly self-seeking, concentrated upon the attainment of positions of power.... The leaders saw that they could be useful to Louis XVIII by ejecting the most glorious of our soldiers from France, and they jettisoned the most faithful and ardent among them, those who stepped forward the first to volunteer." This condemnation of the Liberal party is exaggerated; many of its members had real feelings for the veterans' Texas enterprise. We may note in passing that among those who returned from the Field of Refuge was a law student from Vic-en-Bigorre, Bernard Lacaze, who later became a Liberal leader of Toulouse.

It is not known exactly how Lallemand's colony was financed. The drive launched by Benjamin Constant's paper came too late, and Joseph Bonaparte, it seems, did not loosen his purse strings on its behalf. Certain American papers pointed to Marshal Grouchy as the backer, but the marshal addressed an indignant disavowal to Hyde de Neuville, with a request for publication. That the American government lent support is beyond dispute. It is equally certain that Charles Lallemand drew on the credit of his brother Henri's uncle by marriage, Stephen Girard, for the purchase of both arms and agricultural instruments. Lallemand may also have obtained aid from the Freemasons. General Brice says that the Association Fraternelle Européenne, a Masonic society of which Charles Lallemand was a grand master and which had a French section called Les Amis de la Liberté, publicized the venture.

The funds collected by *La Minerve* did reach New Orleans, and a committee headed by the governor of Louisiana, Jacques Philippe de Villeré, was charged with their distribution. General Charles Lallemand gave up his share in favor of his men, and they gallantly donated it to the poor of the parish of Saint Louis.

When General Rigaud arrived in New Orleans, he and Charles Lallemand had a stormy exchange of words. Each one had his partisans. Lallemand chose to leave the city and lived, somewhat sadly, until the death of Napoleon, on a little farm that he owned near Lake Pontchartrain. Later he had an urge to participate in the European revolutions. Lieutenant Colonel Schultz (of the Polish Lancers stationed on Elba), who had followed Lallemand first to Malta and then to the Field of Refuge, returned to Europe and enlisted in the service of the Italian General Guglielmo Pepe in 1820.

Old General Rigaud, sorely tried by his misadventure, took lodgings with his children in a priest's house. Soon his daughter found a post as governess, and his son took a job as a grocery clerk in Opelousas. In April, 1819, the general went to Washington and called on Hyde de Neuville, who gave the following account to his government: "An old soldier, victim in both France and the United States of men more ambitious than he, and brought down by his weakness to a most unhappy condition, has come to me for help. He has in his favor his poverty, which bears witness to his disinterestedness; his scars, which testify to his valor; his repentance, which calls for pardon, and the weariness and despair that cause him to ask for royal clemency." But the unfortunate general died of yellow fever at New Orleans in 1820.

Several of the persons whom we have met in this chapter are mentioned in Napoleon's will:

> April 15, 1821 [I bequeath to]
> General Brayer, 100,000 francs
> General Lallemand (the elder), 100,000 francs
> April 21, 1821 (codicil)
> From the liquidation of my civil list in Italy:
> To my Dutch aide-de-camp, General Hogendorp,
> now in Brazil, 100,000 francs
> April 24, 1821: I bequeath to General Rigaud, the one who was exiled, 100,000 francs.

It is more than likely that these legacies were meant to recompense men who had tried to help him escape from St. Helena. The Field of Refuge, even in its legendary aspect, could not have interested him, for it reflected ideas of before and after his time, which had for him no immediacy. Before his time, because the rhetoric of Lallemand dated from 1792–93, when Napoleon was a mere artillery captain; after, because the legend of the Field of Refuge was mingled with that of the Liberal party. This party did, as we shall see, plot on behalf of *L'Aiglon*, Napoleon's fledgling son. But the Emperor had reason to detest the Liberals and, above all, their leader La Fayette, who, in order to win political influence, pushed him into his second abdication.

The ideal of Cincinnatus was, of course, quite extraneous to his own. In 1799, as First Consul, in order to assert himself as a peace-lover, he extolled the memory of George Washington, as if to link their two names together as pacifist generals. But at St. Helena it was abundantly clear that the legend he was building up about himself was diametrically opposed to that of Washington.

Equally alien to Napoleon's thinking were the socialistic aspects of the Field of Refuge and the American dream. Napoleon had chosen history. A people that dreamed of reaching a land untouched by history was composed, in his eyes, of "mere tradesmen."

And how did Napoleon size up the feasibility of Lallemand's project for his escape? His judgment was severe. Before Generals Bertrand and Montholon, he said of projects submitted to him:

> All the plans proposed to me so far have been either absurd or degrading. Can you see me disguised as a sailor or a Chinese coolie, lowered onto the beach at the end of a long rope and hidden in a beer barrel in order to be carried in the hold of a ship to Baltimore? The story of an underwater vessel under construction in Jamaica is a fairy tale for children. And General Lallemand's plan is equally fantastic. No one can conquer Mexico with five hundred men.
>
> Moreover, my brother Joseph, a man of common sense, disapproves. He lets Lallemand carry on about it, because there's no way of holding him back, but he wants no part in his doings.
>
> And then, what should I do with myself in America? Live the life of a *petit bourgeois*? I had that passing idea in 1815 when I was very tired.

CHAPTER 7

Echoes of Napoleon in Latin America

For Napoleon, had he exiled himself in the United States, to have any political role was unthinkable. The American Constitution and the political institutions to which it had given birth were exemplary and effectual, the satisfaction and growing prosperity of the people were evident, and there was no field of action for a man who thought of himself as the bearer of a revelation, a liberator, and one who brought that which was unaccomplished to fruition.

If Napoleon had wanted to play a historical and political role in the New World, he would have aimed at Latin America. "If I were in his place," he said at St. Helena, in relation to his brother Joseph, "I'd weld all the Spanish Americas into a great empire." His own achievement, apart from conquest, had been to introduce himself into a revolutionary movement, take it over, channel it, and endow it with order. The liberalism of a constitutional monarchy seemed to him quite inefficacious outside of Nordic countries.

On August 26, 1817, General Montholon noted the arrival of letters from Brazil speaking of insurrection. "All those kings are such fools!" Napoleon exclaimed. "They don't know where constitutional ideas will lead them. They all ape England, without realizing that they've no such class of intelligent aristocrats, who own half the land of the kingdom and have an interest in preserving the monarchy."

In Latin America a Bonaparte was needed. To General Bertrand Napoleon said: "There's still talk of Joseph and Mexico. They say he has 15,000 Frenchmen behind him. If he has only a third this number, or even 2000, as long as there are artillery, cavalry, and engineering officers among them, it's a lot. Officers, you know, make men into soldiers. With them, he could make something out of the Mexicans, who, on their own, amount to nothing."

A constitution of the Anglo-Saxon type did not suit the Latin-American countries, but their independence was to the advantage of the English economy, and the insurgent movements had, for this reason, English support. And, according to Napoleon, both England and the insurgents could make good use of Joseph Bonaparte. He and the officers of the Grande Armée could furnish the military know-how of which there was so great a need. Several times Napoleon enlarged upon the advantages that England could secure over the Bourbons of France and Spain by the presence of Joseph on a Mexican throne. He knew that Joseph was "too attached to bourgeois comforts" to accept the Mexican offer. But, as Napoleon thought out loud before Montholon,

> His acceptance would benefit those unhappy people and save them from the calamities of a long civil war. It would benefit England as well, since it could take over Spanish-American trade. Joseph could not and would not want diplomatic relations with the kings of France and Spain, and since Latin America cannot do without European products it would have to turn to the English market. Besides, Joseph is genuinely fond of me, and he would be in a position to induce the English government to alter my status. Only I don't believe he'll accept.

And to Dr. O'Meara he said:

> I see no feasible method to remedy the distress of your manufacturers except endeavoring by all means at your command to provide the separation of the Spanish South American colonies from the mother country. By means of this you would have an opportunity of opening a most extensive and lucrative commerce with the South Americans, which would be productive of great advantages to you. If you do not adopt steps of the kind, the Americans will be beforehand with you. If you act as I have said, they could trade with no other nation than you. . . . Both Spain and France must be shut to them. . . . By having me in your hands, you could always make advantageous terms with Joseph, who loves me sincerely and would do anything for me.

Aside from economic advantages, the liberation of the Spanish colonies should interest England from a political point of view. According to Las Cases, Napoleon thought that "as long as Spain's policy is aimed at the conservation and administration of its American colonies, it will consider any nation that has command of the seas its natural enemy and will join forces with France to counterbalance England's sea power. But once Latin America is liberated, Spain's policy will be purely continental and it will inevitably clash with France, the only nation adjacent to it and also its only European rival."

In other words, England and the Bonapartes, through the intermediary of Joseph, would join forces. It is true that the Latin-American insurgents called upon both London and the officers of Napoleon's Grande Armée. But their relationship with the Frenchmen was difficult and, at times, violent, and with England mistrustful and even bloody.

The insurgents could not forget the recent past, when both Napoleon and England had covertly aspired to dominate and indeed conquer their countries. It was by virtue of the fear that they inspired rather than their aid that Napoleon and England contributed to the revolutions in Latin America.

Cornelio Saavedra, president of the first Argentinian junta of May 25, 1810, later wrote: "If we look at things in their true light, it seems to me undeniable that the aims of both Napoleon and the English to become masters of this America brought about the May 25, 1810, revolution."

It is true that Mexican insurgents offered the crown of Mexico to the comte de Survilliers and also to Napoleon on St. Helena. But the great leaders of revolutionary Latin America, Bolívar and San Martín, did not care for Napoleon and did not in the least wish for him to interfere in their affairs. On August 22, 1815, when Simón Bolívar heard of the defeat at Waterloo, he wrote the famous letter expressive of his hatred and exaggerated fear of Napoleon:

> At Waterloo the world's future was decided. In this immortal battle Europe was delivered. The consequences will be more important than those of any other in universal history, especially in regard to America, which will witness the transfer to its shores of the theater of war that has ravaged Europe for over twenty years. If it is true that Bonaparte has escaped from France and, as rumor has it, is seeking refuge in America, then whatever country he chooses will be ruined by his presence. With him will come the English hatred of his tyranny and

Europe's jealousy of America. The armies of all the nations will march in his tracks and, if necessary, the whole of America will be blocked by the British fleet.

If Napoleon is welcomed by North America, then all nations will league against it and, as a result, Bonaparte will seek the support of the Independents of Mexico, the United States' neighbor. If South America is stricken by Bonaparte's arrival, woe unto us if our country is the one to take him in! His appetite for conquest is insatiable. He cut down the flower of European youth on the battlefield in order to forward his ambitious plans. Similar plans will lead him to the New World, where he may hope to take advantage of the discords that divide America in order, by shedding what blood remains in our veins, to raise his throne in this vast empire. As if America were not sufficiently unhappy and exhausted by the war of extermination that Spain is waging upon it!

Napoleon's policy in regard to Latin America had three successive stages. The first ended in 1808, when French troops penetrated the Iberian Peninsula and placed Joseph Bonaparte on the throne of Spain. Before this time Napoleon had relied on a Franco-Spanish alliance against England, the long-standing affinity of two continental powers as opposed to an insular nation.

Spain's American colonies were linked to the motherland by a "colonial agreement," by virtue of which they could not trade with any other country. There was the same arrangement between Portugal and Brazil. But the Latin Americans, influenced by eighteenth-century European ideas and the example of the United States, began to aspire to economic and then to political independence. Smuggling activities, shared by Latin Americans and Englishmen, were advantageous to both parties, and common economic interests quite naturally led the Latin American insurgent leaders to seek financial and logistic aid from London. At this point, the revolt of the Spanish colonies was contrary to the policy of Napoleon as an ally of Spain.

In the northern sector of Latin America, two men led the first insurrectionary movements: Francisco de Miranda, known as the "forerunner," and the young Simón Bolívar. Miranda was born in Venezuela in 1750. As an officer in the Spanish army, he fought the British in Florida around the time of the United States' War of Independence and then went to Europe to seek support for his aspirations. He participated in the French Revolutionary wars and, indeed, commanded the Army of the North in the absence of General Dumouriez and was a friend of the Girondin faction and its leader, Jacques-Pierre Brissot. He was expelled from France after the antiroyalist coup d'état of 18 Fructidor, 1797, and again in 1804. Napoleon called him a "Don Quixote" and a "demagogue."

Simón Bolívar was born in Caracas, Venezuela, in 1783. In the early 1800s, he went to Europe for distraction from his widowhood. In France he shared the favors of Fanny de Trobriand with Eugène de Beauharnais,[1] who was asked by Napoleon to break off this connection. Did Fanny, who detested Napoleon, influence the feelings of Bolívar? He was, in any case, indignant over the imperial coronation; he traveled to Rome and thence back to Venezuela.

Shortly afterwards, in 1806, he took part in the first rebellion led by Miranda. The English government, busy putting together a new coalition against Napoleon, was unable to give him effective help, and Prime Minister William Pitt advised him to turn to American President Thomas Jefferson, who did no more than allow him to organize in the American South an expeditionary force directed against Venezuela's Spanish government. The expedition failed, and satirical French sheets portrayed Miranda "dressing to subvert his country" and then, under the Spanish counterattack, "fleeing, like a coward, aboard the *Leander*, and abandoning the rest of his fleet." It was once more the long hand of England, said the French, "up to its old tricks" and "pushing the adventurer Miranda toward the coasts of Latin America."

In the southerly part of Spain's colonial empire, England made the mistake of trying to build up its influence by territorial conquest. For, although the businessmen of the Viceroyalty of La Plata wanted to augment their trade with Britain, they had no wish to fall under its political sway. The viceroy withdrew to the interior in order to regroup his troops and make a plan of defense. The *porteños* of Buenos Aires did not wait for his return before organizing their resistance. All together, whether they favored England or Spain, they joined in driving the British away. A Frenchman, Jacques de Liniers, led the enterprise in the name of the king of Spain. Liniers was the captain of a ship in the service of Madrid. With his brother Henri, he had already sought his fortune outside of France before the Revolution. In the Viceroyalty of La Plata, the brothers started a plant for making an extract of meat, which they sold in tablet form—a forerunner of the modern "bouillion cube." In 1792 they proposed their tablet as a component of French army rations. Henri de Liniers engaged, also, in the slave trade.

When the English, under General Beresford, captured Buenos Aires, Jacques de Liniers, arriving too late to join the battle, hurried to Montevideo, where he gathered together a thousand men, some of them French freebooters, and retook the city. The acclaiming people hailed him as the "Reconquistador," and the city council, without consulting the viceroy, named him a military leader. Thus the future Argentinians acquired a taste for making decisions quite independently of the mother country. The British took Montevideo and attacked Buenos Aires again in 1807. Liniers defeated them in both places, and Madrid named him a squadron leader, captain general, and temporarily viceroy of La Plata.

From this episode the colonials learned a lesson: the viceroy's troops from Spain had been defeated, while the half-breeds and other locals had won. This strengthened their longing for independence. Soon, however, their relationship with Liniers deteriorated. After his victory, Liniers made the grave mistake of writing to Napoleon, expressing admiration and asking his help in the organization of defense against further British attacks. The letter must have reached the Emperor at the beginning of 1808. With this step, Liniers made many enemies, for the colonials, although resentful of the British, had no desire to fall under the rule of the Emperor of the French.

This marks the beginning of the second stage of Napoleon's policy toward the colonies of Latin America. In 1808 he sprang the trap he had laid for King Charles of Spain and his son Ferdinand at Bayonne and put his brother Joseph on the Spanish throne. In theory, the Spanish colonies passed to the Bonapartes. In order to legalize the new government in colonial eyes, it was decided that representatives of the colonies would take part in the vote for a new constitution. But the Creoles attached no importance to the presence of their so-called representatives at King Joseph's court. The constitution, as elaborated in part by Napoleon and signed by Joseph, contained provisions for "the Spanish kingdoms and provinces of America and Asia," which were "to enjoy the same rights as the motherland, and where all forms of agriculture and industry will be free." Moreover, twenty-two deputies "chosen from landowners born in the various provinces" were to represent these provinces to the central government and the Cortes. "They will exercise this function for eight years, and six of them, chosen by the king, will be adjunct members of the Council of State's Indies department and have a voice in all affairs of the Spanish kingdoms and provinces, whether in America or in Asia." Finally—and here we find Napoleon's great design—"the various Spains and Indies will have a single code of civil law."

At the beginning of May, 1808, Napoleon (who had received the letter from Liniers at the beginning of the year) was convinced that to dispatch troops to the Spanish colonies of Latin America would win him the gratitude of the Creoles! On May 8 he wrote to Navy Minister Decrès: "What carries weight in America is the supply of means to combat the English." He decided to send two emissaries, Navy Lieutenant Paul de Lamanon to Caracas and the marquis de Sassenay to La Plata, to sound out the situation. The marquis, who asked for time to put his affairs in order before undertaking this mission, received the following categorical order: "Impossible. You must leave tomorrow, which gives you twenty-four hours in which to make ready. Write out your will, and Maret will convey it to your family. Go at once to [Minister of Foreign Affairs Jean-Baptiste Nompère de] Champagny, who will give you your instructions."

This was not the end of Sassenay's troubles. Like his colleague, Lamanon, at Caracas, he was greeted in Montevideo by cries of: "Down with Napoleon! Long live Ferdinand VII!"

When Liniers, backed by local support, had written to Napoleon, the Spanish dynasty had not yet been overthrown. As soon as the change of dynasty became known, Liniers was suspected of conniving with the French Emperor. A few Creole businessmen were ready to come to terms with Joseph. But most of the Creoles followed the example of the supporters of Ferdinand VII in Spain, creating juntas empowered to govern in the name of an imprisoned king. In short, there was de facto independence. After a cold welcome at Montevideo, which shortly afterwards pledged allegiance to Ferdinand, Sassenay landed, in August, 1808, at Buenos Aires. Foreign Minister Champagny's instructions ran as follows:

> He [Sassenay] will say that an assembly has been called at Bayonne to plan the regeneration of the country, and that it has raised hopes in all the cities and towns of Spain, which are waiting anxiously for the promised sovereign, Joseph Napoleon, king of Naples and Sicily. He will inform America of the glory of present-day France and of the influence exercised by its ruling genius over all Europe, to which he dictates his law. At the same time he will gather all possible information on conditions in Spanish America, particularly in the Viceroyalty of Buenos Aires, observing the effect produced upon the authorities by the news of the happy change in Spain.

Liniers, who found himself in a delicate situation, consented to receive Sassenay officially only in the presence of the junta. "I was told," Sassenay related, "that they wanted no king other than Ferdinand VII. Several members of the junta wanted to use violence and to seize my person. But finally it was decided to send me back to Montevideo, where I would receive an official answer, and then return me on the first ship to Europe."

Liniers did have a secret talk with Sassenay before the latter left for Montevideo. He made his excuses, explaining his dependence on the Cabildo (city council) and giving assurances of his regard for the Emperor. At Montevideo, the unfortunate Sassenay and his accompanying officers and crew were declared prisoners of war. After sixteen months in the jail of the revolutionary junta, they were shipped to Spain and shut up at Cádiz, whence they escaped in 1810.

In Buenos Aires, shortly after Sassenay's departure, there was a solemn oath of fealty to Ferdinand VII, and in 1810 Liniers was sentenced to death and executed. The Argentinian patriots were probably right to suspect that Napoleon had designs on their country and that Liniers had connived with him. It is likely that he had collaborated on a report signed in 1803 by his brother Henri concerning a project for the conquest of Brazil. This report had been presented to the First Consul and received his attention.

Meanwhile, the Creoles' fears were confirmed. As Napoleon

became aware of the violence of the Spaniards' resistance, he thought of sending expeditionary forces to impose his rule on the colonies in Latin America. On June 13, 1808, when Sassenay was on his way across the ocean with news of the "happy change" in the motherland, Napoleon wrote to Decrès: "There's agitation in Spain. ... If it doesn't soon calm down it will spread to the colonies, and in this case I'll need to have several contingents in readiness to go take them over." At El Ferrol, in Spain, Joachim Murat, contacted by the brother of Liniers' mistress, was ready to send three thousand men and money to Rio de La Plata.

Paul de Lamanon, the Emperor's envoy to the northerly colonies, arrived at Caracas, wearing a full-dress uniform, on July 15, 1808. The local authorities were hesitant in their reaction, but on the streets in front of the government palace an excited crowd shouted, "Long live Ferdinand VII! Death to Napoleon!" Fealty was sworn to Ferdinand, and Lamanon fled under cover of darkness.

Not a single Spanish colony recognized Joseph Bonaparte as king; every one subordinated itself to the loyalist junta in Seville. Mexico, Peru, and New Granada (Colombia) obeyed Seville's interdiction of foreign trade; Buenos Aires, Montevideo, Cuba, and Santo Domingo traded with England.

Since Britain did rule the seas, the Emperor saw the futility of trying to bring force to bear on the recalcitrant Creoles and radically switched his policy. For the first time he voiced sympathy for the independence movements, in the hope of winning their leaders' support. This third and last stage of his relationship with Latin America began on December 12, 1809, when he declared to the legislative body that the Latin Americans' independence was "in the necessary order of events." After the reception given to his two emissaries, he realized that direct contact with the insurgent leaders was out of the question and decided to make known his intentions and goodwill through the intermediary of Washington. At the same time, he sought to foil England through a closer relationship with the United States, to which he offered Florida. On December 13, 1810, he instructed Minister of Foreign Affairs Champagny as to his intentions toward the United States and the Latin-American colonies: "You will make it known that I do not oppose the Floridas becoming an American possession and that, in general, I desire everything favorable to the independence of Spanish America. . . . I am happy with the independence of a great country as long as it is not under the influence of England. . . . I shall act as circumstances demand, but in such a way as not to blockade shipping that genuinely originates from an American port."

On August 11, 1811, he communicated to Hugues Bernard Maret (the duc de Bassano), his new minister of foreign affairs, the policy to be followed by Marshal Sérurier, ambassador to the United States:

> To the Duke of Bassano: I am sending you this letter on the United States, of whose contents it seems opportune for you to apprise Monsieur Sérurier with a triple copy, in code, to be dispatched on one of the departing American vessels. You will tell him that it is my intention to encourage the independence of all the Americas, that he should set forth this point of view not only to the president but also to whatever representatives the Latin-American colonies may have in the United States. He should actively try to make contact with them, and he is further authorized to send agents to these colonies and to undertake to supply them with arms and other aid, on condition that their independence is absolute and they have no connections with England. He should use the channel of the American government to convey these intentions. Finally, he should manage to inform us frequently of all that is going on in Latin America. Since the government of the United States must be pleased to see these Spanish colonies acquire independence, Monsieur Sérurier can communicate with them through American agents.

Monsieur Sérurier did convey the Emperor's message to President Monroe, insinuating that "no matter how great was the American Republic's goodwill," it could not foster the Latin Americans' independence all alone, and that, as long as they steered clear of England, France would send them arms through the intermediary of the United States. Monroe's reply was amiable but evasive. "Mere words!" reflected the French ambassador, who was made aware that whatever might be going on was "behind his back."

After Napoleon seized power in Spain, the United States took an attitude of watchful but mistrustful waiting. There was no recognition of Spanish consuls, whether sent by Joseph or by the junta of Seville, between 1808 and 1814, or of the ambassador sent by Joseph in 1810. The proposal of an alliance between France and the United States, when the latter engaged itself in the War of 1812, was turned down. Mistrust, then, in North America and, in South America, hostility—both continents opposed interference on the part of imperial France.

On April 19, 1810, the Venezuelans drove the Spanish captain general from Caracas and installed a revolutionary junta that immediately opened the door to British trade. Bolívar was sent on a mission to London, from which he returned on July 14, 1811, in order to be present at the proclamation of the Republic, with full powers accorded to Miranda, on July 14, 1811. On this occasion Bolívar declared: "We are told that we should wait upon the development of Spanish policy. But what do we care whether Spain sells its slaves to Bonaparte or keeps them for itself, if we are resolved to be free?"

Napoleon tried in vain to charm the Venezuelan leaders. Miranda—who did not forget that he had been imprisoned in the Temple[2] after the coup d'état of 18 Fructidor, 1797—was offered arms by Napoleon, the man responsible for his imprisonment and his subsequent expulsion from France. At this time Miranda was portrayed by one of the wax figures in the Musée Grévin as "Miranda, general of the Spanish Independents of Mexico." Both he and Bolívar preferred to strengthen their ties with England.

On May 25, 1810, the city of Buenos Aires announced the creation of a junta to replace the Spanish viceroy. One of the chief motives for this demonstration of independence was fear of Napoleon's ambition. On June 19, the junta informed the Spanish naval commander of its purpose and reason for being: "a reasonable precaution against the danger of being involved in the ambitious designs of Joseph Bonaparte, the abusive king of Spain." In other words, separation from Spain was a way of escaping the domination of Napoleon. On February 21, 1811, the junta proclaimed: "The government proposes to achieve the great purpose of independence from France." And further on in the text Napoleon was dubbed "the tyrant of Europe."

Here, too, events favored England. The day after the junta took over, ships of the British navy answered the salvos of the local ships with salvos of their own and a display of flags. Trade with Britain was authorized, quite naturally, since the most important members of the junta were two wealthy businessmen, Cornelio Saavedra and Manuel Belgrano.

During the last years of Napoleon's reign, Latin America was ravaged by wars of independence. Their protracted duration was due to the fact that rebel and loyalist forces were much more equally divided than their equivalents in the United States, where the loyalists had been a distinct minority. When Ferdinand VII returned to the Spanish throne, he brutally reconquered a number of the colonies. Belgrano attempted in vain to reach an understanding; in the end Argentina alone kept its independence. In 1812, the Spanish king's troops overturned the Venezuelan government of Miranda, who suffered a miserable death in the prisons of Cádiz a few years later. Bolívar resumed the fight for liberation and reconquered Venezuela. Overturned by the royalists in 1814, he was about to launch another war of independence when Napoleon's empire collapsed. In La Plata, around the same time, General San Martín was organizing an army to safeguard Argentina's freedom and extend it to the surrounding colonies.

The rebel leaders, especially Bolívar and San Martín, tried to enlist veterans of Napoleon's army. Their emissaries made contact with exiles and *demi-soldes* in the United States, and in Europe they set up regular recruiting agencies. The Liberal party made propaganda for the revolutionary Creoles. The Creoles promised generous compensation, and many Frenchmen enrolled directly, without passing through an agency, most of them in the land forces.

Relations between the French veterans and the Creole leaders were often thorny. Bolívar and San Martín had feelings of hatred and fear toward Napoleon. San Martín had begun his military career fighting in the Spanish army against the French invaders, and now French volunteers were bound to feel the repercussions. On the other hand, officers of the Grande Armée, aware of their ability and prowess, found it hard to adapt themselves to subordinate positions.

Navy Captain Maurice Persat, whom we left at Amelia Island, went subsequently to Venezuela to offer his services to Bolívar.

The two men soon fell out, and Persat's *Mémoires* give an unfavorable picture of the Venezuelan leader.

The most important of the Napoleonic veterans engaged in the Creole forces was General Michel Brayer who, as we saw earlier, had promised support for the plan to rescue Napoleon that was based in Pernambuco. Obviously, San Martín could not have tolerated any project of an expedition to St. Helena from Montevideo. Of Brayer, Napoleon said at St. Helena: "I never met a man so definitive and determined in putting his opinions into action." Well built, dark-haired, with pronounced features and a strong character, Michel Sylvestre Brayer disembarked in Baltimore in 1816, at the age of forty-five years. In September of that year, a court-martial had sentenced him to death *in absentia* for having rallied to Napoleon from his post in Lyon upon the Corsican's return from Elba. In Baltimore, the Chilean general José Miguel de Carrera offered Brayer the command of his country's independence army. In December, Michel Brayer, with his son Lucien, his former aide-de-camp Moline Saint-Yon, and several volunteers, set sail for Buenos Aires, where he arrived early in February, 1817. In October of this year, he joined up in Chile with the "United Army of Independents," under the overall command of the Argentinian general San Martín. After the Battle of Talcahuano, on the Pacific shore, General Bernardo O'Higgins, the future "Director" of Chile, noted: Major General Don Miguel Brayer, at the beginning and in the midst of this fiery action, gave many proofs of his military capacity." Brayer had had a brilliant career in the army of Napoleon; wounded more than once in major battles, he attained the rank of Divisional General of the Young Guard. But he could not get on with San Martín, who, perhaps, was jealous of being overshadowed by him. During the Battle of Maipu in April, 1818, he could not tolerate San Martín's critical remarks. He handed in his resignation and returned to Buenos Aires.

An unusually violent controversy ensued. Brayer sent a letter to the Buenos Aires government in reply to the "odious slander" spread about him. San Martín, in his turn, published "several pages filled with insults which," according to Brayer, "left an honest reader with feelings of indignation, pity, and scorn." In 1821, Brayer took advantage of an amnesty to return to France. There he made a reply to the Argentinian, "a man lacking manners, education, judgment, and wisdom, and given to insolent attacks on the well-known honorability and strategic genius of the marshals of France." In short, San Martín could not take lessons from one of Napoleon's generals. And Brayer resented taking orders from a man who, in his opinion, was less versed than himself in the art of war. With emphatic indignation, he denounced the ferocious despotism of San Martín, who had accused him of cowardice and, by his own admission, had thought of assassinating him:

> Know, then, that I have been in more than thirty major battles involving leadership, tactics, talent, and exceptional bravery on both sides. I am not speaking of the encounters to which you pompously and improperly give this name . . . clashes decided by chance, where you had preestablished no plans or troop deployments nor had to judge when to modify them over and over. . . . Know, also, that my body is so riddled with wounds, so furrowed with scars, that bullets aimed by cowardice could have struck no place that did not already bear the imprints of honor.

And he went on to describe San Martín as a hateful tyrant, who threw dissenters into jail or drove them into exile.

Brayer was not the only victim of San Martín's "raging jealousy." Battalion Commander Crammaire, a graduate of the École Polytechnique decorated with the Legion of Honor, had organized a regiment of the Liberation army whose victory at Chacabuco won him the praise of his fellow officers but the implacable resentment of San Martín, who finally sent him away. Brayer, along with many of his contemporaries, thought that Spanish America, unlike the United States, had been so long kept "in chains and in darkness" that it was "ignorant of many things" and could profit from his European military experience. In his mind, the United States was the model of a developing nation, whereas Latin America had a great deal to learn. Michel Brayer died as a Peer of France in 1840, and his name is inscribed on the Arc de Triomphe in Paris.

During the few months he spent with the Liberation movement, Brayer was joined by Bacler d'Albe, a *demi-solde* serving in the Creole armies with the rank of lieutenant colonel in the corps of engineers and one of the few of his rank to retain the native leaders' esteem. Joseph Albert d'Albe was born in 1789 in Sallanches in the department of Haute-Savoie.[3] Graduating as a second lieutenant from the École Militaire, he joined the Army of the North. His topographical knowledge, passed on to him by his father, Napoleon's cartographer, won him highly responsible posts in the map sections of the three general staffs with which he served. A captain, decorated with the Legion of Honor, he was relegated to half-pay status during the Restoration. The fact that he was only a few inches over five feet tall helped him to flee from France during the summer of 1816. Disguised as a woman, he eluded the royal police and reached Antwerp, where General Brayer had set up a departure base whence volunteer *demi-soldes* could sail, via Baltimore, to Argentina. His role in the engineering corps of San Martín's army was considerable; among other things, he effected the cartographical preparations for the crossing of the Andes. After the Battle of Maipu, when San Martín quarreled with Brayer, he covered Bacler d'Albe with praise, voicing in his order of the day his satisfaction with the conduct of "Engineer Major d'Albe, whose knowledge, tireless activity, and bravery have made him universally esteemed." Bacler d'Albe remained in the Chilean army, became a naturalized citizen, and married a girl from Valparaiso, where he died of yellow fever in 1824, when he was only thirty-five years old.

Another noteworthy Frenchman engaged in the Latin-American struggle for independence was Colonel Pierre-Rémy Roulet who, after a stay in the United States, joined the Pernambuco expedition. He was captured, imprisoned, and freed, after which he turned to France but could not regain his military status. He returned to South America and enlisted in San Martín's army in Peru. One of the children borne to him by his Peruvian wife was christened Napoléon Roulet. He went into politics and, as a result, was banished first from Peru and then from Chile.

In the northerly sector of South America, Commander Claude Girardot led a battalion of the British Legion. Captain Eugène Giroust and the Bruix brothers died fighting for the independence movement.

On the slopes of Corcovado, above Rio de Janeiro, amid lush vegetation and superb flowers, there was a little green house, the retreat of an unusual personage. Inside, a visitor was startled to find a small bedroom whose black walls were painted with skeletons. Elsewhere there was an impressive portrait of a French general in full-dress uniform—the house's proprietor, Dirk van Hogendorp.

Hogendorp, scion of a noble Dutch family and a pupil of Immanuel Kant, started his military career in the Prussian army. Resident in Patna, Bengal, for the Dutch East India Company, he frequently sailed the Indian Ocean, was twice shipwrecked, and had a hurricane bring down a house over his head. Subsequently, as governor of Java, he tried to reform the colonial administration, built sawmills and sugar refineries, and promoted the cultivation of indigo. He took in what was left of the Entrecasteaux expedition, which had left Brest in 1791 in search of the lost explorer La Pérouse. By the time survivors landed on Java, France no longer had a king, and Hogendorp decided to treat them as refugees. Among them was the future Admiral Jurien de la Gravière. The Dutch governors of the time lived in regal glory, and when Jurien de la Gravière was invited to the governor's palace he was dazzled by "a luxury of which only that of an Indian rajah's court can give any idea. There we went to parties reminiscent of the fabulous splendors of the Arabian Nights, where an army of uniformed young slaves stood behind the guests at table, waiting to anticipate their every desire."

And what of the governor's coat, with its uncut ruby buttons, when he paraded in a boat made of rare wood, rowed by twenty young Javanese girls "as remarkable for their beauty as for their total lack of clothing"? Later Dirk van Hogendorp became ambassador of Holland (which then called itself the Batavian Republic) to Moscow and Vienna. In 1810 Holland was attached to France, and Napoleon, attracted by Hogendorp's open personality, made him general of a division and subsequently his aide-de-camp. The Emperor still cherished a Far Eastern dream, and perhaps the Dutchman's career in the Orient roused an echo in his imagination.

During the Russian campaign, Hogendorp was named governor of Lithuania. Under the first Restoration, Holland recovered its independence, and Hogendorp resigned from the French army. As soon as he heard of the return from Elba, he hurried to offer the Emperor his services and for several months held the château of Nantes. Stripped of his rank by the second Restoration, he decided to go into exile, and in February, 1817, fifty-six years old and penniless, he settled on the slopes of Mt. Corcovado.

Since the coast of Brazil was the nearest land to St. Helena, suspicion was attached to the presence in this country of anyone connected with Napoleon. We do not know whether Napoleon and Hogendorp exchanged any secret correspondence, but Napoleon had not forgotten his faithful aide-de-camp and tried to get him to St. Helena. In 1820, Grand Marshal Bertrand noted: "The Grand Marshal has sent to the governor [Hudson Lowe] a memorandum to say that by writing to Brazil there could be obtained an 'officer' and a valet for the Emperor, that General Hogendorp, formerly the Emperor's aide-de-camp, who is in Brazil, could make arrangements with the British consul."

But Lowe's answer was negative. We may recall that Napoleon left Hogendorp a hundred thousand francs in his will.

The royal family of Bragança, fleeing before Junot's French army, had left Portugal for its Brazilian colony in 1810 and ruled there until 1821. Dom Pedro, future emperor of Brazil, intrigued by the strange story of the hermit of Corcovado, paid him a visit. But visitors were few and far between. Jacques Arago, brother of the scientist of the same name, accidentally discovered the general's retreat in the course of an excursion to the environs of Rio. Thirst drove him to knock at the door, and behind it he saw, to his amazement, the portrait of Napoleon's general. Finally the subject of the portrait appeared. "Good God! What exile can do to a man!" the visitor noted. "The eyes of the brave defender of Hamburg were dulled, his forehead and cavernous cheeks were furrowed by wrinkles, his hair was sparse, and his skin was burned by the sun. Misfortune had spared neither his spirit nor his body. There was poverty in this high-ceilinged wooden house, which had stood up against so many storms, but a poverty that was noble and worthily endured."

Arago introduced himself, and Hogendorp told him how he had become a dealer in coal and orange liqueur. During a subsequent visit, Hogendorp gave Arago the memoirs that he had written during his solitary exile.

Admiral Jurien de la Gravière, whom Hogendorp had entertained in Java, was sent by Louis XVIII in 1820 on a mission to the new South American republics. During a stopover at Rio, he was told about the hermit of Corcovado and went on muleback to see if he could identify him. We may imagine his feelings when he recognized the former governor of Java in this impoverished old man. Sitting in the shade in front of his house, Hogendorp was looking out over the bay of Rio de Janeiro. Twenty-five years had gone by since the two men had last seen each other. The admiral paid his old acquaintance a second visit on May 5, 1821, the day of Napoleon's death. On October 29, 1822, in the bedroom with the macabre wall decoration, Hogendorp died in his turn. Those who dressed him for the funeral found his body tattooed all over, according to the custom of Java.

When it comes to the southern part of the two Americas, we find little parallel between the Napoleonic and the American dreams. Plainly, the revolutionary theory of Latin America was very different from that of the United States. The North Americans fought to preserve already acquired liberties. They did not tax England with its political principles, which, indeed, they found praiseworthy, but only with the failure to apply them in the colonies. The Declaration of Independence is explicit in this regard.

In Latin America everything had to be created from scratch. The mother country did not merely block economic freedom; it was also a counterrevolutionary force. There was, to be sure, one point in common between the two Americas: economic freedom was closely related to the wars of independence. But, in Latin America, the revolution was philosophical and political as well, and in this way closer to the revolutionary movements of Europe. Indeed, the French Revolution deeply marked the leaders of revolutionary South America. Their situation endowed them with a deeper understanding of the European upheavals than that of most of their North American contemporaries. We have seen that the Venezuelan leader, Miranda, belonged to the French Revolutionary Army of the North. And, in his memoirs, the Argentinian Belgrano writes: "I was in Spain in 1789. The French Revolution so overturned ideas, especially in the literary circles that I frequented, that I was won over to the ideals of liberty, equality, security, and property. I came to consider as tyrants all those who would not allow men in every clime to enjoy peacefully the rights given them by God and Nature and indirectly sanctioned by their institutions and even their societies."

South Americans may have dreaded Napoleon, but his figure and his myth won their admiration. Their Latin blood and Catholic religion, the former motherland's continental vocation, the romantic approach to history, all these emotional factors mitigated the Creole leaders' severe judgment of Napoleon. They could admit that he was marked by his self-proclaimed Destiny and feel his fascination.

After Napoleon had died, Bolívar, delivered of his fear, spoke of him admiringly and with a certain emotion. To General José Antonio Páez he wrote: "Napoleon was great, and unique." To Sir Robert Wilson: "Bonaparte initiated a great reform for the benefit of the human race. It is up to England to carry out the promises of this prophetic conqueror." (Can we imagine a North American calling a conqueror prophetic?) When the Abbé Dominique de Pradt compared him to both Washington and Napoleon, Bolívar replied: "The parallel you draw among Washington, Napoleon, and myself is as audacious as it is inexact. You compare me, sir, to illustrious men! Washington surpasses me in moral and religious virtues, just as he surpasses all men in patriotism and modesty. Napoleon is the man of immensity, and the finite cannot be related to the infinite." Bolívar must have read many books about Napoleon. The character, the military genius, the legend, all enthralled him.

In France, during the Restoration, Bolívar was a hero to the Liberals. In fashionable drawing rooms there was much talk of the Latin-American insurgents. But soon the image of these heroes and their countries was clouded. Didn't Bolívar betray the liberal ideal? The new republics were not exemplary; they were guilty of frequent abuses. Pardo de Leygonier recalls the controversy between the abbé de Pradt and Benjamin Constant on the subject of Bolívar.[4]

De Pradt flattered Bolívar quite shamelessly. And Bolívar, in his turn, used the abbé's encomiums for propaganda purposes in Europe, even if he doubted their sincerity. "My eyes," the abbé wrote to him, "will always be on the hero who has attained the highest fate that heaven can bestow upon a mortal, that of the regenerator of a second universe."

On December 31, 1828, Benjamin Constant published in *Le Courrier français* a virulent article unmasking the South-American "hero":

> I can see why the memory of the services rendered to oppressed peoples and the stubbornly sustained struggle against an unreasonable mother-country should cause certain friends of freedom to judge indulgently the man who is still called the Liberator of South America. But they must forgive me if, in the man who dissolved the legislative body because his supporters formed a minority, who, under the pretext that his fellow citizens were not enlightened enough to govern themselves, took over power and established his dictatorship with murders and executions, I see only a usurper. . . . I know that the man in question attaches importance to the opinion of Europeans, and I want him to know that among them there are some who mourn beside the vulgar and bloody road that he has followed. It is good that sincere voices from afar should interrupt the concert of adulation that doubtless echoes at his side.

And, on another occasion, Constant wrote: "Bolívar, taking advantage of the dismemberment of a few provinces, has endowed them with an imperfect constitution, very little in harmony with genuine freedom." Obviously, Constant used Bolívar as a pretext to defend the Additional Act to the Constitution (1815), to whose composition he had contributed, against extremists.

On January 21, 1829, de Pradt answered Constant with a pamphlet entitled *Bolívar Defended from the Appellation of Usurper.* In defense of his hero, the abbé described the peoples of Latin America with shocking scorn:

> Preachers of liberty, I'd like to see your soapboxes on the banks of the Orinoco, your benches crowded with a horrendous mixture of blacks, mulattoes, whites, and Creoles, all recently issued from the cavern of slavery and barbarism to serve as leaders and legislators! . . . In America everything is division and diversity and lack of civilization. In Europe there is a culture to be enjoyed, in America it has yet to be created. . . . There is no faith; ambition for power causes warriors to devour one another. Spanish blood raises up conspiracies just as trees bear fruit.

Elsewhere the abbé de Pradt wrote: "Before calling Bolívar an usurper we must wait for the end of his career. . . . To us

Paris is everything. We see and carry it with us everywhere. We want liberty to have a palace, and there are places where it has only a frail cradle. Bolívar will have something in his favor when America has some likeness to Europe, when a shapeless society has some shape, when military conflicts give place to law and order."

In apology for the authoritarian rule of Napoleon as contrasted to the liberal principles of the United States, North American society was described as mature, European society as still weighed down by its feudal past. But Latin America, to French eyes, seemed to emerge from the shadows of a terrifying obscurantism. Supporters and detractors of Bolívar agreed on one point: if the North American dream provided a refuge from the calamities of history, this dream did not extend to Latin America. There the historical vices seemed even blacker than in old Europe.

In the following years, an increasingly diversified immigrant group, the search for an Indian identity, and the shadow of United States imperialism created a new, complex image of Latin America. Here, too, there is a dream. But has it anything to do with Napoleon or Washington?[5] Their legends are not without interest in view of the cultural and economic relations among Europe, Latin America, and the United States.

In the Mexican periodical *El Maestro* (1922), there is an article comparing the first American president to the Emperor of the French. "How are they different, these two? One destroyed nations, the other created at least one; one enslaved his people, the other freed them." And Bolívar is presented as belonging to the same family as Washington, as having the same aims and the same democratic ideals.

The admirers of Napoleon are equally present. The number and quality of the commemorations of the two hundredth anniversary of Napoleon's birth and the newspaper articles written about it bear testimony to the vitality of the Napoleonic legend in Latin America. But the presence of Napoleon is more evident in a concrete fact. In an article of the ephemeral Spanish constitution drawn up at Bayonne in 1808, it was stated that both Spain and its colonies would be "ruled by a single code of civil law." And the majority of civil codes in Latin America are inspired by the Code Napoléon.

Here is Napoleon's victory in this part of the world.

CHAPTER 8

At the Canadian Border

Great Britain would never have allowed Napoleon to go to the United States, if for no other reason than that its Canadian colony was so close by. Napoleon might have organized or even led an attempt at conquest or have tried to raise up the French-Canadian population against its ruler. Since the defeat of Montcalm, Canada had been a peaceful province. The English-speaking inhabitants were mostly loyalists who had fled or rejected the American Revolution. As for the French, they were strongly influenced by the anti-Revolutionary Catholic clergy.

The example of the United States seemed, to London, a permanent threat to its New World possessions. On Elba, Napoleon told Major Vivian that Canada was fated to fall into the hands of its growing neighbor. Napoleon, surrounded by his old soldiers, at the Canadian border would have caused England to tremble. He was aware of the British government's nervousness and thought it was justified. On May 26, 1816, Las Cases wrote:

> The newspapers say that his brother Joseph has bought large areas of land in the northern part of New York State, on the Saint Lawrence River, and that many Frenchmen are converging there in such a way as to form an establishment. The choice of this site seems to favor the policy of the United States to the detriment of that of England. In the South, in Louisiana, for instance, French refugees can aspire only to a future of peace and domestic prosperity, while in the North they would eventually attract the French Canadians and form a barrier or even a center of hostility to the English who dominate them. The Emperor said that soon this establishment would group together men with talents in various fields of endeavor. If they do their duty, he added, they will produce excellent writings, powerful

refutations of the system prevailing in Europe today. Already on Elba the Emperor had harbored ideas of the kind.

In March of 1821, as we have seen, there was a short-lived hope on St. Helena that a change of government in England would bring about Napoleon's liberation. On March 10 he said to General Bertrand, "These questions are so complex that it's difficult to have an opinion. If it were up to me I'd go to America. The British are fearful about Canada, which is very French in spirit. In Canada my name must carry considerable weight. For the last twenty years they've heard of little else."

French-speaking Canadians had lived under British rule since 1763. For the most part they were critical of the French Revolution while, at the same time, they unwillingly accepted British domination. The Quebec Act of 1774 guaranteed to Canadians of French origin the preservation of their language, institutions, and religion. Nevertheless, English-speaking Canadians and the London government feared the penetration of "Jacobin emissaries" and watched their French fellow citizens mistrustfully. In 1791 the British set up governments in Upper and Lower Canada (Ontario and Quebec) in order to ward off American and French "democratic excesses."[1]

The French, or some of them, irritated by this display of authoritarianism, began to hope that Revolutionary France, whose victories were more and more publicized, would come to free them from England. The French minister to the United States, Citizen Genêt, who, as we have seen, was never reluctant to take unconsidered action, wrote a call to insurrection, "The Free French to Their Canadian Brothers," called in Canada "The Catechism":

> Man is born free. By what fatality has he become subject to his fellowman? This land belongs to you and must be independent. Break with a daily more degenerate government, one that has become the cruelest enemy of man's freedom. Everywhere there are traces of the despotism, greed, and cruelty of the king of England . . . of a perfidious court that has granted Canada the shadow of a constitution only for fear that it follow the virtuous examples of France and America, by shaking off its yoke and founding a government based on the inalienable rights of man.

The appeal ended with an enumeration of all the advantages that would accrue to Canadians as citizens of an independent nation. This text impressed a number of people in the cities of Quebec and Montreal, who discussed it at secret meetings.

The bishop of Quebec was upset and, at the governor's request, instructed priests to recall to their parishioners their duty to His Majesty the King of England. The clergy, many of whose members had been persecuted by the revolutionaries in France, warned the faithful against French propaganda. There were riots in both Quebec and Montreal in 1794 and again in 1796, but by 1800 calm reigned throughout the colony. The government, however, was still haunted by the fear of French agents. Canadians of English origin (a minority of the total population of 250,000) were grossly insufficient in number for the defense of their large territory.

French citizens were suspect, and their entry into the country was hedged with precautions. In the progovernment sheet, *La Gazette de Québec*, the First Consul was bitterly attacked. The violence reigning in Europe was contrasted with the peaceful happiness of Canada, where people "sang and danced," thereby arousing the "rage" of the French and of Napoleon, the "usurper." This anti-French hysteria inspired a veritable witch-hunt, and various Frenchmen were thrown into prison, to be released only with the Anglo-French Treaty of Amiens in 1802.

In 1800, a tract bearing the seal of the "French Republic" and sent out by the consulate in New York circulated among French Canadians: "The moment of justice has not yet come. Do not despair, but do not rush anything. Submission and prudence should be the order of the day. The time when you can raise your bowed heads cannot be far off."

The Canadian press continued to attack the France of Napoleon Bonaparte. *La Gazette de Québec* published the popular song:

> Under a foreigner's scepter
> France lies low:
> Under the chains she thought to break
> I see her bow,
> Dupe of his ambition.

The Treaty of Amiens was a cause of both rejoicing and disquiet. Canadians heard, somewhat nervously, that French fishing rights were restored to the *status quo ante bellum*. Great Britain, it seemed, had imprudently given Frenchmen an opportunity to come close to the Canadian coast. But the signing of the treaty was enthusiastically celebrated. Bishop Denaut commented on past events: "Religion and humanity mingled their tears with the blood of martyrs, innocent victims of an anti-Christian revolution."

When Jérôme Bonaparte came to the United States, the government followed his movements for fear he might attempt to raise up the French of "Lower" Canada. In 1805 a dozen French-Canadians addressed a letter to Napoleon (quoted by J.-P. Wallot) begging for liberation.

> March 1, 1805. The people of Canada to His Majesty Napoleon I, Emperor of the French:
> Sire, we planned to shake off the English yoke; we were waiting for guns in order to be armed and to strike with assurance of victory. But our hopes have been deceived. The watchfulness of My-Lords and Lords and employees of every kind would crumble before our unity and our efforts if we had a good French general, with a sense of duty and honor. . . . Sire, we trust that, in your fatherly care, you will not make peace until we have recovered the name of Canadian Frenchmen. We are ready for anything at the first sight of Frenchmen, whom we always look upon as brothers.[2]

Trafalgar and the succession of European wars excluded any plan for the "liberation" of Canada. Actually, the writers of the above letter were all of a certain age and had only vague and faraway memories of life in France. Most of them had been born in Canada and heard of events in Europe only through the English-language press. Material well-being, propaganda on the part of government and clergy, and the birth of a certain Canadian nationalism in the face of the growing power of the United States, all these induced the French population to remain loyal to the king of England. All during the struggle against Napoleon, Britain received timber from the forests of its docile North American colony.

In 1785 the northern part of New York State, adjacent to the Canadian border, was visited by a twenty-five-year-old Frenchman, Jacques Le Ray de Chaumont, whose father had taken part in the American War of Independence. Le Ray bought large tracts of land near the Saint Lawrence River and set up important manufacturing plants. He was a friend, after Waterloo, to many French refugees and had with some of them—notably Joseph Bonaparte, Marshal Grouchy, and Comte Réal—business transactions involving the sale of real estate near the Canadian border.

We have already mentioned the comte de Survillier's hunting preserve in this region. The French consul in Philadelphia noted, in a report of December 17, 1816: "General Grouchy has been up North, visiting other generals and local people who gave him a cordial reception. He has bought from Monsieur Le Ray de Chaumont considerable acreage near Lake Ontario, where he proposes to settle." The marshal enjoyed visiting this estate, close to that of Joseph Bonaparte, although he traveled to other parts of the United States as well.

Among the French exiles most stably settled in New York, the most well known was Comte Réal, who had been prefect of police in Paris during the Hundred Days. Fouché, who had long been jealous of him, was suspected of putting his name on the ordinance of proscription of July 24, 1815, which obliged him to leave France.

Pierre-François Réal was born near Paris in 1757. As a lawyer and eloquent speaker, he became an intimate friend of Desmoulins and Danton. After the fall of Louis XVI, his friendship with Danton caused him to be named public prosecutor. His revolutionary enthusiasm did not affect his natural moderation and distaste for cruelty. When Danton fell, Robespierre had Réal jailed and sentenced to death, and only Robespierre's execution on 9 Thermidor, 1794, saved him. After Napoleon's seizure of power on 18 Brumaire, 1799, in which he took part, Réal served him faithfully up until the Empire's last day.

In May, 1816, he decided to go into exile in the United States and landed in New York on August 11. He was received by Joseph Bonaparte at Point Breeze and soon met Le Ray de Chaumont. "Réal," Hyde de Neuville wrote to the duc de Richelieu, "seems to have decided to go live on the Saint Lawrence, where he has bought land. He says that he has no wish to involve himself in politics and aspires only to a life of retirement." Like all those on the proscription list, Réal was an object of suspicion to royalist agents, who were obsessed by the possibility of plots. Why had he chosen the state of New York? In a report from the Philadelphia consul, written around the time of Réal's arrival in the States, we read: "General Scott, governor of the State of New York, who is surrounded by the most dangerous French revolutionaries and friendly with the so-called General Mina, the Regnaults, Clauzel, Grouchy, *et al.*, has opened at the Battery, in New York City, an office for recruiting the most disreputable French, Irish, Spanish, and American types of men willing to sail to join the insurgents of Latin America. Their plan, I am sure, also involves the liberation of the usurper."

In 1817 Réal engaged in a "business operation" with Genêt, former French envoy and author of the "Catechism" designed to subvert French-Canadians. During his stay in the city, a royalist agent wrote ironically to Hyde de Neuville: "Réal plays, once more, the role of the chief of police; he greets new arrivals and enters their name in a notebook." And Hyde wrote to the duc de Richelieu: "Lakanal is presently in New York and almost always in the company of Réal, who is probably his closest adviser and the cleverest of the whole party." Réal's connections with the originator of the "Napoleonic Confederation" was ground for suspicion. And Napoleon left him a legacy of 100,000 francs, as he did to other exiles suspected of having plotted his escape from St. Helena. However, it was never proved that Réal had anything to do with a conspiracy. He owned shares in the Society for the Cultivation of the Grape and Olive, but he would not support Lallemand's Texas project and indeed considered it regrettable.

In 1818, Réal was authorized by the French government to return to France, but he chose to remain at Cape Vincent, near the Canadian border. There he built a highly original dwelling known as "the cup-and-saucer house," because its octagonal shape and construction made it look like a teacup turned upside-down. According to T. Wood Clarke, it was built on an immense foundation containing a well-stocked cellar and had a broad veranda running all around it and two floors.[3] On the ground floor, there were oil portraits of the Emperor and his marshals, elaborately sculpted mantelpieces, superb silver candelabras, a first-class library, and a Stradivarius violin. On the second floor, there were a large number of smaller rooms, separated by panels on wheels, which could be moved around to divide them into varying sizes. In the "cup" part of the house, there were a laboratory and also a sort of sanctuary containing Napoleonic relics. Réal intrigued the local people by his refusal to wear a hat as long as his master was in captivity. He seems to have been the only French refugee inspired by America to go in for a utopian architecture and also for gadgets. An important member of the household was Professor Pigeon, a distinguished astronomer, who had brought from France scientific instruments whose precision probably had no equal in the New World at this time. In Comte Réal's entourage there were such other Bonapartists as General Rollard, Camille Arnaud, Paul Charboneau, and the Peugnet brothers.

Réal's life in America was perhaps the closest to that which Napoleon might have led had he come to the United States. We may recall that, at the moment when he dreamed of going into exile in America, he wrote to Gaspard Monge about the possibility of scientific (including astronomical) studies on the other side of the ocean. Did Pigeon and his equipment foretell Napoleon's escape and arrival? The vicinity of the French-Canadians submitted to British rule would have furnished a perfect excuse for the launching of anti-British and pro-Napoleon propaganda. Even if we do not go as far as the English historian, H. A. L. Fisher, in imagining Napoleon's conquest of Canada from an American base, we may visualize the Emperor at the Canadian border inciting the French-speaking population to echo the cry of "Long Live Free Quebec!"

CHAPTER 9

Itinerary of a Legend

On December 19, 1821, more than six months after his death, a mass was held for Napoleon in the cathedral of New Orleans. Among the veterans of his armies present, General Charles Lallemand, standing a little to one side, found it hard to conceal his emotion.

Shortly afterwards, he heard that he was mentioned in Napoleon's will and set out for France to claim his legacy. Eluding the strict watch of the royal police, he served for a time in the army of the Spanish liberals and, after a brief imprisonment in Portugal, went to Belgium and thence back to the United States, where he remained until the advent of King Louis-Philippe in 1830. During this second stay, he ran a school in New York. And, in 1828, the French ambassador reported: "General Lallemand has become the representative of several English shipbuilding companies, which deal with the insurgent countries of South America. A Greek committee in London gave him 150,000 pounds sterling for the construction and arming of two frigates." When Lallemand returned again to France, Louis-Philippe made him a peer and head of the military command of Corsica. He died in Paris in 1839.

Joseph Lakanal, whose projects had aroused such a furor, went back to France as late as 1837. In 1822 he accepted the presidency of the College of Orleans but resigned fourteen months later because of objections to his being an apostate priest. He went, then, to live near Mobile, Alabama, where he stayed for thirteen years alongside some of the former companions of Lefebvre-Desnouettes in the Alabama grape-and-olive project. His agricultural activities prospered. Disregarding the scruples of Clauzel and Lefebvre-Desnouettes, he became the owner of ten slaves.

Lakanal disembarked in France in 1837, wearing for the occasion the uniform of the French Institute. He married and had a son at the age of seventy-seven. He promised the publication of works on the *Convention* and on the spiritual status of America, but the manuscripts were never found. According to historian Jules Michelet, certain compromising notes on the French Revolution were behind this mysterious disappearance. Lakanal lived modestly but with the esteem of his fellow members of the Institute until his death in 1845.

After the death of Napoleon, the obvious representative of the Bonapartists in the United States was Joseph Bonaparte. On a September Sunday of 1824, the comte de Survilliers had a visit from the official guest of the nation, General de La Fayette. America gave La Fayette a delirious welcome, and Joseph invited him, members of his suite, and the governor of New Jersey to dinner. A sizable crowd gathered around the mansion, asking, so an eyewitness says, for "the blessing of the patriarch of liberty."

The real reason for La Fayette's visit was later revealed by Charles Jared Ingersoll. Before dinner, the two men had a talk in Joseph's study: "The subject of that conference, as often since told by Joseph Bonaparte, was La Fayette's acknowledgment of his regret of what he had done to re-instate the Bourbons. 'Their dynasty,' he said, 'could not last; it clashed too much with French national sentiment. We are all now persuaded in France that the Emperor's son will be the best representative of the reforms of the Revolution.' "[1]

He went on to say that, if Joseph could put two million francs at the disposition of a certain committee, then this leverage would insure that, within two years, the King of Rome could be on the French throne as Napoleon II. But Joseph found this proposal unsubstantial and turned it down. An alliance between Bonapartists and Liberals was suspect from the start. After all, in his will Napoleon had said, "The misfortunes of two invasions of France, when it still had abundant resources, were due to the betrayals of Marmont, Augereau, Talleyrand, and La Fayette." And, on St. Helena, he had repeated over and over that Liberal ideas had been his perdition. "They misunderstood me. I wanted to clamp down on them at first, in order to make them later shine the more brightly."

The part that La Fayette was to play in the advent to power of Louis-Philippe was much more in line with his true feelings.

Joseph Bonaparte, as soon as he heard of the Revolution of 1830, wrote three letters recalling and affirming the rights of Napoleon's son, addressed to General La Fayette, the Chamber of Deputies, and Empress Marie-Louise. La Fayette replied to Joseph that Napoleon was "great and incomparable, but his system, based on despotism, inequality, servility, and war, would only bring back those plagues that are the usual consequences of military glory."

Joseph's long letter to the Chamber was never read to its deputies. There was only mention of the idea that Napoleon II was a legitimate heir to the throne because his legitimacy came from the will of the nation and not from a supposed divine right of kings.

To Marie-Louise, "Madame my Sister and Sister-in-law," Joseph Bonaparte ingenuously offered his services in the preparation of her son's, Napoleon II's, return to France. "If his grandfather, the Emperor, gives him a minimum of support and allows me to present him to the French people, his mere presence will lead to his re-establishment on the throne." But Joseph learned from his devoted friend, Baron Méneval, that, when Marie-Louise received his letter, "she displayed ill-humor and forbade her French correspondent to send her any more communications of the kind."

From this time on, Joseph Bonaparte dedicated himself to the creation of opinion favorable to his nephew and to the memory of his brother. He subsidized several papers and founded *Le Courrier des États-Unis*. In this public relations campaign, he reaped the enthusiastic support of Victor Hugo, who said that fate must, sometimes, be aided by "human hands" and that "the press is the most powerful of all vehicles." In a letter of December 7, 1831, Victor Hugo went on to say:

> It is because I am devoted to France and to liberty that I have faith in the future of your royal nephew. He can render great services to his country. If he were to give, as I am sure he would, the necessary guarantees of emancipation, progress, and liberty, no one would rally with more heartfelt or ardent feelings than mine to his crown. And with me, Sire, I dare to promise in his name, there would stand all the French young people who venerate the Emperor's memory. In my obscure but independent position I have, perhaps, some influence upon them.

Then he says that he presumes to send to "Your Majesty" a copy of his latest book, *Notre-Dame de Paris*: "You'll see that, as in my other writings, I've put the Emperor's name everywhere, because everywhere I see it. If Your Majesty does me the honor to read what I've published previously, you will notice that, with every work, my admiration for your illustrious brother has become deeper, more profoundly felt, and freed of the royalist dross of my early years. . . . As for the heir to the greatest name in the world . . . I think that France must be saved. This I shall say and write and, God willing, print."

When Joseph heard of the grave illness of Napoleon's son, he sailed on July 20, 1832, for Europe. At Liverpool, where he arrived on August 16, he was told that the King of Rome had died in Vienna on July 22, at the age of twenty-one years. He lingered in vain in England in the hope of an authorization to go to his mother and his wife, Julie, in Italy. In 1835 he returned to Bordentown, where he was warmly greeted by his neighbors and many friends.

After Napoleon's death, Joseph was visited in his American exile by several members of his family. His younger daughter, Charlotte, arrived at Philadelphia on December 21, 1821, for the purpose of cheering up her father, who was deeply affected by the death of his brother. Charlotte was not pretty, but she was lively and independent. She had a gift for drawing and several times exhibited American landscapes at the Academy of Fine Arts of Philadelphia.

In 1822, Jérôme-Napoléon Bonaparte, son of Jérôme, Napoleon's youngest brother, and of his first wife, the American Elizabeth Patterson, came for a visit. Napoleon never recognized this first marriage of a brother fifteen years his junior, of whom he said on St. Helena: "Jérôme was a wastrel and given to conspicuous excesses. The only excuses were his youthful age and the company he kept." In 1801, the First Consul had put him into the navy. The young man was in Martinique when he was ordered back to France to take part in a new war against England. He defied his brother's orders, let his ship go back without him, and betook himself to the United States, where he arrived in 1803. Here he soon met the beautiful Elizabeth Patterson, a year older than himself, daughter of a wealthy Baltimore businessman, to whom he quickly announced his engagement. In the First Consul's eyes, an alliance between the Bonaparte family and that of an American businessman was out of the question. Joseph, to no avail, took a kindlier view. Mr. Patterson and the French ambassador both tried in vain to dissuade the young couple from the marriage, which was celebrated by the archbishop of Baltimore on December 24, 1803. Because Jérôme was not of legal age, Napoleon branded the marriage as null and void and ordered his brother to return to France without Elizabeth. The couple stayed on in the United States but, in 1804, when Napoleon became Emperor, Jérôme found himself excluded from the dynasty and made for France, taking his wife with him, in the hope of changing his brother's mind. Napoleon, master of Europe, forbade "Miss Patterson" to land in any country under his control. Jérôme left his wife at Lisbon and went to seek out his brother. Elizabeth went to England, landing there in May, 1805, and giving birth on July 7 to her only son, Jérôme-Napoléon. Jérôme, terrorized by the Emperor, consented to an imperial annullment of his marriage a few months later. Napoleon made regular payments of an annuity to Elizabeth Patterson, even from the island of Elba.

Jérôme-Napoléon lived in the United States between 1808 and 1829, then went to Europe with his mother, visiting Paris, Rome, and Florence. His father's family, particularly Madame Mère and Princess Pauline, gave him a friendly welcome and even thought of marrying him off to Charlotte Bonaparte, then at Bordentown with her father. Madame Mère wrote to tell Joseph of her approval of such a marriage, but to Elizabeth Patterson's disappointment, it did not come off.

In September, 1823, Joseph's elder daughter, Zénaïde, with her young husband Charles-Lucien Bonaparte, son of Lucien, disembarked at New York. The comte de Survilliers built for them the "Maison du Lac," in which they led a quiet and studious existence. Charles-Lucien was an ornithologist and became a member of various American scientific institutes and societies. Soon after her sister's arrival, Charlotte went back to Europe, where she married the older brother of the future Napoleon III; her husband died of a mysterious malady in 1831.

Joseph welcomed, also, his nephews Achille and Lucien Murat, sons of King Joachim of Naples and Queen Caroline. Achille arrived in New York on May 19, 1823, became an American citizen, and, in 1826, married a young widow who was a great-niece of George Washington, Mrs. Catharine Willis Gray. They went to live in Florida, where Achille practiced law. He and his wife had no children and are buried in Tallahassee.

Lucien came to the States in 1825 and in 1831 married a South Carolinian, Caroline Georgina Fraser. With his wife, who for a time ran a girls' boarding school, and his four American-born children, he returned to France in 1848.

It was as a political exile that Louis-Napoléon Bonaparte, the future Napoleon III, disembarked in Virginia on March 30, 1837. After the attempted but unsuccessful coup at Strasbourg, with which he had hoped to seize power, he was arrested and then exiled to America. During his short three-month stay, he must have heard about Charles Lallemand's settlement near the Mexican border and Lakanal's mysterious projects. Did he remember them, we may wonder, when he embarked on his own unfortunate Mexican adventure?

Joseph Bonaparte's last years in the United States were marked by the deaths of members of his family. Madame Mère died in Rome in 1836, and three years later he learned of the deaths of his daughter, Charlotte, and his uncle, Cardinal Fesch. At this point, he returned to Europe. Half paralyzed by a stroke, he was authorized to go to Florence where, after twenty-five years of separation, he rejoined his wife, Julie, and died in 1844.

Other sojourners in America were Pierre Bonaparte, the fourth son of Lucien, whose violent character made a poor impression on New York society, and Napoléon-Jérôme Bonaparte, son of Jérôme and his second wife, Princess Catherine of Wurtemburg, and, in 1861, a witness to the Civil War.

The last Bonapartes established in the United States were the children born to Joseph's mistress, Annette Savage, and the descendants of Elizabeth Patterson.

But the actual presence of members of the Bonaparte family did not put an end to myth-making in other related directions. Not long after World War II, on September 29, 1946, in the graveyard of the Presbyterian Church of Third Creek, North Carolina, there was a religious ceremony and a military procession before the tomb of . . . Marshal Ney. After a false execution, he supposedly came to America and lived there in obscurity until his death, when there was inscribed on his tombstone: "Peter Stewart Ney, soldier of the French Revolution and of Napoleon Bonaparte, died on November 15, 1846, at the age of 77 years."

The American Ney story is strange and even fantastic. Marcel Teissier, delegate to the United States of the Amitiés Internationales Napoléoniennes, believes that many facts and singular coincidences make it believable that Marshal Michel Ney and Peter Ney, North Carolina schoolteacher, are one and the same person. A notary in Topeka, Kansas, named Henderson, remembers his grandfather, an English soldier at Waterloo who had been present at the execution, saying, "Ney wasn't shot. The execution was a farce." Colonels de la Rochejacquelin and de Montigny supposedly slipped Ney a little bag containing a red fluid. The grenadiers of the firing squad had orders to shoot over his head; Ney was seen to strike his chest, bursting open the bag, and fall to the ground in a puddle of blood. Contrary to general usage, the commander of the squad, de Saint-Biais, did not finish him off with a revolver. Organizer of the performance was Comtesse Ida de Sainte-Elme, with the complicity of none less than the duke of Wellington, who was, like Ney, a Freemason. The head sister of the hospital where the body was taken was a friend of the comtesse and arranged for a substitution.

Marshal Ney fled to Bordeaux, where he embarked for Charleston, South Carolina. Hutchinson, the Englishman who engineered his escape, was later to effect that of the comte de Lavalette.[2] In the course of his journey, a soldier of Napoleon definitely recognized the marshal. A few years later, Ney settled at Third Creek as a schoolteacher, taking the first name of his father. The age of the Peter Ney whose name is on the tombstone coincides with that of the marshal. Finally, Marcel Teissier quotes a Boston magazine article of 1920, which says, "Freemasons know about Ney's escape, especially those of the Grand Orient Lodge of France."

In 1950, the American government authorized Mrs. Dorothy Mackay Quynn, holder of a degree from the Sorbonne, to clear up the mystery, and Monsieur Marcel Dunan asked her to communicate her conclusions to the Institut Napoléon.

It seems certain that when Ney was arrested in the department of the Lot on August 3, 1816, he was not going to Switzerland, as it appeared from his passport, but to America, via Bordeaux. For fear of disturbances, the government chose to stage the execution before dawn, near the Palais du Luxembourg, where he was imprisoned. In spite of the atmosphere of secrecy, numerous Englishmen, French peers, diplomats, generals, and other officers came, according to police report, to see and identify the body.

Peter Stewart Ney greatly impressed his pupils and their families at Three Creeks. When he was in his cups, he shouted out orders, like a general on the battlefield, and called for a horse. In company, he talked about the prominent figures of the Empire whom he had known. Once, indeed, he said to a lady: "Don't look at me like that! Madame de Staël used to look at me the same way." The death of Napoleon, followed by that of his son, caused him to drink and then to fall into a deep depression. Dr. Quynn examined Peter Ney's writings and deduced that he had had a classical eighteenth-century English education. Actually, he was angry when one of his pupils asked for French lessons. His comments, in English, on books about Napoleon are full of errors. And he avoided the many prominent Napoleonic exiles in the United States. The conclusion is that he was a Scottish admirer of Napoleon, one who perhaps served in his Grande Armée, and was caught up in the identity that he either claimed or found attributed to him. He played the game to the end, bolstered up, it seems, by alcohol.

Not Marshal Ney alone, but also Napoleon is buried in the United States! Between the Bayou des Oies and Barataria, some twenty-five miles south of New Orleans, Madame Toinette Perrin, in recent years, has shown visitors three graves surrounded by ancient trees and rosebushes. The largest is that of the "Big Boss"— the Emperor—and the other two are those of Jean Laffite and the American naval hero John Paul Jones. In 1928, readers of the New Orleans *States* learned with astonishment that "Napoleon's tomb has been discovered in Louisiana" and "how Jean Laffite helped Napoleon to escape from St. Helena." According to this legend, the famous pirate set off one day aboard the *Comète*, the fastest of his ships, for St. Helena. Pierre Laffite, his brother and accomplice, arrived at the same time at the port of Jamestown on a schooner flying the Spanish flag and landed a Malaysian slave who, one stormy night, managed to convey the escape plan to Napoleon! Napoleon followed instructions; at seven o'clock on the evening of February 28, 1819, he sat, wearing his largest greatcoat, with the collar turned up, on a cliff overhanging the sea. In the shadows someone—Jean Laffite—tugged at his sleeve, then slid a big wooden cross into the coat and put the hat on top of it, while Napoleon glided away, replaced by this dummy, "which is mentioned in some French historical documents." With much difficulty and emotion, Napoleon arrived aboard the *Comète*. But at the end of the voyage he fainted away across the carriage of a cannon, spat blood, and died without saying a word. Jean Laffite buried him in the place he had chosen for his own grave.

Stanley Clisby Arthur, author of *Jean Laffite, Gentleman Rover*, found descendants of the pirate in Kansas City. Although historians wrote of Laffite as dead after his expulsion from Galveston, he lived on for many years under the assumed name of John Lafflin. He became a manufacturer of gunpowder in St. Louis and, at fifty years of age, acquired a second wife, Emma Mortimore, almost thirty years his junior, who bore him two sons.

John Lafflin could not bear to hear mention of his legendary past. An atheist and adept of secret societies, he hoped with a sort of mystical fervor for the advance of a universal communist society. His extraordinary existence was crowned by an amazing episode: a meeting in Germany with Karl Marx and Friedrich Engels. At the age of sixty-five years, he went off to Europe, and enthusiasm for the manuscript of the *Communist Manifesto* caused him to contribute to the financing of its publication. In a letter of 1847, he wrote to a Belgian friend about his historic encounter with the two theorists:

> They discovered that exploitation is at the base of all evil. . . . I am enthused in regard to the manifest [*Communist Manifesto*] and other prospects for the future, as I heartily support the two young men. . . . Mr. Marx advises . . . me not to plunge into all America with the Manifests because there are others of the same kind for New York. . . . I have described my second commune which I was forced to . . . abandon to the *flambeau* March 3, 1821. I then took the resolution to retire without convert. I am no longer aiding those who are opposed to my principles.

These last revelations of Laffite add a new dimension to his legend. From his Louisiana lair, with its heterogeneous and shifting population, he heard, through the bayous, the echo of a new ideology.

A New Orleans tradition had it that Jean Laffite's faithful companion, "Captain Dominique," also organized an expedition to rescue Napoleon. A "long, low, black" ship, the *Séraphine*, was built in secret for this purpose. But the only ship of this name listed as having entered the harbor was built in 1829, eight years after Napoleon's death.

The Napoleonic legend in the United States had, of course, a particularly strong tinge in Louisiana and, above all, New Orleans, where people of French descent mourned a French hero. But, beyond the field of anecdote and provincial nostalgia, the debate between the American myth and the historical dream of Napoleon continued in a vein of ambiguity and passion. The memory of Napoleon was altered, adapted, and reinvented by the New World. And, in France, the image of America was alternately idealized, rejected, and even despised. The two legends clashed or harmonized, according to the political trends of the day.

Until his death in 1834, La Fayette remained the standard-bearer of Liberalism, holding that the liberal and Masonic ideas that should have triumphed in the French Revolution were solidly implanted in the United States. When Bonaparte seized power, the two men were already rivals, both claiming to be the Revolution's spiritual heir. The text of the Declaration of the Rights of Man and of the Citizen (1789) was, we must remember, the joint effort of La Fayette and Thomas Jefferson. It is true that the French Assembly did not adopt it in its original terms, but, as a symbol, it retained its forcefulness and meaning. The American Revolution led the first steps of its younger follower, and La Fayette was seen as a sort of ambassador of the American ideal in France.

But the French Revolution led to Bonaparte. La Fayette returned from Austria to France in 1799, having acquired first-hand acquaintance with the prisons of the anti-Revolutionaries. Bonaparte relegated him to his estate of La Grange and restored his civil rights only the following year, along with those of other *émigrés*. In spite of La Fayette's uncontested prestige, he was not invited to the Paris commemoration of the death of Washington. He voted against the Consulship for life, and from then on relations between him and Bonapart were broken. After the Louisiana Purchase, his friend Jefferson offered him the governorship of the state of this name. La Fayette chose to remain in France as the symbol and chief of the Liberal opposition.[3] Under the Restoration, he maintained the same ideas.

Liberalism and Bonapartism joined in opposing the Bourbons. For the first time, American and Napoleonic ideals met through the intermediary of the Liberals, and the Field of Refuge illustrates their reconciliation. Novelist Honoré de Balzac was a royalist who denounced the partnership of the opposition parties. In 1821, La Fayette conspired with some *demi-soldes*, but his reputation was so great that he was not arrested. The return of the Bourbons caused Americans to forget the despotism of which they had accused Napoleon and to consider him, like La Fayette, an heir to the Revolution. The summit meeting between Liberals and Bonapartists may be identified with La Fayette's visit in 1824 to Joseph Bonaparte in order to propose a movement in favor of the King of Rome.

Actually, only a common enemy could have brought the two parties briefly together. Their principles and politics were still far apart. On St. Helena, Napoleon said that Liberal ideas were responsible for his downfall. In 1830, La Fayette contributed greatly to the accession of Louis-Philippe. He explained his action in a letter to Joseph Bonaparte, quoted by the duc de Castries: "I owe you, as a friend, an explanation of my way of thinking. Despotism is tolerated only under an empire, which there can be no question of restoring." And, referring to Louis-Philippe: "He is a Bourbon, but this name had been more than yours, more than that of republic, a guarantee against war. He does not prevent the statement and the exercise of the sovereignty of the people, the donation of arms to two million citizens who choose their own officers, freedom of the press, and of popular institutions."

According to La Fayette, a high-ranking Freemason, Louis-Philippe's ideas would not conflict with those of the United States, which were in harmony with those held by Masonic societies from the beginning of the French Revolution. The Republic, first, and then Bonaparte had prevented the good start of 1789 from following its normal course of development. At this time, La Fayette was commander of the National Guard and busy editing the Declaration of the Rights of Man and of the Citizen. By coincidence, in 1830, he was again commander of the Guard and immensely popular. He might have become president of the Second Republic, a French Washington, but he chose to put Louis-Philippe on the throne. The letter to Joseph Bonaparte, quoted just above, explains this choice: the Republic and Bonaparte were both linked to war and to the despotism of a central power. This pins down and enlightens La Fayette's judgment of Napoleon: more than himself, Napoleon was heir to the short-lived First Republic, but he, La Fayette, better represented republican principles.

When La Fayette turned down the presidency of the Republic, he was no longer only the ambassador of the American political ethic; he was a man who saw America with European eyes as the country with ideals that Europeans were never able to achieve in Europe. In La Fayette's view, France was not ready to apply the principles that he espoused. Louis-Philippe, the son of Philippe-Égalité, had lived two years in America and admired its Constitution. He was the man for a transition. But La Fayette was soon disillusioned. In 1831, the new king stripped La Fayette of his commandership and blandly removed him from the seat of power. Joseph Bonaparte commented on the news to his friend, Charles Jared Ingersoll: "La Fayette wants to appease his republican conscience and American public opinion; he forgot that he was in France, and you see what happened to him." La Fayette died in 1834, and with him the image of an America just and prosperous, free and moderate, with easy-going ways and manners.

Then, before Europe realized it, America began to change. In 1829, General Andrew Jackson was elected president; for the first time the frontier was in power. Suffrage became almost universal; the old administration was swept away by a new uneducated bureaucracy. The political image of America had nothing more in common with the refined liberalism of the early Virginian presidents, spiritual sons of a bourgeois and liberal Europe. This was the vision of Alexis de Tocqueville, which he transmitted to French public opinion in 1835. America was a laboratory where democracy had reached its "natural limits"; it was no longer an irreproachable political and social model, but the image of a future European society. "I confess," Tocqueville wrote, "that in America I saw more than America. I looked there for a picture of democracy itself, its trends, character, prejudices, and passions. I wanted to know it, if only to find out what it gives us to hope or fear."

Tocqueville observed the strength and weakness of American society objectively. His admirably perspicacious observations apply to the America of today. The pioneer engaged in clearing the wide open spaces, he notes, is no longer the European immigrant, "friendless and resourceless," who hires himself out in the industrial area of the East; he is the American who has capital and credit, however small, at his command and is "broken to the rigor of a new climate." The American dream is no longer a vent for European nostalgia; it belongs to America and its people.

Europe rediscovered an America where a population of three millions had tripled since the Revolution. A great economic boom had changed its aspect, manners, and social relationships, and it bore the marks of capitalism: the self-aggrandizement of financiers, cynical materialism, oppression of Blacks and Indians. No longer did the United States escape the vices of older societies.[4]

Hope deferred or denied often gives way to violent hostility. In France, "leftists" (including, for a time, Bonapartists) decried the heretofore admired American model. Paradoxically, memory of the imperial epic rose up against the myth of America. Louis-Philippe tried to neutralize the forces opposed to his rule with spectacular gestures intended to win over enemies of the Bourbons. The grandiose ceremonies that marked the return of Napoleon's body played on popular emotions. Meanwhile, the federal structure of the American government was criticized, just as it had been during the Empire.

The new king of the French, in spite of his goodwill toward republicans and Bonapartists, did not belong to their political line, as he found out in 1848. The Second Republic, whether in opposition to the feelings current under the July Monarchy or from a desire to return to its own sources, was favorable, momentarily, like the Republic of 1789, to the United States, viewed as its predecessor. But soon the Jacobin and centralizing spirit of the French republicans resumed its ironical criticism of the looser American federal system.

Louis-Napoléon Bonaparte, as prince-president, refused to play the part of a George Washington. He wrote on March 11, 1840, to Deputy Laralut:

> The role which you believe that unexpected events might cause me to play in the future is very fine. I do not know whether I shall ever be called upon to serve my country and be useful to it,

but that would be my ambition. From a historical point of view, I see no chance that anyone in Europe can take the role of Washington. Washington had a single and very great merit: to construct the nation, after the war, in the only way it could be constructed. He confined himself to the possible. Had he wanted to be named king, he would not have succeeded. . . . In other words, if he had done anything but what he did, he would have lost America. . . . A true genius does not build a nation on abstract theory but on the basis of its present state, its real needs, its character and position. . . . To think that people go so far as to say that Napoleon, by an act of will, could have made us into Americans, setting up a federal republic in France, and that Washington, by disguising his colonists as soldiers, could have founded a powerful monarchy! . . . A talent for government consists not of inventing but of making use, as the Emperor said, of the materials at hand.

It was clear that one day the prince-president would take on the title of emperor.

As soon as he had come into power, Napoleon III remembered the soldiers of the Grande Armée who had stayed in the United States. St. Helena medals were sent out to them and delivered in even the remotest regions of Louisiana.[5]

In 1854, the Emperor gave an officer's commission to the grandson of Jérôme Bonaparte and Elizabeth Patterson, then twenty-four years of age. Jérôme-Napoléon Bonaparte distinguished himself in Crimea, Algeria, and Italy. Before leaving for the front in 1870, Napoleon III gave him command of the Tuileries Palace.

Joseph Bonaparte had, by his American mistress Annette Savage, two daughters, of whom the elder, as we have seen, was killed by a falling flowerpot. The younger, Charlotte, separated from her husband, a certain Zebulon Benton, was received by Napoleon III in 1859 and struck him by her resemblance to her father. He gave her a pension and named her daughter, Josephine, lady-in-waiting to Empress Eugénie. After the fall of the Second Empire, Charlotte returned to the United States, where she lived in poverty.

If Napoleon III was generous to his American relatives, French opinion of the United States, under his reign, was severe. Captain Just Girard, one of Lallemand's companions at the Field of Refuge, wrote his memoirs in 1860 and indignantly denounced American "capitalists" and the "essentially mercantile and speculative character of the Yankee race."

America was beginning to be considered imperialistic as well. Already under Louis-Philippe there was fear of "American imperialism" and the idea of supporting an independent Texas.

Napoleon III's involvement in the disastrous Mexican adventure was not due to the bad advice of his immediate circle alone. It was the last stage of a dream that began when Napoleon I was on St. Helena. At that time, the Mexican insurgents against Spain saw from close by that the United States had its eye on their territory. Because they did not share their South-American counterparts' prejudice against Napoleon, they proposed, as we know, the throne of Mexico to Joseph Bonaparte and, according to St. Helena gossip, even to the exiled Emperor. Lakanal's project was, perhaps, less fantastic than it seemed.

In any case, Napoleon III's idea of installing an unwanted Austrian prince on the throne of Mexico, in order to contain the territorial ambitions of the United States, was an error that contributed greatly to the fall of the Second Empire. When the Emperor heard of the reverses suffered by French troops, he called them back and urged Maximilian to abdicate. The short-lived emperor of Mexico rejected this advice and, on June 19, 1867, a prisoner of the insurgents, he was sentenced to death and executed.

The Mexican adventure was advantageous to Prussia. After obtaining a promise of neutrality from France, which was involved in Mexico, the Prussians crushed the Austrians at Sadowa in 1866. This was the beginning of Bismarck's aggressive policy, which led to the Franco-Prussian War of 1870, the defeat and abdication of Napoleon III, and the beginning of the Third Republic.

The development of the Napoleonic legend in the United States is quite independent of that of the American myth in France. Americans learned of the death of Napoleon in July, 1821. Newspapers recounted every detail of his last moments, and the man and his achievements were discussed at length, just as after the Battle of Waterloo.

Napoleon died at a moment when Americans saw the Holy Alliance as helping Spain to recover its colonies and, indeed, two years later came the pronouncement of the Monroe Doctrine. Because he could be considered the Holy Alliance's victim, Napoleon was considered a champion of national self-determination, and his popularity grew rapidly in the following years. Unlike his predecessors and in spite of the critical view of him voiced by the Bonapartists, President Andrew Jackson admired Napoleon and was one of those who asked for a cutting from the willow tree under which he was buried.

Sir Walter Scott's unfavorable biography of Napoleon appeared in the United States in 1827 and caused indignation among many readers. Popular and family-type magazines published highly romantic stories of which Napoleon was the hero. Professor Lee Kennett[6] quotes such titles as *Napoleon and the Red Man*, *A Game of Chess with Napoleon*, and *Napoleon's Advice to Young America*. Between 1830 and 1840, the readers of *Godey's Lady's Book* were regaled with at least twenty stories and poems dedicated to Napoleon's glory.

John S. C. Abbott, a contemporary of Napoleon III, wrote a biography published in installments in *Harper's New Monthly Magazine* and in four volumes in 1869, a wildly Bonapartist panegyric that had considerable success. The theater, too, treated the Napoleonic legend, and it inspired two of the first big American "shows": *The Battle of Waterloo* (1840), with two hundred actors and fifty horses, and *The Exile and Death of Napoleon*, which featured a thirty-foot-high hearse drawn by sixteen horses.

Various explanations have been given for the popularity of Napoleon and the persistence of his legend in the United States. Some historians say that it was due to his being a "self-made man," with a powerful drive for all-out action and efficiency like that of an industrial tycoon. But the most convincing analysis is that of Professor Kennett. Americans, he says, made their own Napoleon. The hero was "de-nationalized" in such a way that he might belong to any people. His ideas, words, and even actions unconnected with war were of no interest; what mattered were feats of arms, battles, and military glory. "The cult of Napoleon was part of another cult, that of chivalry." America lacked soldier heroes and, in a period of romanticism, Napoleon symbolized the romantic warrior.

After this, the fratricidal Civil War, with its murderous battles, went far toward deromanticizing war. At the same time, it gave

America heroes of its own, and it is from this time on that the cult of Napoleon, although it did not disappear, began to decline.

Paradoxically enough, by making their own Napoleon, divorced from historical reality, Americans divined one of the deepest and most enduring aspects—romantic heroism—of the Napoleonic dream. When they set him up as a warrior belonging to all times and places, their vision was the same as Napoleon's own, as embodied in a painting that he ordered from Girodet for Malmaison. Ossian, the legendary blind Gaelic bard, in a somber and tragic lyric vein, welcomes to paradise the dead soldiers—Desaix, Marceau, Kléber—in what Axelle de Broglie calls a "whirlwind of brotherhood."[7] The lyric power of Ossian's verse, playing over a people of ghosts, endows the dead heroes with pagan immortality. And the dead Napoleon became, in America, by virtue of feeling rather than reason, one of the gods of Ossian's pantheon. America forgot ideological differences and instinctively understood the intimate meaning of the Napoleonic dream: military victory and glory, sublimated by legend and endowing their protagonists with immortal life.

The Civil War was to haunt Americans for years to come; they abandoned European models in order to embrace and glorify heroes of their own. Beginning in 1857, says André Maurois, Mark Twain was the "true hope of a genuinely American literature." His satirical treatment of the Old World delighted his readers. Emancipation from Europe and a new sophistication were in the air.

But Napoleonic memories and mementos endure across the country. New Orleans, of course, is the most obvious spot. Eight hundred thousand citizens of French origin, of whom two hundred and fifty thousand speak French, are in part responsible. The Napoleonic Code is still applied in matters of inheritance. At the corner of the Rue de Chartres and the Rue Saint-Louis, in the Vieux Carré, a two-story structure topped by an octagonal belvedere and called "Napoleon House" was built in 1821 by the mayor, Nicholas Girod, who financed a plot to free Napoleon and bring him to New Orleans. Many street names—Napoleon, Milan, Marengo, Iéna, Austerlitz—are loaded with nostalgia. In the Cabildo (now seat of the Louisiana State Museum) there is a room containing a death mask of Napoleon, surrounded by French and American flags, once the property of Antonmarchi, the last doctor who attended him.

Madame Pardee has drawn up a list of all the Napoleonic place-names in the United States. There are six towns called Napoleon, two towns and one Lake Bonaparte, two Marengos, one Iéna.

Joseph Bonaparte's mansion, Point Breeze, has unfortunately been destroyed. Still extant is the Philadelphia house at 260 South Ninth Street, where he lived between 1815 and 1817.

At Tallahassee, capital of Florida, there is the grave of Achille Murat, son of Joachim, King of Naples. The house where his widow lived has been moved to Lake Bradford at the edge of the city, near the Junior Museum, where it is to undergo restoration.

Fort Monroe, Virginia, exhibits a bust of General Simon Bernard, donated by his native town of Dôle in honor of the defense installations that he engineered in the United States. The inhabitants of Demopolis, Alabama, point out olive trees and grapevine roots dating from the time of the French soldier-colonists, several of whom were buried in the area.

In 1837, a French traveler discovered the location of the Field of Refuge in the small town of Liberty, Texas. On the bark of a tree trunk he deciphered the words *Honneur et Patrie*, cut by the followers of Lallemand. After a hundred years of oblivion, the site was rediscovered in 1937 by Professor Marcel Moraud. Thanks to him, the State of Texas put up a marker with this inscription:

> To Generals Charles Lallemand and Antoine Rigaud, the Veterans of the Napoleonic Wars and other French settlers
>
> Who after many trials and adventures came to Texas in the Spring of 1818 to found on the banks of the Trinity River the *Champ d'Asile*, a last refuge for peace and liberty. '*Nous voulons vivre libres, laborieux et paisibles* [We want to live as free men through our labor and in peace.]

In Baltimore, a room of the Maryland Historical Society exhibits mementos of Elizabeth Patterson and her descendants, along with items from the American collection of Joseph Bonaparte. The son of Elizabeth Patterson and Jérôme Bonaparte had, in his turn, two sons. The elder, as we have seen, served under Napoleon III. The other, Charles-Joseph, twenty years his junior, chose American rather than French citizenship. He exercised the profession of attorney-at-law until his friend Theodore Roosevelt,[8] as president of the United States, drew him into public service. In 1905, Charles-Joseph Bonaparte became secretary of the navy and in 1909 attorney general. He died without issue in 1924.

The last male descendant of the American Bonapartes was Jérôme-Napoléon Charles, son of the Jérôme-Napoléon to whom Napoleon III gave a colonel's commission. He made prolonged stays in Europe at the German and Belgian courts, in Biarritz, in Deauville, and in Denmark, where his sister married a count. He, too, died without issue in New York in 1952.

Napoleon remains, for Americans, the best-known figure in European history. Few of them, when visiting Paris, fail to visit his tomb at the Invalides. In 1959, Professor David L. Dowd of the University of Florida drew up for his students a monograph entitled *Was Napoleon the Heir to the French Revolution?* Although the preface reminded readers to take into account the differences of periods and situations, Napoleon was judged by the criterion of an ideal common to both France and the United States—the Age of Enlightenment—and the question posed was: did Napoleon activate this idea, which was the motor of both countries' revolutions, or did he betray it? A few years ago, French television held a mock trial of Napoleon, pitting him against George Washington as his ideological adversary. Might not the real question be that which separates America from the Napoleonic dream? In other words, shouldn't history rather than Napoleon be put on trial?

Napoleon did not choose to apply the revolutionary idea in its complete form, but to take hold of it, cast it into the stream of history, and submit it to fate. America dreamed of a world delivered from history, as we saw when we considered its utopian ventures. In spite of the importance of its role in world affairs, it is still attracted to isolationism.

The survival of the Napoleonic myth is linked to the prophecy of Hegel: with Napoleon history sparkles and then dies. The Emperor, last point of light in the proud and muddy procession of history, passes under the philosopher's window: "I saw the Emperor, that soul of the world, ride through the city streets on horseback."

History did not die with Napoleon, but his prestige has weakened. Present-day liberalism and the ambition to achieve peace and prosperity are in the Jeffersonian tradition. We do not take thought to insert ourselves into a chain of memories supposed to assure a sort of eternity. "Farewell, posterity!" was the title of an article in *Le Figaro* by Valéry Giscard d'Estaing when he was finance minister. "We live in a time that has no memory," he wrote. The American dream is seductive. Shall we see history abandon its stamping ground and find ourselves no longer able to conjure up its tragic mask?

A correspondent of the *Souvenir Napoléonien* told a story about a children's masquerade party. Dressed up as Indians, with the accouterments of American mythology, the little boys wanted to lay siege to St. Helena and free the Emperor. Alas, Hudson Lowe was on guard, and the attackers admitted failure. History remained a prisoner; the children could not or dared not free her. Will she break her chains?

CHAPTER 10

The Napoleonic and the American Dreams Face to Face

When Napoleon went into exile, the Western world was still haunted by the Enlightenment's great enthusiastic dream of the estate and future of man. In 1815 Napoleon's public life ended, and the legend of him as a superman and martyr began. It was possible, at last, to pass judgment on his historical figure and the imprint it left behind it.

At this same moment, after the War of 1812, the United States cut the umbilical cord binding it to the Old World and embarked upon a path of its own. As its real self, it could be defined in terms of the American dream. Both the destiny to which Napoleon Bonaparte aspired and the example of America set themselves up as guideposts rivaling each other in the attempt to capture the world's imagination. The rivalry and at times clash between them were sharpened by the fact that a common vocabulary stemming from common ideological origins and a shared modern attitude toward earlier ideas masked fundamental differences. This confusion is based on a misunderstanding that still unleashes passionate feelings.

When Napoleon's empire fell, Americans did not seem conscious of the rivalry of which we have spoken. They showed sympathy for the heroic proponent of new ideas, overcome by a reactionary coalition. They recalled the day of December 15, 1799, when, in connection with the death of Washington, the First Consul (since November) showed the same sympathy toward the American people and, indeed, proclaimed: "Washington is dead! This great man combated tyranny and consolidated the freedom of his country. His memory will always be dear to the French people as to all the free men of both worlds, especially to French soldiers who, like him and his Americans, fight for liberty and equality."

The flags and pennants of the Republic and its army were hung with black crepe and, on the Champ-de-Mars, amid the trophies of Napoleon's Middle Eastern army, Louis de Fontanes pronounced a funeral oration. Among those present, some must have remembered the famous talk between Franklin and Voltaire, when the two old men delighted witnesses by embracing each other. When the great American ambassador died, the French revolutionary government proclaimed public mourning and called on Mirabeau to be the official speaker. And the bust of Franklin was carried in the funeral procession that escorted the body of Jean-Jacques Rousseau to the Pantheon.

Waterloo furnished such American leaders as Jefferson and Adams, unmoved by the sentimental reactions of the common people, an occasion to state the superiority of the American ideal over the action of Napoleon, who was judged, very harshly, as an amoral, ambitious conqueror, a traitor to republican liberties and the principles of reason, and hence bound to fall. The contrast that Chateaubriand made between Washington and Napoleon is a good illustration of this point of view. Elsewhere, the writer made a pitiless explanation of Napoleon's failure to embark for the United States after his abdication: "His resolution failed when he looked on the French shore. He was averse to the republic; the freedom and equality of the United States were distasteful to him."

On St. Helena, Napoleon saw the American mirage as a dangerous obstacle to the epic dream that he wished to be his legacy. On various occasions he spoke up for his way of doing things over and against the pull of America, all the more powerful inasmuch as it represented the accomplishment of a European dream that had never come to anything in Europe. The most eloquent and efficacious element of Napoleon's dream was the military epic, and it was on this subject that he inveighed most violently against false American ideas: "The example of the United States is absurd. If the United States were in the middle of Europe, it would not stand up two years to the monarchies' pressure. In its last war against England [1812], the blows of a few British frigates humbled this confederation of ten million inhabitants to the point of signing a peace treaty amid the smoking ruins of Washington. And this because the first requisite of a strong national defense is the permanence of its government."

In the last sentence, Napoleon throws light on a long-standing misunderstanding between France and the United States. In France, no government was considered legitimate unless it could assure the defense of the nation. And a nation which, by virtue of its constitution or political structure, had no defensive capacity could not hold itself up as an example. Certainly, America did win the War of 1812, but, Napoleon thought, only because of the weakness of the British. "I've never understood," he told General Gourgaud, "why, in 1814, the British sent 30,000 men. They were too few to conquer the United States and too many to force them to make peace. By blockading the coasts they could have forced the Americans to do what they pleased. . . . The Americans had no army and only a few frigates. . . . They couldn't have resisted a three-year blockade. . . . The Americans amount to nothing."

About a century and a half later, in 1959, General Charles de Gaulle explained the rationale of France's withdrawal from the North Atlantic Treaty Organization and also of the refusal to allow the Americans to store atomic bombs on French soil: "I am showing that, with us, the State has never had and can never have a stronger justification for its being, aside from duration, than the direct assumption of responsibility for its national defense." When André Malraux was in the United States, he insisted to President John F. Kennedy that "before speaking of France's domestic politics, it has to be said that any government of ours that does not assure national defense has no more than an 'apparent' legitimacy."

Today, obviously, no one throws the United States' defensive capacity into doubt. But during the reign of Napoleon, several ambassadors called it into question. Actually, there is a disparity between two ideas. In France, a country often invaded, a government without an army to back it up could only be that of a minor power, doomed to eventual extinction. In the United States, at the beginning of the nineteenth century, the regular army came to only six thousand men, and defense depended on a militia. The choice of a volunteer rather than a conscript army was linked to political institutions. A professional army could have made a victorious or ambitious general into a dictator, and nothing is more remote than a dictator from the American dream. In France, on the other hand, the stability of political institutions depends on an army permanently at the government's disposal.

What characteristics of government are best suited to national defense? "Unity and permanence," said Napoleon, heir to the Republic "one and indivisible" and to the centralized monarchy of the Capets, pronouncing himself against the federal principle of the American Constitution which, in his view, could only weaken the nation at home and abroad. In 1816, Napoleon said to General Montholon that the various states of the American confederation seemed to be united because "they were still influenced by the common interest of their emancipation from the English crown," but that their existence "as a great nation was in its infancy and the federal Constitution impeded its advance." As if foreseeing the Civil War, he spoke of "the dissidence between the northern and the southern states," as an index of the weakness of the federal principle. Either a spirit of conquest and military glory would reenforce the central government and a congressional majority, "or else federal unity will be broken by local interests and commercial rivalries." And how could a nation weakened by internal dissension face up to foreign enemies?

Napoleon had witnessed in France the failure of certain decentralizing experiments by which the budding Revolution had wanted to copy an American model. The weakening of the central organs and the defiance of their power had brought about disorder and insecurity. When he seized power as First Consul, he took care to return to the centralized power of the Capets and the unification brought about by the Revolution and the Republic. Thus he created the Council of State, which revived the former Council of the King; prefects took up the tasks of the former royal intendants, and magistrates were centrally appointed, rather than elected as in the United States and in France under the Constituent Assembly of 1789.

Certain remarks made by Napoleon on St. Helena about the creation of Europe made it seem as if there might be a likeness between the federal structure of the United States and what he had in mind. To Las Cases, Napoleon said he didn't believe that "there is any balance possible in Europe except through the agglomeration and confederation of its peoples," and, in his will, he advised his son to "unite Europe in indissoluble federative bonds." We must not forget that this was a moment favorable to liberal ideals and that he may have spoken in the language of a certain republican liberalism that had allied itself with Bonapartism against the old monarchies. The terms in which he contrasted American ideas with his own are far more revealing. Thus the following passage from Las Cases' *Mémoires de Sainte-Hélène* betrays Napoleon's exasperation at contemporary comparisons of Washington and himself:

> When I came to power, it was hoped that I would be a Washington. Words are cheap, and those who so facilely voiced this hope did so without understanding of time, places, men, and events. If I had been in America, I should willingly have been a Washington, and with no great merit, since there was nothing else I could have been. But if he had been in France, with domestic disorder and the threat of foreign invasion, I defy him to have been himself. If he had, he would have been a fool and prolonged the unhappiness of the country. As for me, I could only have been a Washington with a crown, amid a congress of conquered kings. Only under such circumstances could I have shown his moderation, wisdom, and disinterestedness. These I could attain only by a universal dictatorship, such as, indeed, I strove for.

We note an immediate contradiction: "I could only have been a Washington with a crown."

Although General Washington was not among the American statesmen most hostile to monarchism in its English form, he was, nonetheless, bound to republican principles. American public opinion was shocked and distressed by the proclamation of the Napoleonic Empire. In their newspapers, Republicans were sorrowful and Federalists indignant and sarcastic. "He has destroyed the finest hopes of mankind," said the Richmond *Virginia Argus* of the new Emperor. Napoleon had violated and betrayed the sacred character of the Republic. This accusation weighed all the more heavily on the fallen Emperor in that, on St. Helena, his legend "went republican."

It was not by chance that Napoleon explained to General Montholon that the Empire, as he understood it, was the expression of a "regularized republican principle," facing up to monarchies that were armed "to fight republican propaganda." These words occur in the very conversation in which he treated the American model as absurd because a government without unity and "permanence" could not defend its territory or, obviously, its ideas.

The imperial dynasty was created, in part, in order to assure the permanence and stability of the republican principle and to infuse the threatened young republic with the force and authority of a crown. We may recall the scene at Erfurt in 1808, when Napoleon said, before an assembly of crowned heads, "When I was an artillery lieutenant," and then, seeing his hearers' surprise, added, "When I had the honor of being an artillery lieutenant . . ."

The first article of the Senatus-Consultus, which declared the Empire, ran: "The government of the Republic is entrusted to an Emperor." And engraved on coins were the words: "*République Française, Napoléon Empéreur.*"

When Napoleon took the title of Emperor, he sought to avoid any ambiguity about the principle of heredity, so contrary to republican ideas. "I submit the law of heredity to the sanction of the people." He was elected emperor by the people, and it was as such that he took the crown from the hands of the Pope and put it on his own head. "I created the Empire for the salvation of the Revolution," he insisted.

Here there is the fundamental difference between the French and American republics. In France, the republic was born of a bloody revolution, in defense of national territory and in foreign wars. In America, the proclamation of the republic seemed, at least in part, the defense of an acquisition that a dishonest regent was trying to take away for his own profit. The Declaration of Independence is, in this respect, significant. After a short preamble, the text explains the rupture with Great Britain, which had abolished "the free system of English Laws," whose excellence Americans did not contest. They complain, in these terms, of their "British Brethren": "We have appealed to their native Justice and Magnanimity, and we have conjured them by the Ties of our common Kindred to disavow these Usurpations, which would inevitably interrupt our Connections and Correspondence."

There is no question, in the Declaration, of creating a new body of laws, such as went with the French Declaration of the Rights of Man and the Citizen. In France, a whole system was to be replaced by another; in America, there was the break with a mother country that had abused, in the colonies, its own legislative tradition.

After his abdication, when Napoleon hesitated between exile in England or in America, he was aware of the similarity between them on this score. He had chosen America for its "positive laws," Las Cases tells us, but "since England offered him the same advantages, he didn't mind being obliged to sojourn there."

From the beginning of the French Revolution, many American leaders, Washington included, foresaw the ambiguous nature of the feelings that the American and French republics inspired in each other. The ill-fed and ill-shod citizen-soldiers commanded by Washington were not too different from the ragged French *sans-culottes*. But after the capture of the Bastille, when La Fayette sent General Washington "the main key of the fortress of despotism" (which is still at Mount Vernon), Washington prudently and ironically sent him back a gift that is, to say the very least, prosaic, accompanied by these lines: "Not for the value of the thing ... but as a memorial and because they are the manufacture of the city, I send you herewith a pair of shoe buckles." There could be no clearer sign of the will to keep the United States clear of the French revolutionary tumult.

The American ambassador in Paris, Gouverneur Morris, as hostile as his president to the Terror, wrote to him on December 30, 1794: "In judging the French we must not recur to the feelings of America during the last war. We were in the actual enjoyment of freedom and fought not to *obtain* but to *secure* its blessing."

There were, however, let us not forget, American leaders who responded to the French republicans' enthusiasm for the young American nation, possessed in 1789 of thirteen years of democratic experience. The first draft of the Declaration of the Rights of Man and of the Citizen submitted to the Legislative Assembly was prepared by La Fayette and Thomas Jefferson, ambassador to Paris. Although this exact text was not adopted, its principal tenets endured.

America and its dream had no bloody scenes behind them. The bloody and terrorist course of the French Revolution is due to the fact that, unlike its American counterpart, it was a social upheaval. Let us quote Napoleon from St. Helena: "General rule: no social revolution without terror. Every revolution is, in principle, a revolt that time and success ennoble and legitimate, but which have run through an inevitable phase of terror. How can you say to those who have wealth and public office: Go away, give up your fortune and your employ, unless you have first intimidated them and made it impossible for them to defend themselves?"

No, there was nothing revolutionary in the French memory of Ben Franklin, the rustic philosopher with the picturesque coonskin cap, which he took pains to wear in France ever after he learned of the success it had won one day when he had worn it by mistake. There was nothing warlike in the dark, sober attire of American ambassadors, which stood out democratically amid the glittering panoply of European courts.

Napoleon, on the battlefield, wore the famous gray coat that contrasted with the bright uniforms of his officers. The "Little Corporal's" coat was not only the symbol of republican simplicity, it was also that of revolutionary austerity, which he bore, like a banner, amid the wounded and dead.

For Napoleon, in this regard an heir to Robespierre, military glory was inseparable from the success of a revolution. "You cannot make or stop a revolution. What is possible is that one or more of its children may lead it, by dint of victories." Napoleon recalled that Robespierre had said: "I see no force that can close the revolutionary chasm except the prestige of victory and of great military glory."

Foreign enemies brought together a nation torn apart by the hatreds and dissensions of the Revolution, and military victories were chalked up as Revolutionary victories. Here we have another difference between Napoleonic and American ideas or, perhaps, between continental Europe and the Anglo-American world. Napoleon fought for political reasons; his wars were ideological in character. If the continental blockade was an act of economic warfare, its motivation was not economic. America, on the other hand, was defending its trade; trade and taxation were the prime movers of the War of Independence. And from then on, Americans carried on the British tradition of warring for trade routes, raw materials, and markets. Napoleon pointed up this contrast when he said to Baron Gourgaud in St. Helena, about the Americans: "They're mere tradesmen and glory only in money." Napoleon's ambassadors to the United States had branded the mercantile spirit as corrupting. Beaujour wrote: "Virtue is said to be the mainspring of a republic. But the American Republic's mainspring seems to be love of money." In so saying, he anticipated French opinion after 1830, when the image of a simple and virtuous America gave way to that of a businessman's society. In demythologizing America, Napoleon foretold the era of bad feeling.

Napoleon had scant notions of economics, although he tried to bridge the gap between France and England in the economic domain. Economics, he thought, had to be restrained, lest it corrupt the political state and its citizens. As a general, he was mindful of the profiteering rampant in the domain of military supplies and spoke of the "thievery" of suppliers. His highly orthodox monetary policy stemmed from his aversion to paper money and to all systems of credit. Protectionism was the order of the day.

America, on the other hand, took its ideas from the English merchant class. It was afraid not of the corruption engendered by the mercantile mentality but of the danger of a political power so strong as to infringe upon democratic freedoms, chief among which was the freedom to make money. Going back to the opposite point of view, we note that French ambassador Turreau wrote home: "No State at the same time democratic and mercantile can have a long political existence."

In the United States, the government was called upon to support rather than to regulate industry and commerce. Political action became the handmaiden of the economy; "laissez-faire" was the motto, and modern capitalism was born. Free enterprise was desirable because it limited the power of the government, that sleeping dragon which it was wiser not to awaken.

Jefferson ceaselessly warned his fellow citizens against an expanding and overweening central government that risked turning into a Leviathan too large and complex to be controlled by the people. The agents of an all-powerful government cannot resist the temptation of tyranny and the abandonment of their powers to the most capable or the most ambitious among them. The rights of the individual are obviously threatened. Jefferson wanted to hold off the demons that had dominated Europe and, notably, Napoleon. On January 9, 1816, he wrote from Monticello to his friend Benjamin Austin: "Bonaparte . . . had he used it [the means confided to him as a republican magistrate] honestly, for the establishment and support of a free government in his own country, France would now have been in freedom and rest; and her example operating. . . . Every nation in Europe would have had a government over which the will of the people would have had some control."

Although in France Washington was considered the incarnation of America and was hence set up against Napoleon, actually Jefferson, whose presidency coincided with the Empire, better represented, in his person and philosophy, the America of his time and a certain aspect of the American dream. He was born to an aristocratic Virginian mother and a father who was a planter and surveyor, thereby combining two aspects of the American scene. Until he was eighteen years old he had seen no agglomeration of more than twenty houses; his neighbors were farmers who had fought off the Indians and ran local affairs in the same democratic manner as that with which they ran their farms. Here is the origin of his faith in democracy.

The word *democracy* was and still is a source of misunderstanding between America and France. In America, local government was democratic from the start; the people's will was transmitted from the town to the country to the state and to the national capital. The decentralization of power was the soul of American democracy. Every town or city was an entity, electing its own magistrates possessing its own schools and police, and raising its own taxes. The right to vote was held by parishioners and landowners who formed scattered oligarchies throughout the national territory. If new immigrants disturbed this "wise and frugal" government, as Jefferson defined it in his inaugural address, they were shipped out to the virgin lands of the West. In Jefferson's time 90 percent of all Americans were farmers, neither rich nor poor, who did not live in closed class compartments. The cultural level was not high, but basic education was widespread. Hyde de Neuville, at the time when he was a political exile, wrote: "Here the laborer, the least 'cabin' dweller, is equivalent to the 'gentleman' of our small towns. He reads, writes, subscribes to a newspaper, talks of politics, follows on a map the progress of the European wars, and is never alien to the interests of the nation or to linguistic discussions."

No such situation existed in France, where it was necessary to shatter the local authority exercised by groups with hereditary status. The monarchy of the Capets had pursued a policy of centralization in opposition to the feudal lords. The Revolution sought to break up all the privileged bodies: the magistracy, the guilds, and the town councils, as well as the nobles and clergy who exercised their powers, jealously and on a hereditary basis, at a local level. In so doing, it had to make use of a central apparatus to restructure the provinces into uniform "departments." Officials from Paris were empowered to seize, on the spot, the powers of those who had inherited them from the Ancien Régime.

Napoleon would have subscribed to the opinion of democracy expressed by Robespierre in his speech of February 5, 1794, to the Convention: "Democracy is not a form of government in which the people, gathered in constant assembly, direct public affairs," for if "a hundred thousand fragments of the people" are in opposition, nothing is accomplished. Ambassador Gouverneur Morris wrote to President Washington: "Republican virtues are not of Gallic growth," and "To fit people for a republic a previous education is necessary."

To General Montholon, on St. Helena, Napoleon recalled that, in 1804, 96 percent of all Frenchmen were illiterate and "knew nothing of liberty except the delirium of 1793." "It is not enough," he added, "for people to say: 'We want the liberty preached by the apostles of liberalism'; they must deserve it by their education." The timing of this statement makes it seem a reply to the accusations of despotism that admirers of the United States have brought and still bring against him.

La Fayette, for one, as something like a representative of American ideas in France, did not fail to bring out the superiority of American liberalism over the tyranny of Napoleon. It is interesting to quote the reply made to him in 1831 by Joseph Bonaparte, who was still living in the United States:

> The part of your letter in which you speak of the Napoleonic system and judge it as marked by despotism and aristocracy, deserves a fuller answer on my part. I give credit to your good intentions, but I deplore the particular situation in which you found yourself when you came out of the Austrian prisons, since it did not allow you to judge the effects of the unhappy period of the Terror on the national character and opinion. You saw only the liberal system of America and you condemned the all-powerful man who did not bring it to France. I remember that, one day, my brother, the Emperor, coming from a conversation with you, my dear General, said to me: "I've just had quite an argument with Monsieur de La Fayette about some seditious scribblings of his from various periods brought in by the police to Paris. I said it was in order to assure the peace of mind of respectable men like himself whose continued existence seems to some people one of my crimes. Monsieur de La Fayette doesn't realize the kind of people he's got in with. He was in the prisons of despotism when these people were making France tremble, but France remembers them all too well. We aren't in America."

On St. Helena, Napoleon passed harsh judgment on La Fayette's "limited mentality" and his "dissimulating nature, dominated by vague, ill-conceived, and undigested ideas of liberty."

Napoleon was certainly one with the Revolution in the overthrow of feudal ideas; it is not for nothing that there continued to be talk of the "conquests" of 1789. The Revolution had, by definition, to use force and to act in an authoritarian manner, and it took an authoritarian and military empire to make over the social, administrative, and judicial structures of the countries it conquered. The Empire went under, but modern Europe was born.

In the association of social revolution and terror, Napoleon saw fatality rather than necessity. He had dire memories of the massacres of September, 1792, and thought that "a revolution, no matter what you may say, is one of the greatest misfortunes with which divine wrath can afflict a nation." He doubtless believed in social happiness, assimilated, in his mind, to the happiness of individuals. Terrorism was no more sparing of individual well-be-

The Napoleonic and the American Dreams Face to Face

ing than was feudal privilege; it had to be mastered and channeled. The authoritarian form of the consular and imperial governments was dictated, in large measure, by circumstances.

However, nothing was farther from Napoleon's mentality than the people's control of government favored by Thomas Jefferson. Public opinion in a democracy is one thing, and the public opinion that Napoleon sought not to obey but to mold for his own purposes is another. One of the major reproaches that his envoys made to the American system was the danger of a dictatorship of public opinion.

The United States, following the long-standing praxis of England, fostered public discussion at every level: villages, cities, clubs, and also the caucuses that chose presidential candidates. France was for too long submitted to feudal structures, revolutionary upheaval, and constitutional changes to adopt English forms of discussion. In France, opinion groups are linked to different types of government, and this is why their claims often hark back nostalgically to privileges they have enjoyed in earlier times, and also why the opposition is almost always constitutional. This is what Napoleon meant when he explained why, in England (and we may add, America) the opposition presented no danger: "The men who make it up are not seditious; they regret neither feudalism nor the Terror. They exercise the legitimate influence of talent and seek only to be bought by the Crown. With us it's quite different. The opposition is made up of the formerly privileged and of Jacobins. They aren't after just jobs or money; they hanker after the *ancien régime* or the Jacobin Clubs. There is a great difference between discussion in a country with a stable structure and opposition in a country not yet stabilized."

In America, the people took part in the government through regularly constituted groups. In France, groups and parties were an obstacle to popular participation. The only way to get around this obstacle was the plebiscite or referendum. The French Revolution, under the Convention, submitted the Constitution to a referendum, a process that did not take place in the United States.

American democracy, in 1800, was that of five million largely rural people. Napoleonic France, on the contrary, was, for the times, heavily inhabited, with its population of thirty million. In contrast to America, indeed, Europe was an overpopulated continent, with varied traditions and diverse social classes established in a limited geographical area.

Napoleon accused those who insisted on contrasting him to Washington of doing so "without understanding of time, places, men, and events." He neither could nor would make a clean break with the past and install a new order. His temperament led him not to destroy existing forces but to take them over and channel them in the direction that he thought most suitable for the passage of the Western world and of mankind to better things. In his pursuit, he had to take circumstances into account and the men who were at hand, together with their pasts.

The achievement of this design called for the fusion of all the scattered elements available in Europe. In this context, the word *Empire* has the same meaning as that of the Roman *Imperium*, a form of political organization diametrically opposite to that of a freely consented federative union. The Empire was conceived as the means of impelling the human race along the road to the single planetary civilization that Napoleon considered to be its destiny. This is no new idea. Alexander of Macedonia broke down the barriers between the Greek world and the East in a dream of universal monarchy.

Unlike Washington, leader of a homogeneous people, Napoleon brought the Revolution to "kings convinced or conquered," in a dream of "universal dictatorship." The Napoleonic Empire came into being shortly after the death of the duc d'Enghien, whose blood, says Balzac, wedded Bonaparte to the Revolution.

The Empire created a new aristocracy, with the aim, as Bignon puts it, of "neutralizing, by means of new qualifications, the tenaciously surviving old qualifications,"[1] and of fusing old and new glories into the service of the new monarch and his grand design. Napoleon put this idea of fusion into words in the message that he sent, as First Consul, to the Assemblies in February of 1803: "In the *lycées* as in the École Militaire, the youth of the departments newly incorporated into the Republic will live together with the youth of Old France. Hence a fusion of minds and manners, communication between habits and personalities.... From this mingling of interests, ambitions, and hopes, there will arise a brotherhood that will make of several peoples one people, destined by its geographical location, its courage, and other virtues to be the example and binding element of Europe."

In America, brotherhood stemmed from the similar backgrounds of the founders, most of them middle-class city dwellers who had come to create agricultural colonies in the New World. Later on, as immigrants came to have more varied origins, Americans were bound together by the pursuit of economic gain in their virgin land.

Brotherhood, for Napoleon, was not simply a union among the men of his time in the same political order; it was the solidarity of all men throughout history. He himself was the link of a chain that attached a dying civilization to one in the process of birth. He inserted himself into history; his dream's movement was meant to be synchronized with the movement of history.

America, on the other hand, lay outside history, a gigantic island detached from the world of men and its dramatic tumults, an island where history was never born and never died. Here is the originality of the American phenomenon and the essence of the American dream.

Chateaubriand remarked on the insularity and isolation of the new continent. "The solitude surrounding Americans has influenced their nature; they achieved their freedom in silence." It was the broad expanse of North America, faraway and unknown, with its Indians, its wild nature, its exotic flora and fauna, rather than the nature of its white society that attracted Europeans of the early nineteenth century. America had no historical references, while Napoleon, everywhere he went, attached his actions to a historical reference point. At the start of the Egyptian campaign, he called up the glory of Alexander the Great; apropos a canal between the Mediterranean and the Red Sea, he recalled that the Pharaoh Sesostris had had the same idea. For the brief moment when he dreamed of going to America, he thought, instead of forests and prairies to be explored, of botanical and astronomical studies.

It was distance that made isolationism a dominant feature of American foreign policy. The Declaration of Independence was concerned with America and its problems alone, whereas the Declaration of the Rights of Man and the Citizen was addressed, as its title states, to all mankind. The Napoleonic Code has been adopted in many parts of the world because it is widely adaptable.

America meant to give an example to the world, but at the same time it could not but stand alone, since Europe was marked by corruption. In Washington's Farewell Address, there is already a call to isolationism: "Why, by interweaving our destiny with that of any part of Europe, entangle our peace and prosperity in the toils of European Ambition, Rivalship, Interest, Humour or Caprice?" America should concentrate on its own development, indifferent to others. "The Nation which indulges towards another an habitual hatred, or an habitual fondness, is in some degree a slave."

America gave birth to a nation, but one that was born fully developed, like Adam. Hyde de Neuville remarked that the United States had no past and no infancy, and these lacks deprived it of poetry. It was the paradise lost that men hoped to rediscover, evoking the simplicity of a newborn world untroubled by the complexities of intertwined civilizations.[2] Although Western myths live on in America, it is at an early stage, before they are full-blown. There is, in America, a state of precivilization.

Rome, for instance, is in the Western tradition. It is conventional to compare the mothers of both Washington and Napoleon to Roman matrons, because the Western hero has to stem from Rome. Napoleon's Rome was that of Augustus, because the Napoleonic Empire was nostalgic for Augustus' *Imperium*, the period of peace that Jefferson considered decadent, as a peace of slaves. The American Rome is that of the simple Roman beginnings; it calls up the picture of Cincinnatus, the soldier-farmer, to whom Washington was so often compared.

In order to recognize and support religion, Napoleon had himself consecrated amid the pomp of the Roman Catholic church. The Bible was sacred to America's Founding Fathers, and its people considered themselves the Children of Israel marching toward the promised land. This biblical notion was reflected in the sacred quality that Americans attributed to their continent, to the annoyance of many foreign visitors. America provided a baptism; anyone choosing to settle there could feel that he had thrown off Original Sin. Many Europeans were drawn by the idea of making a fresh start, passing a sponge over their past errors. American thinking is fundamentally optimistic, viewing man, like Rousseau, as by nature good. To which Napoleon answered: "Until I was sixteen I'd have fought for Rousseau against all the friends of Voltaire. Today it's just the contrary. After I had seen the Near East, I was disgusted with Rousseau. Natural man is a dog."

Progress, in the American view, hinges from the perfectibility of human nature; man's superior character is verified by his victory over natural elements. Napoleon, a pessimist or realist, thought that progress had to be organized and imposed by legislative structures. Original Sin caused man to be driven out of Paradise, but America exorcised the ancestral curse. As the seat of a paradise regained, America gave birth to a civilization based on the possibility of happiness. This prospect was brought back to France by French officers who fought in the American Revolution.

We may recall the famous sentence of Saint-Just: "Happiness is, in Europe, a new idea." The American Declaration of Independence for the first time numbered among man's unalienable rights the pursuit of happiness: "We hold these Truths to be self-evident, that all Men are created equal, that they are endowed by their Creator with certain unalienable Rights, that among those are Life, Liberty and the Pursuit of Happiness."

The Declaration of the Rights of Man and the Citizen lays claim to liberty and equality, but the word *happiness* has no place in it. This does not mean that the French revolutionaries rejected the idea of the legitimacy of happiness. To Saint-Just, as to Robespierre, social justice was one with the idea of a happy, pre-industrial society made up of small landowners and farmers, shopkeepers and artisans, a petty-bourgeois world without great inequalities of fortune. In this sense, the ideal of Robespierre was not unlike that of Jefferson. But the French Revolution, as opposed to the American, was bourgeois and urban. Robespierre came from the middle class, and the French Revolutionary idea of happiness was concerned with the happiness of the petty bourgeoisie.

Jefferson was a gentleman farmer who cared for neither the citified middle class nor the very poor. The American Revolution was agrarian, and its concept of happiness applied to those who tilled the soil. Never in history had corruption made inroads among farmers, who represented a sort of chosen people. In America, happiness associated itself with the virtue of the Puritans, mitigating their austerity with an amiable rustic frugality. Since the state of nature was considered the most desirable, it was obvious that the most virtuous civilization should be agricultural in character.

In 1810, when Lucien Bonaparte, on bad terms with his brother, asked for asylum in the United States and was captured on the way by the British, he composed, while under house arrest, an *Ode to America*. His picture was that of a new laborious and virtuous Arcadia:

> On the cultivated banks of its many rivers
> The peaceful laborer exploits his domains.
> . . . .
> Near him his children share his work.
> They grow up without fear; no edict of terror
> Is pasted onto their rustic walls.
> . . . .
> Does the son attain the age of Spring?
> He carefully follows his father's example.
> When it is time to wed he builds with his own hands
> A cottage near to that of his parents.
> His ax lets light into the forests,
> And soon new fields
> Increase the abundance of his father's village.
> The trees he has cut down will cross the seas;
> Busy trade transports the opulence
> Of American fields to twenty different climes.
> On every side new villages are formed
> Where once there was a thick forest.
> Thus the bee spreads its useful work
> In the golden contours of its fertile hive.

To Napoleon, social happiness was not a value sacred per se, but the offshoot of an order and a harmony among men who, in a European framework, obviously did not live in a state of nature. As early as 1791 he wrote: "Physical self-preservation is the first law of nature. Second is the desire to be happy. But what is happiness? It is the reason for our being here on earth, the true enjoyment of life. But don't men lose their way looking for it? This is usually the case. No, I am not happy!"

The Napoleonic and the American Dreams Face to Face 217

And, on St. Helena, he said to Gourgaud in 1817: "All men have the same dose of happiness. Certainly I wasn't born to become what I am. I'd have been just as happy as Monsieur Bonaparte as I am as the Emperor Napoleon. Workers are just as happy as other men. Everything's relative."

No, to him, happiness was neither an essential value nor a goal to be pursued. To contrast the unhappy end of Napoleon and the serene end of Washington is to mix one frame of reference with another.

George Washington and Napoleon Bonaparte: two personalities, two worlds, incarnations of two different dreams that both kindle human imagination. The abrupt and brutal fall of Napoleon and the sad conditions of his exile call up the collapse of a giant's dream. The peaceful and honored death of Washington seems the just recompense of a modest and virtuous hero.

> When I put together my memories, [wrote Chateaubriand] when I remember seeing Washington in his modest Philadelphia house and Bonaparte in his palaces, it seems to me that Washington, having retired to his Virginia countryside, could never have felt the remorse that stung Bonaparte as he waited in the gardens of Malmaison to go into exile. In Washington's life nothing had changed; he fell back upon his modest ways, having never raised himself above the happiness of the laborers he had freed. In Napoleon's life everything was turned upside down.

These two ends have been analyzed with the criterion of immanent justice. A life respectful of moral principles is rewarded; one lived outside the limits of morality is punished. In the 1816 letter quoted above, where Jefferson passed a severe judgment on Napoleon, he underlined the sentence that states that "chagrin and mortification are the punishments our enemies receive." In other words, there were good men and bad.

Some time after, when he had read Dr. O'Meara's *A Voice from Saint Helena*, he spoke stringently of Napoleon's lack of morality. This book, he says, goes to show that

> Nature had denied him the moral sense, the first excellence of well-organized man. If he could seriously and repeatedly affirm that he had raised himself to power without ever having committed a crime, it proves that he wanted totally the sense of right

and wrong. If he could consider the millions of human lives that he had destroyed or caused to be destroyed, the desolations of countries . . . the destitutions of lawful rulers of the world without the consent of their constituents, to place his brothers and sisters on their thrones, the cutting up of established societies . . . and all the numberless train of his other enormities; the man, I say, who would consider all these as no crimes, must have been a moral monster, against whom every hand should have been lifted to slay him.

Aside from its passionate character, this judgment opens the essential debate between the ethical American concept of civilization and Napoleon's esthetic vision of history. "I am not like other men," said Napoleon, "and the laws of morality and good behavior cannot be applied to me." Even Madame de Staël, who suffered under the imperial authority, wrote that "his character cannot be defined in conventional terms; he was neither good nor violent, gentle nor cruel like persons of our acquaintance." He was no common mortal.

Misfortune and martyrdom were no longer a punishment but a metamorphosis. The suffering on St. Helena brought about the metamorphosis of a god. "I must die here unless France comes to fetch me. If Jesus Christ hadn't died on the Cross he wouldn't be God." And again: "My son mustn't avenge my death, he must take advantage of it."

His constant preoccupation with posterity expresses his profane vision of eternity: the future life is survival in the memory and history of man. "What will history say? What will posterity think?" To his brother Jérôme, he confided: "To die young . . . without leaving a trace of your existence . . . is not to have existed."

Art expresses and proves the divinity of human nature; morality and religion are merely useful supports of the social structure. The Concordat reconciled traditionally royalist Catholics with the Consular Republic. "My gendarmes, my prefects, my priests . . . " To Comte Pierre-Louis Roederer, he said: "I love power. . . . I love it as a musician loves his violin. . . . I love it in order to extract from it sounds, chords, and harmonies; I love it as an artist."

God is inscribed in the American Declaration of Independence, whereas the French Declaration of the Rights of Man and the Citizen speaks only of "the auspices of the Supreme Being," a mere

The Napoleonic and the American Dreams Face to Face 219

formula with no religious significance. One declaration is religious, the other secular.

Among the seventeen articles of the Declaration of the Rights of Man and the Citizen, which proposes itself as a universal compendium, eight are dedicated to the role and definition of the law, as if the tablets of Moses were once more presented to the world. Americans were content with their morals and manners and with reading the Bible, of which every household had a copy. Gouverneur Morris remarked, in 1792, that the metaphysical philosophy with which Frenchmen intended to replace religion could not serve as a solid moral basis. The Founding Fathers brought to the New World the idea of a democratic Church, and it is the democratic structure of the churches that makes for the tone of American democracy. In America, there is no separation between public and private morals; institutions stem from the morality that they protect.[3] George Washington liked to quote from Addison: "The post of honor is a private station." Twice he was called to the highest public post, and twice, when his task was done, he returned, with disconcerting ease and exemplary humility, to private life. The private and the public man were one.

Freedom of conscience in America made for a total separation between Church and State, something unknown in Europe, although Napoleon, on St. Helena, voiced to Dr. O'Meara a very broad tolerance: "My system was to have no predominant religion, but to allow perfect liberty of conscience and of thought, to make all men equal, whether Protestants, Catholics, Mahometans, Deists, or others; so that their religion should have no influence in getting them employment under government."

But when he added, "I made everything independent of religion," the connection with American ideas became hazier and, indeed, the mocking indifference that he sometimes displayed toward religion is completely at variance with the American respect for it.

Napoleon believed that the world was run by a hidden power reminiscent of the Fate of the ancient Greeks, a power above the gods, which allotted to superior men roles in a great design known to it alone, a design that had no moral element. He himself was one of these godlike men, like Alexander the Great and Julius Caesar:

> The day when I was so lucky as to become acquainted with Bossuet, when I read his *Discours sur l'histoire universelle*, what

he says so magnificently about the conquests of Alexander and about Caesar who, at the moment of his victory at Pharsala, seemed to stand out before the universe, I thought that the veil of the temple was rent from top to bottom and I could see the gods on the march. That vision has never since left me, in Italy, Egypt, Syria, Germany, on my most historical days.... Bossuet's thought came back, ever more shining, to my mind as my destiny grew before me.

Obviously, everyday morality cannot be applied to a god. America has no place here with a Napoleon who confessed to having lost his faith when he was eleven years old. "I heard a sermon in which the preacher said that Cato and Caesar would be damned... and from that moment I had no more religion."

The divine role with which he believed that Destiny had endowed him runs throughout his heroic trajectory. He was a link in the chain of geniuses, and he had to leave concrete traces of his genius on the fresco of history. Art was to preserve them. When David protested against Napoleon's refusal to pose for a portrait, he answered, "No one asks whether the portraits of great men are good resemblances. It is enough that their genius lives in them." Art is not just an ornamentation of life that devours government money; America knows that. But Americans could not understand the sacred mission that Napoleon attributed to it, the mission of furthering the cult of his epic. "I must tell you that my intention is to direct the arts toward subjects such as to perpetuate what happened in the last fifteen years." Art was to raise up the ghost of the giant before posterity. "Greatness is the only beauty." Art, then, was to make his greatness eternal; by means of art he would be God's rival. We may recall Victor Hugo's telling sentence: "His fall was inevitable. He was a nuisance to God."

Napoleon knew that in America grandeur was in the wide open spaces of the continent and not in the historical will of its leaders. He was busy creating his own legend and presenting his story to his contemporaries and their descendants. To painters, he dictated a description of battle scenes. From his very first *Bulletins de l'armée*, Frenchmen learned that, in the Italian campaign, "Bonaparte flies like lightning, strikes like thunder." He identified his personal fate with history.

History imposed itself on George Washington, and he did not

The Napoleonic and the American Dreams Face to Face 221

resist it. He was to remain, among his contemporaries and their descendants, a man without faults, irreproachable because he was a product of America, a blessed land whose inhabitants, according to Jefferson, were "the sole depositaries of the remains of human liberty." Here there was total identification between the man and his country. Washington was chosen because he incarnated values that existed before and outside him. Already, as a living man, he was made into a statue. The opposition group in Congress smothered him with compliments before attacking certain points of his policy, because to criticize Washington would have meant to criticize America. His legend has something static about it, the quality of an immobile perfection. It is linked to the cultivation of land, for agriculture evokes permanence.

Chateaubriand compared the silence and deliberateness of Washington to the tumult and haste of Napoleon: "Something silent envelops the actions of Washington. He moves slowly as if he felt responsible for the future of freedom and feared to endanger it. . . . Bonaparte has no likeness to this grave American; he fights noisily in an old land . . . seeming to realize that his mission is a short one, that the rushing stream from a high place will soon be exhausted. He hastens to enjoy his glory as if it were a young fugitive."

The silence that envelops Washington is like a cosmic silence, remote from the deafening tumult of epic actions. His deliberation was that of a country that had no knowledge of the acceleration of history and the flight of time.

The tumult of Napoleon's actions is that of history. He strove to catch up with history in order to insert himself in and identify himself with it. His legend is in constant motion: the revolutionary general, the emperor of a new Rome, the martyr, the demigod. He was the man of the *Blitzkrieg*; his military strategy was characterized by mobility and rapidity. Paul Morand called him "a man in a hurry. . . . Born of speed, he was condemned to acceleration." He was like a meteorite whose briefest pause must precipitate its fall.

Washington meditated at length before coming to a decision. He was a methodical man, even in his moments of reflection. The wisdom of his reasoning was that of a philosophical America, born of the Age of Reason. Both John Adams and Thomas Jefferson violently chased Napoleon out of the temple of Reason.

"He says," writes John Adams, "he was the creature of the

principles of the Age. By which no doubt he means the age of Reason; the progress of Manilius' Ratio, of Plato's Logic, etc. I believe him. A Whirlwind raised him and a Whirlwind blowed him a Way to St. Helena. He is very confident that the Age of Reason is not past; and so am I; but I hope that Reason will never again rashly create such creatures as him. Liberty, Equality, Fraternity and Humanity will never again, I hope, blindly surrender themselves to an unbounded Ambition for national Conquests, nor implicitly commit themselves to a custody and Guardianship of Arms and Heroes. If they do, they will again end in Saint Helena . . . and Sacred Ligues."

As for Thomas Jefferson, when he had read O'Meara, he recognized, after recalling the "unworthy passions" of Bonaparte, that: "The flashes, however, which escaped from him in these conversations . . . prove a mind of great expansion, although not of distinct development and reasoning. He seizes results with rapidity and penetration but never explains logically the process of reasoning by which he arrives at them."

"Imagination rules the world," said Napoleon. Brilliance and insecurity of Napoleon's creative imagination . . . Security of Washington's methodical and dull reasoning . . . Still, there is something touching about the insecurity of Napoleon, as he feels his way through the darkness of enigmatic and capricious history. "It is known that I didn't try to bend circumstances to my ideas, but that I let myself be led by them. And who can answer for chance circumstances, for unexpected accidents? How many times I have had to make drastic changes! Thus I have lived on general ideas rather than on definitive plans. The agglomerations of general interest, that which I thought advantageous to the majority, these are the anchors to which I remained attached. But I floated around them, most of the time, quite haphazardly."

"I didn't know where I was going," said Napoleon elsewhere. Ambitious men know, but "I have no ambition," he explained to Comte Roederer.

In his haste, there are the outsize proportions of genius. "He governed more in three years than the kings in a hundred," Roederer says. It took a superman to break down the old structures; only the fascination of a legend, the belief in an exceptional destiny could force a fusion of the old order and the new upon the French people; only the physical charisma of the man, with his larger-than-life virtues and defects, could induce whole nations to follow him on the path of an unpredictable story.

In America, the lack of governmental restrictions made for involuntarily rapid and imaginative development. A spectacular economic growth was spurred by the government's hands-off policy. Hyde de Neuville remarked on the speed with which roads and waterways were constructed: "It's true that the government neither pushes nor restrains; in France we make big plans and set up bureaucratic machinery, but we never bring anything to a conclusion." Because there were, for a long time, no social problems and no foreign wars, America became a land of utopias, in which it gave free rein to its dreams and inventive spirit. But utopian imagination of the American brand was far removed from the imagination of Napoleon. It had an experimental character unlike that of the structured and channeled Napoleonic dream. The American dream was based on an experience outside history; the Napoleonic dream on a destiny bound up with history.

Napoleon fascinates us by his epic wars, his life drama; Washington is revered for his pacific bravery, stemming from the eighteenth century rather than the nineteenth, which, indeed, he did not live to see. Voltaire says that the only great men are "those who have done something outstandingly useful or pleasing; those who sack provinces are merely heroes."

Washington has the coldness and severity of a Protestant—actually an Anglican—unacquainted with the "mythology" of Catholicism. He has been dehumanized in order to be shown as an abstract model, the incarnation of an idea. Marcus Cunliffe remarks that no one, not even the British, has been able to give him a nickname.

Napoleon was a romantic hero, the offshoot of a romantic revolution. Gouverneur Morris wrote to Washington from Paris in 1789, apropos the members of the National Assembly: "They have all that romantic spirit, and all those romantic ideas of government from which, happily for America, we were saved before it was too late." And, in 1799, he wished that the United States might again confide "the helm of her affairs to your steady hand."

Bonaparte, as a Revolutionary general, already conveyed the romantic image so well described by Talleyrand: "Twenty victories on the field of battle go well with youth, splendid eyes, a pale face, and a sort of weary air." Napoleon's language was persuasive by virtue of its sentimental tone: "I didn't usurp the crown; I picked it up from the river. The people placed it on my head. . . . I felt myself to be a republican at heart. Men don't change, and I'm still a republican. . . . Democracy can rage, but it has visceral feelings; aristocracy remains cold and unforgiving." On Napoleon, ideas exercised an affective appeal. The *Bulletins de l'armée* influenced writers and readers of the Romantic period. "Our teachers read us the frontline dispatches of the Grande Armée," says Alfred de Vigny, "and we interrupted Tacitus and Plato with our cries of 'Hurrah for the Emperor!' "

Washington's example was that of a father figure. People even said that, if he had no children, it was because he was the father of his country. He is thought of as an old man, a sage. Napoleon was young and had the seductiveness of a lover. "I have only one passion, one mistress, and that is France. I go to bed with her." He revealed nations to themselves and seduced them, charged energies, stirred men through their passions. With his paradoxes he was upsetting: imaginative and realistic, warlike and peace-loving, tyrannical and liberating, a man of the Enlightenment and a romantic hero. "Everyone loved and hated me, took me up, let me go, and came back to me. I think it may be said that there is no Frenchman whom I didn't stir up, one way or another."

In America, the continent was revealing. Men outdid themselves in the struggle with nature, in the labor of cutting down trees and clearing the land. There might have been a tacit dialogue between Napoleon and the American continent. Napoleon spread himself out in order to break the constrictive structures of a narrow space; Americans kept themselves under control in order to face up to an unlimited geographical expanse. Historical dizziness on the one side, geographical dizziness on the other. A romantic hero, and the romantic nature of a continent.

But Americans' thrust across the continent does not have the same meaning as the conquests of Napoleon. Americans took over a promised land. When they rolled back the frontier of monarchical Spain, they had a feeling that they had finally expelled the Old World from their virgin territory.

Napoleon conquered men, peoples, and civilizations. This spectacular advance was effected by a drive for overachievement. He elbowed his way through history, pulling people toward what he hoped was a better order. There was drive in America, too, but it was expressed in discreet philanthropy for the benefit of individuals drawn into moral reform. American optimism gave to each and every one the possibility of a better life.

Napoleon had an aristocratic view of his achievement. He was at the head of his army and his country because he had the gift of leadership. "It wasn't for love of power that I commanded," he told General Bertrand on St. Helena; "I felt that I was better equipped, more farsighted, better than the others." Every advance called for a brain that pulled the body after it. Thus he attached more importance to higher education than to elementary schooling, which he was willing to leave in private, that is, religious, hands. "I have two ambitions: first to develop France's military power and consolidate its conquests, second to develop its intellectual side to a point that hasn't been reached since Louis XIV. . . . Frenchmen respect culture. I knew what I was doing when, as an army general, I became a member of the Institute. I knew that even the littlest drummer boy would understand me."

Washington was no intellectual and not a brilliant talker, but his fellow citizens did not think of holding this against him. Americans were said to have a philosophical bent because they had been inspired by the Enlightenment and the Age of Reason. But, as René Rémond says, their reasoning was strictly "reasonable" and their philosophy homespun wisdom rather than the intellectual elucubrations of their French contemporaries. We may quote John Adams' negative answer to the Directory, which had requested visas for a delegation from the French Institute: "We have had too many French philosophers already, and I really begin to think or rather to suspect that learned academies . . . have disorganized the world and are incompatible with social order."

The authors of the successive French constitutions are political thinkers and philosophers in search of an absolute that they have not yet discovered. The American Constitution was drawn up by businessmen and lawyers, working in an empirical spirit and without feeling the necessity of adding to it a body of laws. The importance that Protestantism attributes to personal judgment incites individuals to discern on their own, without the aid of constitutional laws, what should be their social and political behavior.

There is a deep-laid difference between Napoleonic and American individualism. Napoleon had been called "the father of individualism." This he may have been, in a romantic sense. But he was the opposite of a prototype, and his individualism consisted of the fact that his personality was like no other.

American individualism is anonymous, based on the theories of John Locke, the English philosopher who so greatly influenced American thinkers. Individuals are considered separate mental substances, with no other bonds among them than those of reason. The Aristotelian or Thomistic concept of a society as a superior spiritual order that agglomerates individuals but has a life of its own, independent of them, is rejected.

Napoleon's planetary dream was of a new order that should gather all men together, bypassing the individual level. The only part of the world that he gave up and excluded from his dream was America.

Notes

Introduction

1. On the lid, there was a detachable portrait by Isabey of Josephine, who had superstitiously added to it a second lid bearing another similar portrait by the same artist.
2. The American government later assumed the same prudently neutral attitude toward Joseph Bonaparte when he took refuge in the United States after the fall of Napoleon. We may reasonably suppose that, had Napoleon himself reached American soil, he would not have been given a chance to meet the country's leaders.

Chapter 1

1. By the Treaty of Paris of 1763, England obtained not only Canada but also that part of Lousiana lying east of the Mississippi. Spain received all that lay west of the river, and this was what Napoleon bought back in 1800.

Chapter 2

1. Muiron died in the Battle of Arcola (1796), where he shielded Napoleon's body with his own.
2. This episode, taken from the *Mémoires* of General Bertrand, is discussed by André Malraux: "Napoleon, who was so knowledgeable, seems to forget that the summer and winter skies are not the same."
3. Donald D. Horward, "American Opinion on Napoleon's Downfall," *History Today*, XVI (December, 1966), 832-40.
4. A minority opinion, mostly Federalist, had always been opposed to the Emperor. A Connecticut editor wrote, "The injuries of Europe, the spirits of thousands he has murdered and the future peace of the world demand his life forfeited."
5. Édouard de Montulé, *Voyage en Amérique, en Italie, en Sicile et en Égypte* (2 vols.; Paris, 1821).—TRANS.
6. This letter is in the personal archives of Monsieur Gabriel Girod de l'Ain, author of *Joseph Bonaparte, le Roi malgré lui* (Paris, 1970).
7. A plot against the Bourbons engineered by Paul Didier in May, 1816, ostensibly in favor of Napoleon's son, but actually serving the interests of Louis-Philippe, then duc d'Orléans.—TRANS.
8. Charles IV and Ferdinand VII, kings of Spain from 1788 to 1808 and 1814 to 1833 respectively.—TRANS.

9. Abbé Dominique de Pradt, *Des colonies et de la révolution actuelle en Amérique* (Paris, 1817).—TRANS.

Chapter 3
1. René Rémond, "Les États-Unis devant l'opinion publique française, 1815–1852" (Doctoral thesis, University of Paris, 1962).—TRANS.

Chapter 4
1. Quoted in Jesse Siddall Reeves, *The Napoleonic Exiles in America: A Study in American Diplomatic History, 1815–1819*, Johns Hopkins University Studies in Historical and Political Science, Series 23, Nos. 9–10 (Baltimore: Johns Hopkins University Press, 1905).—TRANS.

Chapter 5
1. *Moeurs et voyages: Récits du monde nouveau* (Paris, 1835).—TRANS.
2. Thomas Jefferson, *Writings*, edited by Andrew A. Lipscomb *et al.* (Memorial Edition. 20 vols.; Washington, D.C., 1903–1904), XV, 100. —TRANS.
3. Since the publication of the French edition, the author has learned that Colonel Roul and the Colonel Nicolas Raoul mentioned earlier as a ferryboat operator in Démopolis were two different persons, frequently confused by historians. The text of this translation therefore corrects an error in the original edition.—TRANS.

Chapter 6
1. Just Girard, *Les Aventures d'un capitaine français, planteur au Texas, ancien réfugié du Champ d'Asile* (Tours, 1860).—TRANS.
2. *Ibid.*—TRANS.

Chapter 7
1. Son of Empress Josephine by her first marriage and one of Napoleon's most trusted lieutenants.—TRANS.
2. A fortified monastery in Paris built by the Knights Templars. It served as a prison during the French Revolution, notably for Louis XVI, and was razed in 1811.—TRANS.
3. M. Bacler d'Albe-Despax, "Un officier de Napoléon au Chili," *Revue de l'Institut Napoléon* (No. 94, January, 1965).
4. G. F. Pardo de Leygonier, "Bolivar, de Pradt, Benjamin Constant," *Revue de l'Institut Napoléon* (No. 94, January, 1965).—TRANS.
5. In his library on St. Helena, Napoleon had several books, mostly travel accounts, about South America. His few political treatises on this subject, probably sent to him by Lady Holland, arrived around 1820.

Chapter 8
1. Robert R. Palmer, *The Age of the Democratic Revolution: A Political History of Europe and America, 1760–1800* (Princeton, N.J., 1964).
2. J.-P. Wallot, *Intrigues françaises et américaines au Canada, 1800–1802* (Montréal, 1965).
3. T. Wood Clarke, *Émigrés in the Wilderness* (New York, 1941).

Chapter 9

1. *History of the Second War Between the United States of America and Great Britain* (2 vols.; Philadelphia, 1852–53), I, 386.—TRANS.
2. Antoine Marie Chamans, comte de Lavalette, Napoleon's postmaster general, was married to Émilie de Beauharnais, a niece of Josephine's first husband.—TRANS.
3. Monsieur Charles Braibant, in his preface to the catalogue of the La Fayette exhibition at the Hôtel de Rohan in 1957, reported an anecdote told by the general's granddaughter: "One day when I was playing on the Champs-Élysées, there was a sudden movement among the crowd. I wanted to join it, but my governess faced me up to a wall and said, 'The Emperor is passing by. But you're not to see him; that's an order from Monsieur de La Fayette.' "
4. Balzac wrote *La Rabouilleuse* during the reign of Louis-Philippe. Here is his account of the bad impression that New York made upon Colonel Philippe Brideau, who had lost his all at the Field of Refuge: "His misfortunes in Texas and his stay in New York, a city where speculation and individualism are carried to the highest degree, where the brutality of self-interest leads to cynicism, where an isolated man has to show his muscle and to plead his own cause, where good manners are nonexistent, in short, all the petty events of his travels had developed in Philippe all the worst traits of a trooper. He had become a brute, a drunkard, a smoker, an egotist, and an oaf."
5. After the death of Napoleon, Louisiana poets wrote many imitations of the panegyrics of Béranger and Victor Hugo. But, under the influence of the latter, Napoleon III did not win the Louisianians' favor.
6. Lee Kennett, "Le Culte de Napoléon aux États-Unis jusqu'à la Guerre de Sécession," *Revue de l'Institut Napoléon* (No. 125, October, 1972).
7. Axelle de Broglie, "Ossian le fanomatique," *Connaissance des Arts* (No. 264, 1974), 82–91.
8. When the French historian Louis Madelin mentioned to Theodore Roosevelt the age at which Napoleon had died, the president exclaimed, "Lucky man! He died at fifty-one years, after living for two hundred."

Chapter 10

1. Baron L. P. E. Bignon, Napoleonic diplomat, author of the *Histoire de France, depuis le 18 Brumaire (novembre 1799), jusqu'à la paix de Tilsitt (juillet 1807)* (14 vols.; Paris, 1829–50).—TRANS.
2. Rémond, "Les États-Unis devant l'opinion publique française, 1815–1852."
3. *Ibid.*

Bibliography

Manuscript Sources

Archives diplomatiques du Ministère des Affaires Étrangères.

Correspondance politique États-Unis: Vols. 72, 73, 74, 75, 76.

Correspondance consulaire (1815–21): La Nouvelle-Orléans, Philadelphie, Boston, New York, Charleston, Baltimore

Bibliothèque Thiers.

Fonds Masson: Dossier Brayer

Printed Sources

Mexico (City), Colegio de México. *Correspondencia diplomática franco-mexicana (1808–1839)*. México, 1957.

Brazil, Ministerio da Justiça e Negocios Interiores. *Os Franceses residentes no Rio de Janeiro (1808–1820)*. Arquivo Nacional, Series 1, Vol. 45. Rio de Janeiro, 1960.

Books

Adams, Henry. *History of the United States of America During the First Administration of Thomas Jefferson*. 9 vols. New York, 1889–91.

Adams, John Quincy. *Memoirs of John Quincy Adams Comprising Portions of His Diary, 1795–1848*. Edited by Charles Francis Adams. 12 vols. Philadelphia, 1875.

——. *Writings of John Quincy Adams*. Edited by Worthington Chauncey Ford. 7 vols. New York, 1916.

Advielle, Victor. *La Bibliothèque de Napoléon à Sainte-Hélène*. Paris, 1894.

Arthur, Stanley Clisby. *Jean Laffite, Gentleman Rover*. New Orleans, 1952.

Aubry, Octave. *Sainte-Hélène*. Paris, 1954.

Baldensperger, Fernand. *Le Mouvement des idées dans l'émigration française (1789–1815)*. Paris, 1925.

Balzac, Honoré de. *La Rabouilleuse*. Bibliothèque de la Pléiade. Paris, 1952.

Barbagelata, Hugo D. *L'Influence des idées françaises dans la révolution et l'évolution de l'Amérique espagnole*. Paris, 1917

——. *Napoléon et l'Amérique espagnole*. Paris, 1922.

Bean, Ellis Peter. *Memoirs of Colonel P. Bean, Written by Himself About the Year 1816*. Edited by W. P. Yoakum. Houston, Tex., 1930.
Bertin, Georges. *Joseph Bonaparte en Amérique*. Paris, 1893.
Bertrand, Henri Gratien, Comte. *Cahiers de Sainte-Hélène*. Edited by Paul Fleuriot de Langle. 3 vols. Paris, 1949–59.
Billington, Ray Allen. *The Far Western Frontier*. New York, 1956.
———. *America's Frontier Heritage*. New York, 1966.
Boisson, Jean. *Napoléon était-il franc-maçon?* Cholet (Maine-et-Loire), 1967.
Bonaparte, Joseph. *Lettres d'exile inédites*. Paris, 1912.
Bonnel, Ulane. *La France, les États-Unis et la guerre de course (1797–1815)*. Paris, 1961.
Brice, Raoul. *Les Espoirs de Napoléon à Sainte-Hélène*. Paris, 1938.
Calhoun, John C. *The Papers of John Caldwell Calhoun*. Edited by Robert L. Meriwether. Columbia, S.C., 1959.
Casse, Albert du. *Mémoires de Joseph Bonaparte*. Paris, 1858.
———. *Le Général Vandamme et sa correspondance*. Paris, 1870.
Castries, René de la Croix, Duc de. *La Fayette, pionnier de la liberté*. Paris, 1974.
Chandeau, Robert. *Napoléon à Fouras—La journée du 8 juillet 1815*. La Rochelle, 1958.
Chateaubriand, François-René de. *Mémoires d'Outre-Tombe*. Bibliothèque de la Pléiade. Paris, 1956.
Clarke, T. Wood. *Émigrés in the Wilderness*. New York, 1941.
Constant, Benjamin. *Opinion de M. B. Constant sur la pétition à demander le rappel des bannis*. Paris, 1819.
Cunéo-d'Ornano, Ernest Jules Alfred. *La République de Napoléon*. Paris, 1894.
Cunliffe, Marcus. *George Washington, Man and Monument*. Boston, 1958.
Damas, Hinard. *Dictionnaire ou Recueil alphabétique des opiniones et jugements de Napoléon*. Paris, 1964–65.
Didier, E. *La Vie et les lettres de Mme. Bonaparte*. Paris, 1885.
Doher, Marcel. *Proscrits et exilés après Waterloo*. Paris, 1965.
Dowd, David. *Napoleon: Was He the Heir of the Revolution?* New York, 1959.
Duhamel, Jean. *Les Cinquante Jours de Waterloo à Plymouth*. Paris, 1963.
Girard, Just. *Les Aventures d'un capitaine français, planteur au Texas, ancien réfugié du Champ d'Asile*. Tours, 1860.
Girod de l'Ain, Gabriel. *Joseph Bonaparte, le roi malgré lui*. Paris, 1970.
Godechot, Jacques. *L'Europe et l'Amérique à l'époque napoléonienne*. Paris, 1967.
Gomard, Philippe. *Les Origines de la légende napoléonienne*. Paris, 1906.
Gourgaud, Général Gaspard, Baron. *Journal de Sainte-Hélène, 1815–1818*. Edited by Octave Aubry. 2 vols. Paris, 1944.
Guillon, Édouard. *Les Complots militaires sous la Restauration d'après les documents des Archives*. Paris, 1895.
Guillot, Lucien. *Lefebvre-Desnouettes, 1773–1822*. Doctoral thesis, no location, 1961.
Hartmann, L., and Millard. *Le Texas, ou Notice historique sur le Champ-d'Asile*. Paris, 1819.

Hogendorp, Général Dirk van. *Mémoires*. La Haye, 1887.
Humboldt, Alexander von. *Voyage aux contrées equinoxales du Nouveau Continent*. Paris, 1814.
Hyde de Neuville, Jean Guillaume, Baron. *Mémoires et souvenirs*. 3 vols. Paris, 1888–92.
Imbert, Auguste, et Benjamin-Louis Bellet. *Biographie des condamnés pour délits politiques depuis la Restauration des Bourbons en France jusqu'en 1827*. Brussels, 1827.
Jefferson, Thomas. *Papers of Thomas Jefferson*. Edited by J. P. Boyd et al. 90 vols. Princeton, N.J., 1950–71.
Jolly, Pierre. *Du Pont de Nemours, soldat de la liberté*. Paris, 1956.
Jouin, Henri Auguste. *Lakanal en Amérique, d'après sa correspondance inédite (1815–1837)*. Besançon, 1904.
Lachouque, Henry. *Les Derniers jours de l'Empire*. Paris, 1965.
Lagny, L. *La Cession de la Louisiane selon des documents inconnus*. Paris, 1968.
Lapouge, Gilles. *Utopie et civilisations*. Geneva, 1973.
Larrey, Dominique Jean, Baron. *Madame Mère*. 2 vols. Paris, 1892.
Las Cases, Emmanuel, Comte de. *Mémoires de Sainte-Hélène*. Bibliothèque de la Pléiade. Paris, 1956.
La Souchère-Deléry, Simone de. *À la poursuite des Aigles*. Paris, 1950.
La Tour du Pin, Henriette Lucie, Marquise de. *Journal d'une femme de cinquante ans*. Paris, 1914.
L'Héritier, L. F. *Le Champ d'Asile, Tableau topographique et historique du Texas*. Paris, 1819.
Louis-Jaray, Gabriel. *L'Empire français d'Amérique*. Paris, 1938.
Lucas-Dubreton, Jean. *Le Culte de Napoléon, 1815–1848*. Paris, 1959.
Madelin, Louis. *Fouché*. Paris, 1900.
Madison, James. *The Papers of James Madison*. Edited by William T. Hutchinson, et al. 9 vols. Chicago, 1962–73.
Malraux, André. *Les Chênes qu'on abat*. Paris, 1971.
Marchand, Louis. *Mémoires de Marchand, premier valet de chambre et exécuteur testimentaire de l'Empereur*. Edited by Jean Bourguignon and Henry Lachouque. 2 vols. Paris, 1952–55.
Martin, Thomas Wesley. *French Military Adventurers in Alabama, 1818–1828*. Birmingham, Ala. 1940.
Martinescu, Gilbert. *Napoléon se rend aux anglais*. Paris, 1969.
Maurois, André. *Histoire des États-Unis*. 2 vols. Paris, 1959.
Mélon, Pierre. *Le Général Hogendorp*. Paris, 1938.
Monroe, James. *The Writings of James Monroe*. Edited by Stanislaus Murray Hamilton. 7 vols. New York, 1898–1903.
Montchenu, Claude Marin Henri, Marquis de. *Extrait de la lettre écrite de l'île Sainte-Hélène*. Bordeaux, n.d.
Montholon, Général Charles-Tristan, Comte de. *Récits de la captivité de l'Empereur Napoléon à Sainte-Hélène*. Paris, 1847.
Montlézun, Barthélémi Sernin Du Moulin de la Barthelle, Baron. *Voyage fait dans les années 1816 et 1817 de New York à la Nouvelle Orléans et de l'Orinoque au Mississippi*. Paris, 1818.
Montulé, Édouard de. *Voyage en Amérique, en Italie, en Sicile et en Égypte, pendant les années 1816, 1817, 1818 et 1819*. 2 vols. Paris, 1821.

Morris, Gouverneur. *A Diary of the French Revolution.* Edited by Beatrix Cary Davenport. Boston, 1939.
──────. *An Oration, upon the Death of General Washington, Delivered . . . on the 31st Day of December, 1799.* New York, 1800.
──────. *An Oration, Delivered June 29, 1814, in Celebration of the Recent Deliverance of Europe from the Yoke of Military Despotism.* New York, 1814.
Neveu, Charles. *L'Énigme du Nouveau Monde.* Paris, 1846.
Nigoul, Toussaint. *Lakanal.* Paris, 1879.
O'Meara, Barry Edward. *Napoleon in Exile, or A Voice from St. Helena.* London, 1822.
Palmer, Robert R. *The Age of the Democratic Revolution: A Political History of Europe and America, 1760–1800.* Princeton, N.J., 1964.
──────. *Twelve Who Ruled: The Year of the Terror in the French Revolution.* Princeton, N.J., 1968.
Parrington, Vernon Louis. *Main Currents in American Thought.* 3 vols. New York, 1927–30.
Parrington, Vernon Louis, Jr. *American Dreams: A Study of American Utopias.* Brown University Studies, Vol. 11. Providence, R.I., 1947.
Persat, Maurice. *Mémoires du Commandant Persat, 1806–1844.* Edited by Gustave Schlumberger. Paris, 1910.
Philips, Edith. "Les Réfugiés bonapartistes en Amérique, 1815–1830." Doctoral thesis, University of Paris, n.d.
──────. *Louis Hue Girardin and Nicholas Gouin Dufief.* Paris, 1926.
Poniatowski, Michel. *Talleyrand aux États-Unis, 1794–1796.* Paris, 1967.
Pradt, Abbé Dominique de. *Des colonies et de la révolution actuelle de l'Amérique.* Paris, 1817.
──────. *L'Europe et l'Amérique depuis le Congrès d'Aix-la-Chapelle.* Paris, 1821.
Reeves, Jesse Siddall. *The Napoleonic Exiles in America: A Study in American Diplomatic History, 1815–1819.* Johns Hopkins University Studies in Historical and Political Science, Series 23, Nos. 9–10. Baltimore, 1905.
Rémond, René. "Les États-Unis devant l'opinion française, 1815–1852." 2 vols. Doctoral thesis, University of Paris, 1962.
Renaut, François Paul. *La Question de la Louisiane, 1796–1806.* Paris, 1918.
Rhodes, Harold V. *Utopia in American Thought.* Tucson, 1967.
Riencourt, Amaury de. *L'Ère des nouveaux Césars.* Paris, 1959.
Robert, Avocat. *Les Ministres, duc Decazes, Maréchal Gouvion Saint-Cyr et Marquis Desnolles, ou les conspirations civiles et militaires. Un Bourbon sur le trône de Buenos Aires.* N.p., 1820.
Roederer, Pierre-Louis, Comte de. *Mémoires sur la Révolution, le Consulat et l'Empire.* Edited by Octave Aubry. Paris, 1942.
Rousseau, Jean-Jacques. *Discours sur l'origine et les fondements de l'inégalité.* Bibliothèque de le Pléiade. Paris, 1964.
Schalck de La Faverie, Alfred. *Napoléon et l'Amérique.* Paris, 1917.
Saint-Denis, Louis Étienne. *Souvenirs du Mameluck Ali sur l'Empereur Napoléon.* Introduction by G. Michaut. Paris, 1926.
Shulim, Joseph I. *The Old Dominion and Napoleon Bonaparte: A Study in American Opinion.* Columbia University Studies in History, Economics,

and Public Law, No. 572. New York, 1952.
Silvestre, Jean. *De Waterloo à Sainte-Hélène.* Paris, 1904.
Soulié, Maurice. *Autour de l'Aigle enchaîné.* Paris, 1929.
Thiry, Jean. *La Seconde abdication de Napoléon.* Paris, 1945.
———. *Les Débuts de la seconde Restauration.* Paris, 1947.
Tocqueville, Alexis de. *De la démocratie en Amérique.* Paris, 1835.
Veron, Louis Désiré. *Mémoires d'un bourgeois de Paris.* 6 vols. Paris, 1853–55.
Vidalenc, Jean. *Les demi-solde: étude d'une catégorie sociale.* Paris, 1955.
Wallot, Jean-Pierre. *Intrigues françaises au Canada, 1800–1802.* Montréal, 1965.
Washington, George. *The Writings of George Washington, 1745–1799.* Edited by John C. Fitzgerald. 39 vols. Washington, D.C., 1931–44.
Wilson, Beckles. *America's Ambassadors to France, 1777–1927.* London, 1928.

Periodicals

Bacler d'Albe-Despax, M. "Un officier de Napoléon au Chili." *Revue de l'Institut Napoléon,* 94 (January, 1965), 36–38.
Baulny, Olivier. "La Naissance de l'Argentine et l'entreprise ibérique de Napoléon." *Revue de l'Institut Napoléon,* 112 (July, 1969), 169–80.
Beaunier, André, "Lakanal conspirateur." *Le Figaro,* October 29, 1910.
Belgrano, Mario. "Napoléon et l'Argentine." *Napoléon,* I (1925).
"The Bonaparte Family and the United States." Embassy of France, *Service de Presse et d'Information,* No. 1307.
Bourdon, Léon. "Un français au Brésil à la veille de l'indépendance: Louis-François de Tollenare (1816–1818)." *Caravelle,* 1 (1963), 29–49.
Broglie, Axelle de. "Ossian le fantomatique." *Connaissance des arts,* 264 (February, 1974), 82–91.
Brunet, Michele. "La Révolution française sur les rives du Saint-Laurent." *Revue de l'histoire de l'Amérique française,* II (1957–58).
Cazenave, Georges. "Émigrés 1815 aux États-Unis." *Revue de l'Histoire diplomatique,* 43, No. 1 (1929).
"Le Champ d'Asile." *Chercheurs et Curieux,* 75 (1957).
Champion, Jean-Marcel. "Napoléon et Saint-Domingue." Lecture at the Institut Napoléon, January 13, 1973.
Da Costa, J. Augusto. "Napoléon Ier au Brésil, d'après des documents inédits." *Revue du Monde latin* (February, 1966).
Dansette, Adrien, ed. "Napoléon par Napoléon." *Plaisir de France,* 364 (February, 1969).
Delalande, Jean. "Napoléon en Louisiane." *Miroir de l'Histoire,* 217 (January, 1968).
Desfeuilles, André. "Refugiés politiques à New-York (1814–1816)." *Revue de l'Institut Napoléon,* 72 (July, 1959), 125–34.
Devaux, Pierre. "Napoléon et Fulton." *Le Figaro,* March 26, 1969.
Dupuy, Aimé. "Un épisode assez peu connu de notre histoire coloniale: les soldats-laboureurs du Champ d'Asile." *Revue de la Méditerranée* (March-April, 1951).
Fleuriot de Langle, Paul. "Le général Simon Bernard, créateur du fort Monroe en Virginie." *Le Ruban rouge* (December, 1964).

Foyer, Jean. "Ses lois ont franchi les siècles et les océans." *Le Figaro littéraire*, No. 1186 (January 27–February 2, 1969).
Gavoty, André. "Laure Regnaud de Saint-Jean-d'Angély et Napoléon." *Revue des Deux Mondes*, June 15, 1966, pp. 531–46.
Gonnard, Philippe. "Légende napoléonienne dans la press libérale." *Revue des Études Napoléoniennes*, I (1912).
Gun, Nerin E. "Les Bonaparte ont deux patries: la France et les États-Unis." *Le Figaro littéraire*, No. 1186 (January 27–February 2, 1969).
Horward, Donald D. "American Opinion on Napoleon's Downfall." *History Today*, XVI (December, 1966), 832–40.
Joxe, Louis. "Napoléon, parent terrible de l'Europe." *Le Figaro littéraire*.
Kennett, Lee. "Le Culte de Napoléon aux États-Unis jusqu'à la guerre de Sécession." *Revue de l'Institut Napoléon*, 125 (October, 1972), 145–56.
Lallemand, Général. "Napoléon refuse de passer en Amérique. Extrait du journal du général Charles-Frédéric-Antoine Lallemand, juillet-août 1816." *French-American Review*, II (1949), 63–80.
La Souchère-Deléry, Simone de. "Some French Soldiers Who Became Louisiana Educators." *Louisiana Historical Quarterly*, XXXI (1948), 849–55.
———. "Le Thème napoléonien dans la poésie louisianaise." *French-American Review*, II (1949).
"Lettre de Mme Regnault de Saint-Jean d'Angély à son mari, 1817." *Revue Rétrospective*, X (1889).
"Mission Bourquenay aux États-Unis." *Revue de l'Histoire diplomatique*, 69, No. 1 (1955).
Moraud, Marcel. "Le Champ d'Asile au Texas." *Le Courrier de l'Amitié, Bulletin des Amitiés internationales napoléoniennes*, Special Number (July, 1967).
"Napoléon, Empereur des Arts." *Connaissance des Arts*, 203 (January, 1969), 30–41.
"Napoleon y Bolívar." *El Maestro—Revista de Cultura Nacional* (Mexico), II, No. 6 (1922).
Nouvion, Jacques de. "Elisabeth Patterson." *Revue des Revues et Revue d'Europe et d'Amérique*, 32 (1900).
Pardo de Leygonier, G. F. "Napoléon et les libérateurs de l'Amérique latine." *Revue de l'Institut Napoléon*, 82 (January, 1962), 29–33.
———. "Bolivar, l'Abbé de Pradt, et Benjamin Constant." *Revue de l'Institut Napoléon*, 87 (April, 1963), 62–68.
"Participation des Français au soulevement des colonies espagnoles d'Amérique du Sud." *Revue historique de l'armée*, 16, No. 1 (1960).
Pérez, Parra. "Bolivar et Napoléon." *Annales de l'Idée Latine*, 1963.
"La Plata faillit devenir française." *Revue historique de l'armée*, 14, No. 1 (1958).
"Une prédication sur Napoléon (lettre de Dupont de Nemours à Regnault de Saint-Jean d'Angély (24 avr. 1798)." *Souvenirs et Mémoires*, II (1899), Variétés historiques.
Quynn, Dorothy Mackay. "La Liquidation d'une légende: la survivance de Ney en Amérique." *Revue de l'Institut Napoléon*, 125 (October, 1972), 157–60.
Renaut, S. P. "États-Unis et Amérique espagnole sous Joseph Bonaparte, roi

d'Espagne (1808–1814).″ *Revue des Sciences Politiques*, February 15, 1918.
Rousseau, François. "Une tentative de colonisation française au temps de la Restauration: le Champ d'Asile." *Revue d'histoire des colonies*, 3rd Trimester (1916).
Senti, Louis. "La déplorable affaire méxicaine." *Le Courrier de l'Amitié, Bulletin des Amitiés internationales napoléoniennes*, Nos. 140–41 (January–February, 1975) and Nos. 142–43 (March–April, 1975).
Shulim, Joseph I. "Napoleon as the Jewish Messiah: Some Contemporary Conceptions in Virginia." *Jewish Social Studies*, VII (July, 1945).
Tartary, Madeleine. "Souvenirs napoléoniens aux États-Unis." *Revue de l'Institut Napoléon*, 49 (October, 1953), 122–23.
Teissier, Marcel. "Est-ce-que le Maréchal de France Michel Ney est mort aux États-Unis?" *Le Courrier de l'Amitié, Bulletin des Amitiés internationales napoléoniennes*, Nos. 134–35 (May–June, 1974) and Nos. 136–37 (July–August, 1974).
"El Temor a Napoleon en Buenos Aires." *Boletín de la Real Academia de la Historia* (Madrid), 134 (1954), Ch. 1.
Tulard, Jean. "Napoléon écrivain." *Souvenir Napoléonien*, 13, No. 240 (February, 1969).
Vallaux, Camille, "La Légende napoléonienne aux États-Unis." *Le Mercure de France*, 177 (1925).
Vauthier, Gabriel. "Notes sur les Français retirés aux États-Unis à l'issue des Cent-Jours de 1818, par M. de Maud'hui." *Revue des Études Napoléoniennes*, 32 (1931).
Warren, Harris Gaylord. "Documents Relating George Graham's Proposals to Jean Laffite for the Occupation of the Texas Coast." *Louisiana Historical Quarterly*, XXI (1938), 213–19.

Index

L'Abeille américaine, 60, 70, 76, 87, 133
Adams, John, 7–8, 9, 10, 200, 221–22, 225
Adams, John Quincy, 15, 32, 56, 111, 112, 113, 121, 140
Agriculture: French exiles in Alabama and, 76–77, 81, 85–100 *passim*
Aigleville (Ala.), 76, 85–100 *passim*
L'Aiglon. *See* Napoleon II
Alabama: French exiles in, 76–77, 81, 82, 84–100 *passim*, 110, 144, 179
Alexander I (Czar of Russia), 37, 45, 50, 71
American dream: effect of Louisiana Purchase on, 4; Hamilton's view of, 9; and *demi-soldes*, 54; and Bonapartist exiles in U.S., 63; and Bernard, 68; and Dupont de Nemours, 72–73; and Field of Refuge, 127, 145; and utopian ideas, 129; Napoleon's view of, 150; and Latin America, 168; in France, 188–93; and Tocqueville, 191; mentioned, vii, 16, 37, 48, 197, 198, 199–226 *passim*
American Revolution: France's aims in, 5; causes of, 207; agrarian character of, 215–16; mentioned, 96, 172, 188, 191
Amiens, Peace of, 11, 174–75
Archambault (Napoleon's groom), 32, 34, 38, 105
Argentina, 158. *See also* Buenos Aires; La Plata
Association Fraternelle Européene, 148
Aury, Louis, 119, 120, 121, 122–23, 124

Balzac, Honoré de, 54, 145, 147, 189, 212, 229
Bassano, Hugues Bernard Maret, Duc de, 44, 45, 160
Béranger, Pierre Jean de, 146, 147, 229
Bernard, Simon, 64–69, 197
Bertrand, Henri, 44

Bolívar, Simon, 114, 118, 153–54, 155, 161, 162, 169–71
Bonaparte, Caroline. *See* Murat, Caroline Bonaparte
Bonaparte, Charles-Joseph, 196–97
Bonaparte, Charles-Lucien, 183
Bonaparte, Charlotte, 44, 182, 183, 184
Bonaparte, Elisa, 44
Bonaparte, Jérôme, 44, 45, 175, 182–83, 184, 192, 196, 218
Bonaparte, Jérôme-Napoléon, 182, 183, 192, 196, 197
Bonaparte, Jérôme-Napoléon Charles, 197
Bonaparte, Joseph: Napoleon's view of, 26–27, 151–53; as aide to Napoleon, 3, 10, 20, 24; as King of Spain, 114, 154, 156–57, 158, 159, 161; mentioned, 71, 74, 89, 109, 110, 148, 192, 196
—exile of, in U.S., 22–46 *passim*, 56–57, 67–68, 69, 73, 92, 102–104, 105, 112, 115, 116–17, 120, 150, 151–53, 172, 176, 180, 181, 182–84, 189, 190, 210, 227
Bonaparte, Julie Clary, 25, 26, 27, 33, 44, 182, 184
Bonaparte, Louis, 44
Bonaparte, Louis-Napoléon. *See* Napoléon III
Bonaparte, Lucien, 3, 18, 40, 45, 112, 183, 184, 216
Bonaparte, Maria Letizia Ramolina (Madame Mère), 17, 25, 29, 34, 35, 36, 182, 183, 184
Bonaparte, Napoléon. *See* Napoléon
Bonaparte, Napoléon-Jérôme, 184
Bonaparte, Pauline, 11, 13, 18, 44, 183
Bonaparte, Pierre, 184
Bonaparte, Zénaïde, 44, 46, 183
Brayer, Michel Sylvestre, 116, 117, 149, 163–64, 165
Brazil, 151. *See also* Pernambuco
Buenos Aires, 92, 114, 156, 158, 159, 161

240 Index

Buisson, Pierre Benjamin, 64, 69

Calhoun, John C., 16, 96
Caracas, 157, 159
Catherine of Würtemberg, 44, 184
Champagny, Jean-Baptiste Nompère de, 157, 158, 159
Champ d'Asile. *See* Field of Refuge
Chateaubriand, François René de, 37–38, 49, 55, 56, 118, 200, 213, 217, 221
Chaudron, Simon, 60, 85, 87
Chilean insurgents. *See* Insurgents, Chilean
Clary, Julie. *See* Bonaparte, Julie Clary
Clauzel, Bertrand de: exile in U.S. of, 89–90, 91, 93–95; career prior to exile, 90; mentioned, 57, 61, 71, 85, 88, 93, 99, 117, 177, 179
Code Napoléon. *See* Napoleonic Code
Colonial Society of French Émigrés, 82
Colonization: contrasting American and French ideas on, 77–81
Constant, Benjamin, 147, 148, 169–70

D'Albe, Joseph Albert, 164–65
Declaration of Independence, 168, 204–205, 213, 215, 218–19
Declaration of the Rights of Man and of the Citizen, 188, 189, 205, 213, 215, 218–19
Decrès, Denis, 11, 19, 157, 159
Demi-soldes: in aftermath of Hundred Days, 52–54; in Latin America, 54, 162; as mercenaries, 54; professions of those exiled in U.S., 74, 75; mentioned, 38, 139, 147, 165, 189
Democracy: contrast in French and U.S. ideas of, 208–209
Democratic party (U.S.). *See* Republican party (U.S.)
Démopolis (Ala.), 76, 82, 85, 86, 228
De Pradt, Dominique, 169–71
Dupont de Nemours, Pierre Samuel, 58–60, 70, 72–73

Federalist party: view of Napoleon, 10, 14, 15, 203, 227; mentioned, 9, 12, 13
Fesch, Cardinal (uncle of Napoleon), 36, 43, 88, 184
Field of Refuge, 79, 121–50, 192, 196, 229
Florida, 119–20, 142–43, 159
Fortress Monroe (Va.), 64, 66, 196
Fouché, Joseph, 18, 19, 20, 51, 176
Franklin, Benjamin: French image of, 206; mentioned, 45, 56, 57, 60, 200

Freemasons. *See* Masons
French Revolution: Americans' views of, 6, 9–10, 12, 61, 96; and Dupont de Nemours, 59; and Field of Refuge, 132; impact on Latin America, 168; Canadians' views of, 173; La Fayette on, 188, 189; relation to Napoleonic Wars, 206–207; Napoleon's view of, 210–11; mentioned, 4, 47, 53, 55, 95, 97, 98, 156, 180, 202–15 *passim*
French Revolution of 1830. *See* Revolution of 1830 (France)

Galveston Island: and Field of Refuge, 122–23, 125, 141, 143–44; occupied by Lafitte, 123, 124–25, 142; mentioned, 114
Garnier de Saintes, Georges, 85, 86–87
Genêt, Edmond, 6, 173–74, 177
Girard, Just, 122, 137–38, 139, 142, 192
Girard, Stephen, 32, 58, 60, 66, 92, 109, 148
Gourgaud, Gaspard, 34, 105, 108, 117, 201, 207
Grouchy, Emmanuel de: career prior to exile, 69–70; exile in U.S., 70–71; mentioned, 30, 56, 57, 62, 85, 93, 109, 148, 176, 177
Guadaloupe, 99

Haiti. *See* Santo Domingo
Hamilton, Alexander, 7, 9, 12, 48
Hogendorp, Dirk van, 118, 149, 166, 167–68
Hugo, Victor, 181–82, 220, 229
Hyde de Neuville, Jean Guillaume: exile of, in U.S., 49, 50; as French ambassador to U.S., 29, 38, 39, 61, 62–63, 71, 88, 92, 93–94, 103–105, 106, 107, 111, 115, 118–19, 125, 126, 140–41, 142, 149, 176, 177, 209, 214; mentioned, 31, 52, 60, 73, 81, 90, 115, 118, 148, 177, 223

Independents: Mexican, 90, 154; of Buenos Aires, 92; Latin-American, 118, 151–71 *passim. See also* Insurgents
Ingersoll, Charles Jared, 32, 180, 190
Insurgents: Latin-American, 28, 33, 54, 63, 90, 123, 151–71 *passim*, 177; Mexican, 29, 103, 104, 113, 114, 122, 125, 153; Chilean, 114, 163. *See also* Independents

Jackson, Andrew, 16, 65, 119–20, 124, 190, 194

Jefferson, Thomas: ideas of, 12; on Napoleon, 13, 15, 208, 217–18, 221, 222; and Louisiana Purchase, 13, 14; and Grouchy, 70; and French colonists in Alabama, 82–83, 84; on America's vacant lands, 129; and Declaration of the Rights of Man, 188, 206; reaction to Waterloo, 200; on central government power, 207–208; mentioned, 24, 48, 59, 60, 61, 68, 87, 155, 208, 211, 214, 215, 221
Joachim (King of Naples), 107, 159, 183, 196

La Fayette, Marie Joseph, Marquis de: and Masons, 57; attitude toward slavery, 99; as leader of Liberals, 145, 188–90; and Napoleon's second abdication, 149; Napoleon's view of, 149, 180; visits Joseph Bonaparte in U.S., 180; and Revolution of 1830, 180–81; and Declaration of the Rights of Man, 188, 206; view of Napoleon, 190, 209–10; sends Washington key to Bastille, 205; mentioned, 5, 10, 70, 229
Laffitte, Jacques, 18, 66, 91
Lafitte, Jean: on Galveston Island, 123, 124–25, 126, 142, 143; life and career of, 123–24, 187; as Spanish agent, 142; and legend of Napoleon's escape from exile, 186–87; mentioned, 144, 188
Lafitte, Pierre, 123, 124, 142, 186
Lakanal, Jacques: career prior to exile, 101–102; exile in U.S., 102, 179; letters to Joseph Bonaparte of, 102, 103–104, 111, 112, 118; and Lallemand, 109; returns to France, 178–79; mentioned, 113, 177, 184, 193
Lallemand, Charles: career prior to exile, 108–109; in New Orleans, 110–11; proposed Mexican expedition of, 111–12, 113, 114, 150; and J. Q. Adams, 113, 121; and Latapie, 117; as leader of Field of Refuge, 122–50 *passim*, 196; and Napoleon's will, 149; returns to France, 179; mentioned, 56, 57, 85, 86, 89, 111, 114, 119, 121, 177, 184, 192
Lallemand, Henri: career prior to exile, 109–10; as exile in U.S., 109, 110; mentioned, 60, 89, 112, 148
Lamanon, Paul de, 157, 159
La Plata, 155–56, 157, 162
Las Cases, Comte Emmanuel de, 26, 105
Latapie, Paul de, 115–18
Latin America: wars of independence in, 114, 118, 162
Latin-American independents. See Independents
Latin-American insurgents. See Insurgents
Leclerc, Charles, 11, 13, 90, 98, 109
Lee, William, 62, 82, 83, 84, 111–12, 121
Lefebvre-Desnouettes, Charles: career prior to exile, 88–89; as exile in U.S., 88, 90, 93–95; and plot to free Napoleon from exile, 91–93; mentioned, 30, 56, 57, 61, 85, 88, 93, 99, 109, 110, 117, 144, 178
Le Ray de Chaumont, Jacques, 35–36, 176
Liberal party (France): and Masons, 57; and Field of Refuge, 145, 147, 149; Balzac on, 147, 148; Napoleon's view of, 149, 189; view of Bolívar, 169; mentioned, 41, 99, 118, 162, 180, 188, 189
Liniers, Jacques de, 155–56, 158, 159
Livingston, Robert, 13, 14, 40
Louis-Philippe (King of France), 48, 69, 71, 179, 189, 190, 191, 193, 227
Louisiana: as French exiles' favorite state, 58; dispute over boundaries of, 113, 139–42
Louisiana Purchase, vii, 3–4, 7, 10–11, 13–14, 188
Lowe, Sir Hudson: as governor of St. Helena, 101, 106–107, 117; as governor of Capri, 107; mentioned, 37, 167, 198

MacGregor, Gregor, 119, 121
Madison, James, 15, 23–24, 29, 124, 129
Marie-Louise (Empress of France), 44, 181
Martinique, 97, 98, 99
Masons: aid to French exiles, 57; attitude toward slavery, 99; in Brazil, 115; and La Fayette, 188, 189; mentioned, 20, 100, 148, 185
Mauritius, 97, 195
Mexican independents. See Independents
Mexican insurgents. See Insurgents
Mexico: and *demi-soldes*, 38; and Lakanal's scheme, 103–105, 193; Lallemand's proposed expedition to, 111–12, 117, 125, 150; Napoleon's view of, 151–52; Napoleon III's venture in, 193; mentioned, 139, 144, 154, 159
Mina, Francisco Javier, 33, 114, 122–23, 177
Miranda, Francisco de, 119, 154–55, 161,

162, 168
Monge, Gaspard, 6, 17, 178
Monroe, James: and Louisiana Purchase, 13; and Skinner Affair, 62; and Bernard, 65-66; and Field of Refuge, 143; mentioned, 15, 23, 31, 111, 112, 160
Montevideo, 114, 156, 157-58, 159
Montholon, Charles Tristan de, 105
Montulé, Edouard de: on New York City, 22, 23; on Philadelphia, 24-25; visits Joseph Bonaparte, 30-31; on New Orleans, 58; on Regnault, 73; on Garnier de Saintes, 86-87; mentioned, 28, 67, 68, 111
Morris, Gouverneur, 6, 205, 209, 219, 223
Murat, Achille, 45, 183-84, 196
Murat, Caroline Bonaparte, 45, 183
Murat, Joachim. *See* Joachim (King of Naples)
Murat, Lucien, 45, 183, 184

Napoleon: considers exile in U.S., vii, 5-6, 17-18, 213; first abdication of, 16; second abdication of, 17-22, 51, 72, 149; Hundred Days, 50-51; will of, 149, 167, 177, 179, 180, 203; impact on Latin America of, 153, 171; image in Canada of, 174-175; return of remains to France, 191; contrasted to Washington, 200, 203, 212, 217-25 *passim*
—as emperor: U.S. reaction to coronation of, 14; and War of 1812, 15-16; Latin-American policy of, 154, 156-62; and French-Canadians, 175
—as First Consul: and Louisiana Purchase, vii, 3-4, 13-14, 139; commemoration of Washington's death by, 9, 39, 149, 199-200; and Leclerc expedition, 11, 13; and Hyde de Neuville, 49; and slavery, 97-99; and Bolívar, 155; and brother Jérôme, 182-83; and La Fayette, 188-89; and centralized power, 202; message to Assemblies, 212-13
—exile on St. Helena: impact on Napoleonic legend of, vii, 106, 149-50, 199; health of, 26, 35; plans to liberate, 29, 63, 90-93, 105-106, 109, 115-18, 120, 125, 139, 149, 150, 163, 177, 186-87, 188; imagines brother Joseph's life in U.S., 29-30; investments in U.S., 30, 35; seeks publication of correspondence with European rulers, 36-37, 40, 42, 44; messages to Joseph, 38; thinks of going to America, 38-39, 41, 100, 150, 178; hopes of being freed, 41, 118, 173; death of, 44, 193; relations with Lowe, 106-107; difficulty of escape, 107-108
—opinions of, on America, 5-6, 27-28, 38-39, 44, 55, 200-201
Napoleon II (King of Rome): La Fayette's proposal concerning, 180; death of, 182; mentioned, 35, 42, 44, 72, 91, 149, 181, 189, 218, 227
Napoleon III: in U.S., 134; as prince-president, 191-92; in power, 192-93; mentioned, 183, 194, 196, 197, 229
Napoleonic Code, 171, 195, 214
Napoleonic legend: and Field of Refuge, 127, 139; and Latin America, 169, 171; and Victor Hugo, 181-182; in U.S., 186-87, 188, 193-97; mentioned, vii, 37, 68, 106, 149-50, 198, 199-226 *passim*
New Orleans: Jefferson on importance of, 13; Battle of, 16, 124; description of, 58; and French exiles, 58; street names associated with Napoleon, 69; Napoleonic legend in, 188, 195-96
Ney, Michel. *See* Ney, Peter Stewart
Ney, Peter Stewart, 30, 184-86

O'Meara, Dr. Barry Edward, 36-45 *passim*, 57, 100, 106, 152, 217, 219, 222
Onís, Don Luis de, 113, 140, 141

Patterson, Elizabeth, 45, 182, 183, 192, 194, 196
Pénières, Jean-Augustin, 87, 102
Pernambuco, 114-15, 116, 163, 165
Persat, Maurice, 120-21, 122, 162-63
Poussin, Guillaume-Tell, 64, 66-67

Quinette, Nicholas-Marie, 73-74

Raoul, Nicolas, 86, 228
Réal, Pierre-François, 85, 176-78
Regnault de Saint-Jean-d'Angély, Comte Michel, 56, 57, 72-73, 177
Republican party (U.S.): opinion of French Revolution, 12; views of Napoleon, 13, 14, 15, 203; view of Bourbon Restoration, 24; opinion of French exiles in U.S., 61
Revolution of 1830 (France), 68, 181, 189
Rigaud, Aimée, 110, 132, 139, 141, 148
Rigaud, Antoine: career prior to exile,

110; and Field of Refuge, 121, 122, 123, 125, 126, 144; life after Field of Refuge, 148–49; mentioned, 89, 109, 141, 143, 196
Rome, King of. *See* Napoleon II
Roul, Colonel, 91–92, 117, 228
Roulet, Pierre-Rémy, 165
Rousseau, Jean-Jacques, 47, 48, 78–80, 82, 83–84, 136–37, 200, 215
Rousseau (steward on St. Helena), 32, 34, 38, 105, 117

Saavdra, Cornelio, 153, 162
St. Helena. *See* Napoleon—exile on St. Helena
San Martín, José de: and Latin-American wars of independence, 114; view of Napoleon, 153, 162; and controversy with Brayer, 163–64; mentioned, 116, 165
Santo Domingo (Haiti): revolt of blacks on, 11; Leclerc's expedition to, 13, 90; refugees from revolt, 50, 58, 85, 90, 142; and slavery question, 96, 98; under Toussaint L'Ouverture, 98; mentioned, 109, 123, 124, 159
Sassenay, Marquis de, 157–58, 159
Savage, Annette, 46, 184, 192
Slavery: in U.S., 95, 96; Napoleon's attitude toward, 95–99
Society for the Cultivation of the Grape and Olive, 81, 177
Soldier-farmer, legend of the, 53, 76, 100, 145, 214
Survilliers, Comte de. *See* Bonaparte, Joseph

Talleyrand-Périgord, Charles Maurice de: and French agreement with U.S., 7–8; and Louisiana Purchase, 13; on Americans, 48; on Napoleon, 52; mentioned, 6–7, 18, 23, 55, 180, 223
Texas: dispute over boundaries of, 113, 139–42; described, 141; as location of Field of Refuge, 127
Tocqueville, Alexis de, 190–91
Toussaint L'Ouverture, François Dominique, 11, 96, 98

Utopian ideas: in France, 55; and America, 127, 128–31, 135–36, 137, 223; and Field of Refuge, 131, 132, 136–37

Vandamme, Dominique-René: exile in U.S., 71–72; mentioned, 56, 69, 110, 112
Venezuela, 155, 161, 162. *See also* Caracas
Viol, Adrienne, 132, 139
Voltaire, François Marie Arouet de, 200, 215, 223

War of 1812: significance for U.S., 16, 130, 199; Napoleon on, 200–201; mentioned, 15, 32, 64, 113, 124, 161
Washington, George: as president, 6–7; Paris commemoration of death of, 9, 188, 199–200; legend of, 76, 135, 169, 171, 221; Napoleon III on, 191, 192; contrasted to Napoleon, 200, 203, 212, 217–25 *passim*; mentioned, 5, 8, 22, 23, 39, 45, 56, 57, 67, 149, 150, 184, 190, 197, 205, 208, 209, 214
Wellington, Arthur Wellesley, Duke of, 16, 18, 185
Waterloo, Battle of, 21, 69, 70, 200

You, Dominique, 124, 188